HIDDEN®
Disneyland
and Beyond

HIDDEN®
Disneyland
and Beyond

**Including Disney's California Adventure,
Universal Studios Hollywood, Six Flags
California, Knott's Berry Farm, SeaWorld,
and the San Diego Zoo & Wild Animal Park**

Lisa Oppenheimer

SECOND EDITION

Ulysses Press®
BERKELEY, CALIFORNIA

Published by:
ULYSSES PRESS
P.O. Box 3440
Berkeley, CA 94703
www.ulyssespress.com

ISSN 1527-7437
ISBN 1-56975-306-7

Printed in Canada by Transcontinental Printing

10 9 8 7 6 5 4 3 2

MANAGING EDITOR: Claire Chun
PROJECT DIRECTOR: Lynette Ubois
COPY EDITOR: Lily Chou
EDITORIAL ASSOCIATE: David Archer
TYPESETTER: Lisa Kester
CARTOGRAPHY: Pease Press, Ulysses Press
COVER DESIGN: Sarah Levin, Leslie Henriques
INDEXER: Sayre Van Young
COVER PHOTOGRAPHY:
    FRONT: Francisco Cruz/SuperStock
Illustrator: Glenn Kim

Distributed in the United States by Publishers Group
West and in Canada by Raincoast Books

Write to us!

If in your travels you discover a spot that captures the spirit of Disneyland, or if you live in the region and have a favorite place to share, or if you just feel like expressing your views, write to us and we'll pass your note along to the author.

We can't guarantee that the author will add your personal find to the next edition, but if the writer does use the suggestion, we'll acknowledge you in the credits and send you a free copy of the new edition.

ULYSSES PRESS
P.O. Box 3440
Berkeley, CA 94703
E-mail: readermail@ulyssespress.com

✳

Ulysses Press would like to thank the following readers who took the time to write in with suggestions that were incorporated into this new edition of *Hidden Disneyland*: Carol and CJ Craddock of Foothill Ranch, CA; Darin Wilson of Seattle, WA; and Emily Fagan via e-mail.

What's Hidden?

At different points throughout this book, you'll find special listings marked with a hidden symbol:

◄ HIDDEN

This means that you have come upon a place off the beaten tourist track, a spot that will carry you a step closer to the local people and natural environment of Southern California.

The goal of this guide is to lead you beyond the realm of everyday tourist facilities. While we include traditional sightseeing listings and popular attractions, we also offer alternative sights and adventure activities. Instead of filling this guide with reviews of standard hotels and chain restaurants, we concentrate on one-of-a-kind places and locally owned establishments.

Our authors seek out locales that are popular with residents but usually overlooked by visitors. Some are more hidden than others (and are marked accordingly), but all the listings in this book are intended to help you discover the true nature of Disneyland and Southern California and put you on the path of adventure.

Contents

Maps

OUTDOOR ADVENTURE SYMBOLS

The following symbols accompany national, state and regional park listings, as well as beach descriptions throughout the text.

	Camping			Surfing
	Hiking			Windsurfing
	Biking			Canoeing or Kayaking
	Horseback Riding			Boating
	Swimming			Boat Ramps
	Snorkeling or Scuba Diving			Fishing

Games to Play While Waiting in Line

The lines at Southern California's theme parks can try anyone's patience. Fortunately, if you know how to create your own entertainment, the wait can be painless (well, almost).

Kids and adults alike can while away the time, use their creativity and even get a few laughs by playing the games described below. Some of these games relate to specific theme parks, others are appropriate for particular age groups. I have also added trivia questions for extra fun.

If you really want to speed up those waiting lines, create some games of your own!

GAMES FOR ALL AGES

RHYME TIME

Everybody loves to make up rhymes. It's even more fun when you do it together. Begin with a line of poetry. The next player adds a rhyming line, the next player contributes another and so on. The player who rhymes the fourth line gets to start a new rhyme. Example:

I read about Disneyland in a book,
And decided I'd go take a look.
I left the dog, but my family I took.
All because of that silly book.

"SENSITIVE" POETRY

Compose a poem that you can see, smell, taste, feel and hear. Give it a try, using the following example as a guideline:

I love the smell of old socks.
I love the taste of ham hocks.
I hate feeling blue,
But I love hearing something new.
As you can see I'm a very good poet, too.

A IS FOR...

Look around you and choose objects that begin with particular letters. Start with "A" and proceed alphabetically. For example: animal, bus, carousel, dirt, exit, etc. Each player must come up with a nearby object that begins with the next letter in the alphabet.

HAVE YOU EVER, EVER, EVER?

Begin this game by reciting the first three lines of the following ditty and inserting an animal or object in the last word of the third line. The next player then provides a rhyming word for the last word in the fourth line:

Have you ever, ever, ever?
Have you ever, ever, ever?
Have you ever seen a MOUSE
Eat a HOUSE?
OH! NO! We never saw a MOUSE eat a HOUSE!

The last line of the verse is said in unison. The second word doesn't need to be a "real" one; in fact, the sillier it is, the more fun you'll have with the children! Some other examples are:

Have you ever seen MICKEY
Be real PICKY?
Have you ever seen a MANGO
Do the TANGO?

STUPID QUESTIONS

Making a fool of yourself is easy. Just ask the stupidest question you can think of. Then have everyone decide whose question is the dumbest. The stupid one is the winner!

PINK FLAMINGOS

Everyone poses a question that has to be answered with the phrase "Pink flamingos." Such as "What did you wear to bed last night?" Pink flamingos. "What did you barbecue for dinner?" Pink flamingos. If you giggle when you ask the question, you're out. The last remaining person is the winner.

SILENCE IS GOLDEN

Here's a game guaranteed to leave your group speechless. (Parents will love this!) Everyone pledges not to talk for a certain time period, say ten minutes. Only sign language can be used. It's a fun way to be imaginative with body language and visual communication. The last person to speak wins.

NUMBER STORIES

Storytelling is even more fun when you use numbers. Begin by using the number "one." The next person adds the word "two," etc. Example: Once upon a time . . . Two frogs went on a date . . . They swam across three lakes . . . Then they saw four speedboats headed for them . . . But they escaped with five seconds to spare. . . .

PICK A NUMBER

One player picks a number between 1 and 100, but doesn't reveal it to the other players. Each person takes turns trying to guess the number. When someone guesses incorrectly, the player will say "higher" or "lower" depending on whether the guess is above or below the secret number. The person who guesses right gets to pick the next secret number.

BODY MOVES

A leader starts the game with a body move, such as winking an eye. The next player performs that move and adds another, like nodding his or her head. For example, they might wink and nod their head. The game continues with each player performing the previous body moves—in the correct order—and adding a new one. Someone who forgets a move, is out of the game.

RHYME, RHYME, RHYME

One player begins the game by saying a simple word, such as "mouse." The next player must say another word that rhymes, like "house." Each person takes turns rhyming the original word. When no one can think of a new word that rhymes, the group goes on to a new word.

SEE AND TELL

A leader asks each person about what they see while waiting in line. Some sample questions: What is the smallest thing you see? What is the prettiest thing you see? What is the brightest thing you see? Other things to look for: tallest, shortest, fattest, skinniest, strangest, funniest, saddest, etc.

STORYTELLING

Children are born storytellers. Encourage kids in your group to create tales based on park characters, rides or situations. If you saw Cinderella yesterday, let your child tell you what Cinderella is doing today while you're visiting SeaWorld—or what a visit to SeaWorld would be like with Cinderella.

COMMON FEATURES

How many people can you find wearing Mickey Mouse ears? How many people have braces? Count them. If you're in line at a ride, count the number of people with black hair, children with cameras, people with hats on. . . . You get it? Add to the fun by guessing the number of people you'll find in each category in five minutes.

HANG LOOSE

Here's an easy way to loosen up while standing in line. Have every player rub their head and pat their leg at the same time. Then have them touch their nose and their back at the same time. Next, have them lift their right leg and grab it with their left hand. Improvise other variations on this theme. Another familiar version is "Simple Simon Says."

QUESTIONS, QUESTIONS

What better way to pass the time than by discussing the highlights of your trip? One player asks the others a variety of questions such as: What is the best beach you've seen? Where is the prettiest place you've been? What is the best ride in all the parks?

COLOR ME PURPLE

One player picks a color and other members of the group try to identify it by asking questions. Each player is allowed to ask up to three questions before making their choice. Example: Do you see lots of people wearing this color? Are there fruits this color? Is it the color of a grape?

CHALLENGES

Create challenges for your children. Here are four examples: Take ten hops with the left foot then another ten with the right. Count backward from 20. Take as many steps as possible to get from one place to another. Hold your breath for the duration of the song "Zip-A-Dee-Doo-Dah."

20 QUESTIONS

The first player chooses an object. The other players then have (surprise) 20 questions to figure out what the object is. Each question has to be answerable by "yes" or "no." And remember, guesses count toward the 20 questions! A good strategy is to ask general questions in the beginning, such as: Is it alive? Is it very big? Is it soft? As a variation on this classic game, limit the object to things within the theme park. Another alternative is to allow each person five questions. After five tries, the next player takes a turn. The game continues until one of the players comes up with the correct answer.

I SPY

This old favorite is a great guessing game. A player says "I spy something purple," referring to an object clearly visible to the other players. Then the other players ask questions to try to determine what the object is. I Spy can also be played by initially describing the shape, dimensions, smell or sound of an object.

GAMES FOR KIDS 6 TO 90

ODD MAN OUT

The object of this counting game is to avoid saying a particular number. To begin, pick a two-digit, odd number like 25. Go around the circle. The first player can count "1" or "1, 2"; then the next player picks up the count, adding one or two numbers to the progression. For example, the first participant says "1." The next says "2, 3." The third person can say either "4" or "4, 5." Continue until someone (the loser) ends up saying "25."

SWITCH HITS

Pick a simple word. The first player must either change a letter in the original word to make another word or create an anagram. For example, start with "BAT." The next player says "BAR" or "TAB." No repeating words!

Extra challenge: After completing a round, try reciting the sequence of words from last to first.

ALPHABET SOUP

When hunger pangs begin to strike, try moving down the food chain alphabetically. Each player repeats the choices of the previous person. Begin at "A" and continue until you get all the way down to "Z." Here's how: First player: "I'm fond of asparagus." Second player: "I'm dying for asparagus and beets." Third player: "I want asparagus, beets and chicken soup."

HINKY PINKY

This word game begins with a player selecting a secret rhyming phrase like "fat cat." The player then defines the phrase—with a clue like "obese feline" or "tubby tabby"—and tells how many syllables are in the rhyming words by saying "Hink Pink" for one syllable, "Hinky Pinky" for two syllables or "Hinkety Pinkety" for three syllables. The other participants try guessing the rhyming couplet.

How about these? What Santa would say during Christmas: "Remember December." An insane flower: "Crazy daisy."

PATTERN WORK

Players of this game use clues to discover a pattern. For example, you choose "double letters" as the pattern. Some clues you could give are: "Look at the crook" or "Poodles love noodles." Another example, a little easier for younger children, could be the letter "C": "He likes cats and canaries, cars and cartoons."

LINKING UP

Here's a way to bring everyone together. The first player mentions a film, book, celebrity or city. Successive players offer a concept linked to the previous one. Example: First player: Teenage Mutant Ninja Turtles. Second player: Pizza. Third player: Cheesy. Fourth player: Smelly. First player: Socks.

BUZZ

Here's a chance to review your multiplication tables. Pick a number between one and nine. That's the buzz-number. Start counting in sequence around the circle of players. When the multiple of the buzz-number comes up in sequence, the number must be replaced by the word "buzz." Players are out if they forget to say "buzz" or if they say it at the wrong time. Example: Pick multiples of 5. When 10, 15, 20, 25, etc. come up they should be replaced by "buzz."

THE POWER OF NEGATIVE THINKING

One person thinks of a funny activity like trying to catch a greased pig. Only negative hints can be used to describe the activity: "It really smells." "You slip and slide around a lot." "There's a lot of squealing." The player who comes up with the right answer suggests the next mystery activity.

ALPHABET MEMORY

Another fun game involves picking words alphabetically. For example, the first player chooses an "A" word, the second player selects a "B" word and the third player picks a "C" word. Each player must name all the words chosen previously. The game continues through the alphabet, with players being eliminated when they forget the sequence of words.

INTERNATIONAL GEOGRAPHIC

See how well you know your way around. The first player names a country. The second player must come up with a city that begins with the last letter of the previously named country. For example, Greenland might be followed by Denver and Portugal could be followed by London. Continue in sequence through your group.

SPELL CHECKER

Here's an easy game that's a great way to build vocabulary. Pick a word like "Lazy." Then have the players run through the alphabet. When you hit a letter that is in the designated word, say "check." For example: Instead of saying "A" the player will say "check." If you forget to say "Check" for the appropriate word you are out of the game.

COCONUTTING AROUND

Coconut is a noun, not a verb. But you can have a lot of fun with this word when you substitute it for a secret verb. Here's how: The contestant goes out of hearing range or covers his or her ears. Other members of the group pick a verb such as "swim." The contestant returns, and can ask up to 12 questions aimed at discovering the verb but must always use "coconut" in the question. For example: "Can you coconut at the beach?" or "Do kids like to coconut in the bath?" After the first contestant finishes, give everyone else a chance to guess other mystery verbs.

NAME THOSE RIDES

The first player starts by naming a theme park ride, such as Space Mountain, It's A Small World, etc. The next player must name a different ride, and the game continues with each person naming a new ride. Players have ten seconds to answer. A stumped player is excused from the game. The last person left wins!

You could also try naming Disney characters (Mickey Mouse, etc.), California cities (Los Angeles, San Diego) or movies (*The Lion King, Mulan*).

FANTASYLAND SEE AND TELL QUESTIONS

So you're waiting in line in the Magic Kingdom's Fantasyland. Ask your kids the following questions as you wait with anticipation for the line to move forward:

At Peter Pan's Flight

❖ In the scenes outside the ride, what color are the clouds?

❖ In the same scene, how many tepees are on the island?

❖ How many totem poles?

At It's A Small World

❖ How many of the following things can you find in the colorful panels outside this ride? Windmill. Flower. Castle tower. Archways. Nutcracker's face. Tree.

At Dumbo the Flying Elephant

❖ Each Dumbo is wearing a different color hat. How many colors can you spot?

❖ Can you find the little animal that befriends Dumbo?

❖ What do you see that made Dumbo think he could fly?

At Snow White's Scary Adventure

❖ In Snow White's forest scenes, what plant is sprinkled around the base of the big tree?

❖ What shape are the trees near the castle steps?

❖ Who is obviously missing from the forest?

TRIVIA CONTEST

1. Who follows the White Rabbit down the hole?
2. What makes Alice shrink and grow?
3. The butterflies Alice meets are shaped like what food?
4. Who was Dumbo's mother?
5. What's the merry tune you hear on the Dumbo ride?
6. Who was Captain Hook's bumbling sidekick?
7. Who are the children Peter Pan takes to Never-Never Land?
8. What did the crocodile swallow in Peter Pan?
9. Who was Mr. Toad's horse?
10. What did Mr. Toad trade his family mansion for?
11. What was the name of Mr. Toad's mansion?
12. Why was Mr. Toad arrested?
13. Who sang "When You Wish Upon a Star" in Disney's *Pinocchio*?
14. Princess Aurora is better known by what name?
15. What was the name of the boy who loved Woody and Buzz Lightyear in *Toy Story*?
16. Where does the DNA come from in the movie *Jurassic Park*?
17. What was the password for the D-Day invasion?
18. Who was the first voice of Mickey Mouse?
19. What kind of television characters were Britney Spears, Christina Aguilera and *NSync's Justin Timberlake?
20. Name Snow White's seven dwarfs.
21. How many natural enemies do killer whales have?
22. How many feathers do penguins have per square inch?
23. How many hairs per square inch does a sea otter have?
24. How many hours a day do pandas spend eating?
25. How many films has Universal Studios produced?

Answers:

1. Alice.   2. Eating or drinking.   3. Bread. They are called Bread and Butterflies.   4. Mrs. Jumbo.   5. "You Can Fly, You Can Fly, You Can Fly."   6. Mr. Smee.   7. Wendy, Michael and John.   8. A clock.   9. Cyril Proudbottom.   10. A stolen car.   11. Toad Hall.   12. For driving that stolen car!   13. Jiminy Cricket.   14. Sleeping Beauty.   15. Andy.   16. Mosquitoes fossilized in amber.   17. Mickey Mouse.   18. Walt Disney.   19. Mouseketeers.   20. Sneezy, Sleepy, Dopey, Doc, Grumpy, Happy and Bashful.   21. None.   22. Seventy.   23. 600,000.   24. Sixteen.   25. More than 8000.

ONE

Disney Dreaming

Decades old now but still a timeless wonder, Disneyland beckons as a real-life passage to Never-Never Land for the ever-ever young at heart. This purveyor of storybook illusions and cotton candy moods remains one of the most popular travel destinations in the world, drawing millions every year through the Disney door to indulge in its fountain of fantasy, to drink its dreams. Disneyland truly is the ultimate escape.

That Disney is a world unto itself is undisputed: The 85-acre park has dozens of shops, restaurants, a hotel and even its own fire department. But more than this, Disneyland is a state of mind. The Magic Kingdom has placed its stamp on the American psyche of three generations, sharing the dreams of one man with an entire nation. For here, in 1955, Walt Disney launched the world's first fantasy playground and started a Southern California phenomenon.

Disney sparked a fantasyland fever that spread throughout the Southland. Knott's Berry Farm, which first opened in 1920 as a modest roadside stand hawking berries and rhubarb, has evolved into a 150-acre theme park with 165 rides and attractions. And Six Flags California in Los Angeles made a name for itself with its acclaimed collection of thrill rides, including 11 hair-raising roller coasters.

Universal Studios Hollywood saw the potential in a Hollywood-style theme park where star-struck tourists could get a behind-the-scenes glimpse of television and film production. Today, Universal is a mammoth 420-acre complex complete with sound stages, theaters, exhibits and live-action shows that give audience members a chance to be sound engineers for a day or even star in a mock television drama.

Of course, Southern California is much more than amusement parks. You can supplement your theme-park tour with visits to many of the region's other attractions. Don't miss seeing the quintessential SoCal burgs of Newport Beach, Laguna Beach and Santa Monica. For healthy doses of history and culture, visit a historic Spanish mission, colorful Olvera Street and the Griffith Park observatory in Los Angeles. And for a bit of the eclectic and downright bizarre, don't forget Hollywood.

Then there is San Diego, which may well be the area's best-kept secret. The city boasts fine museums, award-winning restaurants, superb shopping and a thriving nightlife in downtown's renovated Gaslamp District. Just outside the burgeoning downtown lies more scenic reality. Blessed with an ideal climate and miles and miles of beautiful beaches, bays and parks, sunny San Diego is a year-round playground for both locals and tourists alike.

San Diego is also home to some of the best theme parks in the region. SeaWorld, the renowned aquatic wonderland, has called San Diego home since 1964. And the city also boasts not one, but two of the best collections of wild animals in the world: the San Diego Wild Animal Park and the famous San Diego Zoo.

This book, *Hidden Disneyland and Beyond*, takes you through Walt Disney's fantasy world, then shows you the beauty outside it. The focus throughout is on quality and value, the exemplary and the unique, while always keeping families in mind. Why families? Because every day, more and more travelers are choosing the family experience as parents and kids look to share what is offered here.

▼▼▼▼▼▼▼▼▼▼▼▼
Where to Go

Throughout this guide you'll discover the best of Southern California's "family friendly" establishments and attractions. You'll also find plenty of tips on saving time and money, as well as on special family needs such as babysitters, breast-feeding and stroller rentals. And the book's short feature articles and one-liner teasers give you insider information, providing local trivia and history and little-known hints at a glance.

Each of Southern California's major theme parks is featured in a separate chapter. There's *Disneyland*, the supreme fantasy factory. The place that children love best, this park of all parks features fanciful rides and scenes and happy vibes. Then there's the more down-home *Knott's Berry Farm*, where you can pan for gold or shoot the whitewater rapids.

But the unfolding chapters of this tourist extravaganza don't stop here. There's *Universal Studios Hollywood*, a dazzling fantasy park fashioned with thrilling movie scenes and rides and fabulous special effects. *SeaWorld* delves deep into the mysteries of the ocean and its inhabitants. The world's most popular oceanarium, it puts humans in touch with 16,000 creatures both big and small.

When you're waiting to try all those theme-park rides, you'll undoubtedly want to use *Games to Play While Waiting in Line*. This special fun section, which you'll find near the front of the book, features an assortment of games, poems and theme-park trivia to help pass the time in line.

Recommendations on lodging, campgrounds, dining, shopping and nightlife in and around the theme parks are found at the end of each of the theme park chapters.

Away from the parks, the *Orange County Day Trips*, *San Diego Day Trips* and *Los Angeles Day Trips* chapters span the entire Southern California coast, taking in the San Diego Zoo, San Diego

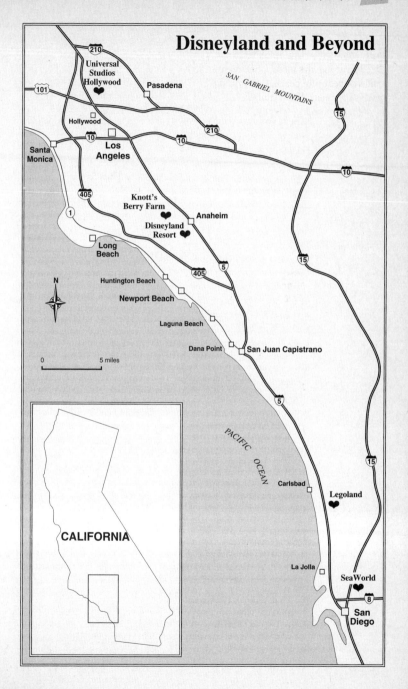

Disneyland and Beyond

Wild Animal Park, Six Flags California, picturesque towns and glorious scenery.

Travel here and you'll find yourself poised on the cusp of reality, a place where, on the same day, you can explore a castle with Cinderella and take a moonlight stroll on a wide, sandy beach. Where you can fly through anytown suburbia with E.T., then stroll a city street lined with postmodern restaurants and surreal shops. Where you can cruise through a concrete lagoon with brightly painted fish and spy dolphins at play in their natural habitat—the waves of the Pacific.

The ultimate paradox, Southern California is the keeper of both manmade empires and natural treasure. The treasure was there long before the empires. With a little luck and a lot of work, it just may stay a permanent part of the landscape.

SAMPLE ITINERARIES You'll be hard-pressed to see all of Disneyland in a single day. To get the most out of your trip, we recommend a three-day visit. Ideally, a Disney vacation should last seven days. Since Southern California has much to offer in the way of side trips, you can spend the remaining four days spent sightseeing along the coast or visiting other theme parks in Orange County, San Diego and Los Angeles. Don't make yourself crazy, though. There's nothing wrong with a casual afternoon spent lounging around the pool. Even the most energetic visitors get tired of pounding pavement ten hours a day. And the day spent at home will give drivers a break from the notorious Southern California traffic.

However long you stay, rarely do two visitors agree on how to see Disneyland and its neighboring theme parks. Still, there are good and bad ways to spend your days, and following a few touring guidelines can help make your vacation less of a hassle.

❖ **Arrive early.** Arriving as much as a half-hour before the official opening time, particularly if you don't already have park passes, is a good way to see the parks without crowds. But if you're a family of late sleepers, don't kill yourself. Too many folks approach the task of "seeing it all" as a job. But this is a *vacation*. Rousing the kids at the crack of dawn might get you on Dumbo faster. But it won't matter if the kids are already shedding tears of exhaustion.

❖ **Be realistic.** Don't try to cram too much in. Decide what you'd really like to see—and then cut that in half. Realize that it's impossible to see everything on your trip. That said, make sure to get everyone's "must do" attractions in so nobody feels cheated in the end. This guide's five-star rating system can help you decide what goes at the top (and bottom) of your list.

❖ **Be flexible.** The most miserable visitors are usually the ones trailing behind a devout itinerary wielder who marches the troops in formation from one ride to the next. Have a general idea of the order in which you'd like to do attractions, but don't be so glued to the schedule that you lose sight of the task at hand—having fun.

❖ **Accommodate the children.** Letting the little ones lead (instead of the grownups) can ease the stress factor enormously. On our first trip (when my children were 1 and 3), my husband and I decided to forego the big rides, instead enjoying the girls' delighted expressions and joyful imagination at the characters and scenery. Now that they're older, we revel in first rides on coasters and thrill rides. That's not to say you shouldn't have any fun.

> Take your children to the restroom before getting in a long line, especially at Dumbo!

❖ **Don't equate fun with finances.** Getting your money's worth means everybody had a good time. Resist the urge to pressure a child to experience a thrill ride (been there, done that—big mistake!). Equally important—avoid the common misstep of tearing a crying child away from something he's delighted with in order not to miss the "fun" of the event next on the schedule.

❖ **Feed the body as well as the soul.** Arriving with a full stomach will keep everybody happier. Eat meals in the park off peak. If you're splurging on a character breakfast (which usually involves vast amounts of food), make your reservation toward the later end of the meal (often 11 a.m. or so), which will carry you through the frenzied lunch hour (this will require, however, grabbing an earlier snack at the hotel).

To help you along, below are itineraries for a family spending four days at Disneyland and other theme parks, along with suggestions for fifth, sixth and seventh days if you have time for them.

For the first few days, we've given two choices: Disneyland for families with young children three to five years old, and Disneyland for families without young children. We've also provided two choices for the fourth day: Universal Studios Hollywood or SeaWorld.

These itineraries are guidelines, not marching orders. You may decide, for instance, to visit Disneyland for only one day. All itineraries assume you're staying at one of the three Disney hotels, or at a hotel just a few miles outside. If you're staying more than five miles away, you can take midday breaks at a Disney restaurant or Downtown Disney. And, however you plan your days, remember the Golden Rule of vacationing (with my apologies to the armed forces)—it's not a job, it's an adventure.

DAY ONE: DISNEYLAND
(with toddlers)

Early Morning Be on Main Street early—as soon as the park opens—to pick up maps, strollers and other touring essentials. Then proceed through Sleeping Beauty Castle to the heart of Fantasyland and ride, in this order:

Dumbo the Flying Elephant
King Arthur Carrousel
Snow White's Scary Adventure (may be scary for some youngsters)
Alice in Wonderland
Peter Pan's Flight (may be scary for some youngsters)
It's a Small World

Lunchtime   Head back to the hotel for lunch and a nap.

Afternoon   Return to Disneyland and take the *Disneyland Railroad* to Toontown station. Enter Mickey's Toontown and visit *Mickey's House, Minnie's House, Roger Rabbit's Car Toon Spin* and other attractions.

Late Afternoon to Early Evening   Board the *Disneyland Railroad* at the Toontown station. Ride to Tomorrowland. Disembark and check out the attractions around the *Astro Orbitor* queue area. Proceed to *Redd Rockett's Pizza Port* for a casual dinner.

If you have time after dinner (and aren't too exhausted), take the kids for a twinkling night ride on the *King Arthur Carrousel*.

DAY TWO: DISNEYLAND
(with toddlers)

Early Morning   Be on Main Street early again. When Disneyland opens, hop aboard the *Jungle Cruise* in Adventureland. Walk across to Tomorrowland and ride *Astro Orbitor* and *Autopia*. Head over to Fantasyland and ride the *Mad Tea Party* (no spinning the teacups). Then repeat other Fantasyland rides the kids like.

Lunchtime   Go to Frontierland and take a raft over to *Tom Sawyer Island*. Relax while the kids burn off some energy. Ride the raft back to the mainland, have a hot dog or a hamburger at the *Hungry Bear Restaurant*.

Afternoon   After lunch, exit Disneyland and take an afternoon break. Arrive back in time to see the live show at Frontierland (check the schedule for show times) in the late afternoon or early evening.

Evening   Here are some suggestions for the evening: (1) see a performance at the *Golden Horseshoe Stage* in Frontierland (2) have dinner at the *Blue Bayou* overlooking the *Pirates of the Caribbean*.

DAY ONE: DISNEYLAND
(without toddlers)

Early Morning   Be on Main Street early—as soon as it opens—to pick up maps and touring essentials. Head to Frontierland and make an afternoon reservation for the *Golden Horseshoe Stage*. Then make a mad dash to ride *Space Mountain*. Next head to Adventureland and ride *Indiana Jones Adventure* and *Jungle Cruise*.

Lunchtime   In New Orleans Square, enjoy an early lunch at the *French Market Restaurant* then try to beat the lines at *Pirates of the*

Caribbean and *Haunted Mansion*. Then exit Disneyland, and spend the afternoon relaxing.

Early Evening   Around 5 p.m., have dinner outside Disneyland, then return to the park.

Evening   Walk over to Fantasyland and go on *Mr. Toad's Wild Ride*, *Mad Tea Party*, *Matterhorn Bobsleds* and other rides. After *It's a Small World*, continue into Mickey's Toontown, tackling *Roger Rabbit's Car Toon Spin*, visiting *Mickey's House* and taking in the general atmosphere of this whimsical community. Lastly, go to Frontierland and ride *Big Thunder Mountain Railroad*—a great finale to any evening!

If it's during the summer or the holiday season, stay in the park for the fireworks display.

DAY TWO: DISNEYLAND
(without toddlers)

Early Morning   Arrive on Main Street early. Go directly to Tomorrowland and ride *Space Mountain* again. Then ride *Star Tours* and *Autopia*.

Mid-morning   Walk to New Orleans Square, stopping to repeat *Pirates of the Caribbean* or any other rides you'd like. Then stroll to Critter Country for *Splash Mountain* action.
Afterwards, hop aboard the nearby *Mark Twain Riverboat* in Frontierland for a relaxing cruise on the Rivers of America.

Lunchtime   While in Frontierland, see a performance at the *Golden Horseshoe Stage*. Then grab a bite to eat at the nearby *Stage Door Café*.

Afternoon   After lunch, ride the *Matterhorn Bobsleds* or re-ride favorite Fantasyland attractions. At 2 p.m., head over to Main Street for the character flood from the current parade. Afterwards, exit Disneyland.

> Walt Disney's private apartment was built above the fire station on Main Street. It is still used by the Disney family and as a VIP tea room.

Evening   Some options are: (1) to dine at the *Blue Bayou* overlooking those outrageous Caribbean pirates (2) have a candlelight dinner at Frontierland's *River Belle Terrace*.

DAY THREE: CALIFORNIA ADVENTURE
(with toddlers)

Early Morning   Be on the Sunshine Plaza early—as soon as the park opens—to pick up maps, strollers and other touring essentials. Stop by the Junior Explorer desk to obtain special maps designed for the kids. Visit Guest Services to get a priority seating for *Avalon Cove* (character dinner). Turn left into the Hollywood Pictures Backlot and visit:

Who Wants to Be a Millionaire—Play It! (if not show time yet, pick up FastPasses)

Jim Henson's Muppet*Vision 3D
Disney Animation

Grab a snack as you cross the Sunshine Plaza to Condor Flats.

Pick up FastPasses (or alternate riding singles) on *Soarin' Over California* (mom and dad should definitely do this ride, even if the kids are too small).

While waiting for FastPass time, visit *Redwood Creek Challenge Trail*.

Then visit *Soarin' Over California*.

Lunchtime   Head back to the hotel for lunch and a nap.

Afternoon   Head straight on into Flik's Fun Fair and visit:

Flik's Flyers
Tuck & Roll's Drive 'Em Buggies
Heimlich's Chew Chew Train
Francis's Ladybug Boogie
Princess Dot's Puddle Park

Walk across the Golden State and visit *Golden Dreams*.

Late Afternoon to Early Evening   Head to Paradise Pier. Then ride:

King Triton's Carousel
Golden Zephyr

Have dinner at *Avalon Cove*. If you're not too tired after dinner, take in *Disney's Electrical Parade*.

DAY THREE: CALIFORNIA ADVENTURE
(without toddlers)

Early Morning   Be on the Sunshine Plaza early—as soon as the park opens—to pick up maps, strollers and other touring essentials. If you have any kids with you, stop by the Junior Explorer desk to obtain special maps designed for younger visitors. Make

AFTERNOON DELIGHTS

On those hot summer afternoons, the last place you want to be is rubbing sweaty elbows in a crowded theme park. Instead, head for:

❖ Your air-conditioned hotel room (the children can nap while you catch an in-room movie).

❖ The Disneyland Hotel swimming pool where you can lay prone in the shade and slurp an icy drink.

❖ A Disneyland hotel restaurant. They're cool and uncrowded in the afternoon.

❖ The air-conditioned comfort of the Country Bear Playhouse, Pirates of the Caribbean, Haunted Mansion or a performance at the Golden Horseshoe Stage.

a priority seating dinner reservation at *ABC Soap Opera Bistro*. Turn left inside the park and head to Condor Flats. Grab a Fast-Pass for *Soarin' Over California*. Ride once. Use FastPass and ride again. Walk straight back through the park to Paradise Pier. Ride:

California Screamin'
Maliboomer
Mulholland Madness
Sun Wheel

Lunchtime Walk across the Pacific Wharf Bridge and enjoy lunch at any one of the counter-service eateries.

Afternoon Head to Hollywood Pictures Backlot. Pick up a Fast-Pass for *Who Wants to Be a Millionaire—Play It!* Digest lunch at *Disney Animation*. Head back for *Millionaire*. Visit *Jim Henson's Muppet*Vision 3D*.

Late Afternoon Head to *Grizzly River Run*. Dry off in *Golden Dreams*. Grab dinner at *ABC Soap Opera Bistro*.

Evening If you've still got energy, grab another ride on *Soarin' Over California*. And stick around for *Disney's Electrical Parade*.

DAY FOUR: KNOTT'S BERRY FARM

Early Morning Get to the park before it opens and as soon as the gates open head for *Boomerang*, then *Montezooma's Revenge*.

Mid-morning Stroll Camp Snoopy with small children. Older kids can do the rides in The Boardwalk section of the park, including *Supreme Scream* and *Perilous Plunge*, then head to the rides in Fiesta Village, including *Jaguar*.

Lunchtime Just before noon, head back toward the entrance and get in line at *Mrs. Knott's Chicken Dinner Restaurant* located outside the main gate in the *California MarketPlace*. There should not be more than a half-hour wait.

Early Afternoon If tots are tuckered out, take them for a whirl on the *Merry-Go-Round* or a relaxing circuit or two on the *Denver & Rio Grande Railroad*. This will constitute a full day for them. Others can walk over to Ghost Town, starting at the Wild Water Wilderness theme area and moving on to *Bigfoot Rapids,* possibly stopping by the *Wilderness Scramble*. Then, check out nearby *Mystery Lodge*.

Late Afternoon On a weekday, crowds will begin to thin, so head to any rides you haven't been on. On a Saturday, crowds will be at their peak so ride *Kingdom of the Dinosaurs* and stroll Camp Snoopy, which will be fairly empty. Then set off for The Boardwalk and ride *HammerHead*.

Evening Grab a tostada at the *Cantina* and watch the *Edison International ElectroBlast* show before you leave. If you have energy left, the shops in the *California MarketPlace* will remain open after the park closes.

DAY FIVE:
UNIVERSAL STUDIOS HOLLYWOOD OR SEAWORLD

UNIVERSAL STUDIOS HOLLYWOOD

Early Morning Plan on arriving at the park 30 minutes before it opens in order to purchase your admission ticket. This way you'll be on the first tram for the Studio Tour.

Mid-morning Hop off the tram and dash to the *Back to the Future* ride and then move on to a show at *WaterWorld* (schedule permitting).

Lunchtime Order a burrito from the *Hollywood Cantina* and stroll with it to *Mel's Diner* to hear the Doo Wop singers.

Afternoon Kids won't want to miss the *Rugrats Magic Adventure*. Those looking for a different adventure may want to ride *Jurassic Park*. Adults and older children should also work *E.T.* and/or *Backdraft* into their schedules.

Late Afternoon Take in any show you've managed to miss and check the *TV Audience Ticket Booth* for shows that might be taping that evening or the next day.

SEAWORLD

Early Morning Arrive just before the park opens. Once inside, pick up strollers, maps and other touring essentials at the Information Center. Look carefully at the show schedule to plan your day, but first head for either the *Dolphin Show* or the *Shamu Show*, depending on which one offers the earliest starting time. Be at the stadium 20 minutes early to secure seats up close.

Spend a day in a theme park and you've walked three to four miles. If you're not in good walking shape, better get moving!

Morning If you saw the *Dolphin Show* in the early morning, now see the *Shamu Show* (and vice versa). En route to that show stop by *Rocky Point Preserve* to feed the dolphins and watch the playful sea otters. Also swing by the *Forbidden Reef*, where you can feed bat rays and view moray eels.

Lunchtime Have a leisurely lunch at nearby *Mama Stella's Italian Kitchen* or over at the pleasant *Shipwreck Reef Cafe*.

Afternoon After lunch follow the path that circles the outer part of the park. Again, check your show schedule and plan to be at the other shows you want to see, as *Cirque de la Mer*, the *Sea Lion and Otter Stadium* and *Pets Rule!* are all along this path. Along the way you can beat the afternoon heat by spending time inside the cool buildings that house the aquariums and walk-through exhibits including the *Penguin Encounter* and *Shark Encounter*. Cool off also at the park's water ride, *Shipwreck Rapids*. If you're with toddlers who are getting antsy, take them for a romp through *Shamu's Happy Harbor*.

Evening If you visit during the summer season, get your hand stamped and leave the park for dinner. After dinner return to Sea-

World for *Mystique de la Mer*. Stroll through the park, enjoying the bands and acrobats and catch any shows you missed during the day. Stick around for the fireworks spectacular between 10 and 11 p.m. If you're visiting in the off-season, head to *Seaport Village* near downtown San Diego for dinner, then stroll through the shops and beautifully landscaped grounds.

OPTIONS FOR
DAYS SIX AND SEVEN

❖ In Orange County, explore the oceanfront towns of *Laguna Beach* and *Newport Beach*.

❖ Spend the day at the *San Diego Zoo*, the *San Diego Wild Animal Park* or *Legoland*. In the evening, head to San Diego's *Gaslamp Quarter* for dinner, then stroll through *Horton Plaza*.

❖ Visit *Griffith Park*, *Olvera Street* and other Los Angeles sights. Or go to Six Flags California and try the wild rides at *Six Flags Magic Mountain*. Then cool off and splash around at *Hurricane Harbor*.

When to Go

SEASONS

Timing is the key to a successful Disneyland visit. If you go during the busy season, you'll spend much of your vacation standing in lines and sitting in traffic. Plus, you'll pay top dollar for everything. One family who went to the Magic Kingdom on Easter Sunday (a peak day) calculated they spent six hours in line and only 35 minutes riding. By contrast, if you go when it's slow, your experience will be the opposite—a *real* vacation.

Unfortunately for families, the summer months—when the children are out of school—are high season. Holidays are also a bad time to visit. Disneyland has its worst crowd crunch from Christmas Day through New Year's Day. Thanksgiving weekend takes a close second, followed by the weeks surrounding Easter. During these frenzied days, Disneyland and Universal Studios are packed by mid-morning. Waits for rides and attractions run a minimum of 45 minutes and a maximum of two hours—not a pretty picture, especially when you have restless children who want to be entertained.

The very best time to visit Disneyland is after Thanksgiving weekend up to the week before Christmas. Other slow times: September and October and the second week of January through May (excluding holidays). As a rule, try to plan your visit in midweek; Tuesday, Wednesday and Thursday are the slowest days. Fridays through Mondays attract far more visitors.

CLIMATE

Southern California has an ideal Mediterranean climate with mild temperatures year-round. While the mercury rarely drops below 40 or rises much above 80, some months are more pleasant than others. August and September are the hottest and January and

February the coolest. And while rainfall is a rarity in this region, you can expect some showers from December to March. Smog is a big factor in Southern California. If you're sensitive to pollution, you may want to avoid visiting in August and September when it tends to be in greater concentration.

AVERAGE TEMPERATURES

	Avg. High Temp. (°F)	Avg. Low Temp. (°F)
January	65	47
February	67	49
March	68	50
April	70	53
May	72	56
June	77	60
July	82	64
August	83	65
September	81	63
October	77	59
November	73	52
December	67	48

CALENDAR OF EVENTS

JANUARY   **Los Angeles**   The **Tournament of Roses Parade** kicks off the **Rose Bowl** game in Pasadena on New Year's Day.

FEBRUARY   **Los Angeles**   The **Chinese New Year** celebration includes a spectacular Golden Dragon parade that snakes its way through Chinatown.

MARCH   **Orange County**   The **Fiesta de las Golondrinas** commemorates the return of the swallows to Mission San Juan Capistrano. Meanwhile, along the coast crowds gather for seasonal **grunion runs**.
San Diego   Kids of all ages flock to a grassy park by the sea for the **Ocean Beach Kite Festival**.

APRIL   **Knott's Berry Farm**   Special entertainment, food, and arts and crafts highlight the annual **Easter EggMazeMent** festival.
San Diego   **Lakeside Western Days** features a parade and a carnival.
Los Angeles   **Easter Sunrise Services** are marked at the famed Hollywood Bowl. In Little Tokyo **Buddha's Birthday** is celebrated; along nearby Olvera Street the **Blessing of the Animals**, a Mexican tradition, is re-enacted.

San Diego In Old Town, the **Cinco de Mayo** celebration is highlighted by mariachis, traditional Mexican folk dancers, Mexican food and displays. The **Pacific Beach Block Party** features food booths, artisans and live music.

MAY

Los Angeles Dancers, revelers and mariachi bands around Olvera Street and East Los Angeles mark **Cinco de Mayo**, the festival celebrating the Battle of Puebla in the French-Mexican War. The UCLA **Mardi Gras** offers games, entertainment and food. Little Tokyo honors kids with **Children's Day**, a two-day festival with arts, crafts and a parade.

San Diego The city kicks off the summer season with several events including the four-month-long **Festival** at the Old Globe Theater, where you can see classic and contemporary plays, and the wacky **Ocean Beach Street Fair and Chili Cookoff**.

JUNE

Los Angeles The Queen Mary Park in Long Beach comes alive with Cajun music, dance, food and family-friendly fun at the **Long Beach Bayou Festival**.

Orange County The **Arts Festival and Pageant of the Masters**, one of Southern California's most notable events, is in Laguna Beach.

JULY

Los Angeles The **Hollywood Bowl Summer Festival** explodes with a Fourth of July concert.

San Diego Concerts, festivals and special events mark **America's Finest City Week**.

AUGUST

Los Angeles Little Tokyo's annual **Nisei Week** honors Japanese-American culture with parades, dances, music and martial-arts demonstrations.

San Diego Downtown rocks to the sounds of more than 50 bands during **Street Scene**, the city's largest street festival. In Point Loma, the **Cabrillo Festival** commemorates the discovery of the California coast by Europeans.

SEPTEMBER

Los Angeles The **Los Angeles County Fair**, the nation's largest, offers music, food, carnival rides, livestock competitions and just about everything else you can imagine.

Knott's Berry Farm The entire park, rides and all, is transformed into one big spookhouse for a **Halloween Haunt** festival.

OCTOBER

San Diego In the San Diego area, the **La Mesa Oktoberfest** features Bavarian bands, beer gardens and arts and crafts.

Los Angeles Kids of all ages don masks of many cultures for a colorful parade highlighting the **International Festival of Masks**, held at Hancock Park.

San Diego In the San Diego area, families flock to El Cajon for the whimsical **Mother Goose Parade**.

NOVEMBER

Los Angeles   Santa arrives early at the **Hollywood Christmas Parade** and is joined by TV and movie stars. In Pasadena, the rollicking **Doo Dah Parade** parodies the city's more traditional Rose Parade.

DECEMBER   **Disneyland**   The Magic Kingdom hosts a month-long holiday celebration that includes a **Candlelight Procession** and the **Christmas Fantasy Parade**, starring 1000 carolers and a celebrity narrator.
Knott's Berry Farm   Seasonal events include the **Christmas Crafts Village** and the ice show **It's Christmas, Snoopy**.
Elsewhere   Several coastal communities, including San Diego, Huntington Beach, Long Beach and Marina del Rey, mark the season with **Christmas Boat Parades**. Latino communities in San Diego, Los Angeles and throughout the Southland celebrate the Mexican yuletide with **Las Posadas**.

▼▼▼▼▼▼▼▼▼▼▼▼
Before You Go

Nothing makes a trip more enjoyable than a little prep work. This goes for every family member. Parents can learn the layout of the theme parks and what each has to offer, thus avoiding confusion and hurried decision-making after they arrive. Preteens and teens who plan to sightsee on their own should definitely know how to get around. And young children can prepare (and get wildly excited) by reading Disney stories and watching the classic animated films. This helps acquaint them with characters and rides they'll see after they arrive. Some families rent Disney videos before their trip and hold movie nights. A few entertaining movies to rent: *Cinderella*, *Peter Pan*, *Alice in Wonderland*, *Dumbo*, *The Little Mermaid*, *Beauty and the Beast*, *Aladdin*, *The Lion King*, *Pocahontas*, *Tarzan* and *Mulan*.

Children should also be told about height restrictions. Certain rides require minimum heights, including Disneyland's Star Tours, Space Mountain, Splash Mountain and Big Thunder Mountain (all 40 inches) and Indiana Jones Adventure (46 inches). The theme parks strictly adhere to these rules. If your kids are too short to ride, it's best they know *before* you leave.

◆◆

BEST SEAT IN THE HOUSE

Riding in the front of the Disneyland Monorail is by far the best spot because you get wonderful views out the curved-glass windows as you're cruising through the air. Just as fun, you can sit with the driver and watch him work the control panels. The drivers are extra-friendly, offering Disney anecdotes and information on their favorite rides. To ride up front, just ask any attendant. If the crowds aren't too heavy, he or she will escort you to your own special waiting area. Happy monorailing!

There are two important rules to remember when packing for a **PACKING**
"Disneyland and Beyond" vacation: Pack light and pack casual.
Unless you plan to spend your trip dining in ultra-deluxe restaurants, all you'll need in the way of clothing are some shorts, lightweight shirts or tops, jeans or casual slacks, a sweater or sweatshirt for cool afternoons and evenings, a bathing suit and coverup and something relatively casual for any special event that might call for dressing up.

The rest of your luggage space can be devoted to a few essentials. These include a good hat and high-quality sunglasses. You should also take along plenty of strong sunscreen. Even the cloudiest winter days bring out that classic tourist look: scorched skin. A light jacket is a good idea for chilly nights.

Soft, comfortable, lightweight shoes are critical for foot survival. A theme-park visitor walks an average of four miles a day (often on blazing-hot concrete, no less), so you're going to need sole support. Tennis shoes are ideal for sightseeing; save the sandals and flip-flops for poolside.

If you're driving and have extra room, bring plenty of baby formula and disposable diapers. You can buy them inside the various theme parks, but you'll pay dearly. For those afternoon munchies, pack some snacks in ziplocked bags. Crackers, granola bars, the kids' favorite cereal and popcorn are a few that will hold up well. Juiceboxes are also great substitutes for carbonated soft drinks sold in the theme parks.

DISNEYLAND RESORT

VISITOR INFO

General Information: Disneyland Admissions Department, 1313 Harbor Boulevard, Anaheim, CA 92803; 714-781-4565; www.disneyland.com.

Disneyland Hotel Reservations: Disneyland Hotel, 1150 Magic Way, Anaheim, CA 92802; 714-778-6600; Paradise Pier Hotel, 1717 Disneyland Drive, Anaheim, CA 92802; 714-999-0990; Grand Californian Hotel, 1600 South Disneyland Drive, Anaheim, CA 92820; 714-635-2300.

KNOTT'S BERRY FARM

General Information: Guest Relations, Knott's Berry Farm, 8039 Beach Boulevard, Buena Park, CA 90620; 714-220-5200; www.knotts.com.

UNIVERSAL STUDIOS HOLLYWOOD

General Information: Guest Relations, Universal Studios Hollywood, 100 Universal City Plaza, Universal City, CA 91608; 818-508-9600; www.universalstudioshollywood.com.

SEAWORLD

General Information: Ticket Information, SeaWorld, 500 SeaWorld Drive, San Diego, CA 92109; 619-226-3901; www.seaworld.com.

SAN DIEGO ZOO
General Information: San Diego Zoo Guest Relations, P.O. Box 120551, San Diego, CA 92112; 619-234-3153; www.san diegozoo.org.

SAN DIEGO WILD ANIMAL PARK
General Information: San Diego Wild Animal Park Guest Relations, 15500 San Pasqual Valley Road, Escondido, CA 92027; 760-747-8702; www.sandiegozoo.org/wap.

SIX FLAGS CALIFORNIA
General Information: Guest Relations, Six Flags Magic Mountain, 26101 Magic Mountain Parkway, Valencia, CA 91385; 661-255-4100; www.sixflags.com.

PARK HOURS

Theme-park operating hours seem to change more often than the California tides, but this is to your advantage. Disneyland, Universal Studios Hollywood and SeaWorld all base their opening and closing times on the seasons. In general, operating hours are as follows:

❖ During the summer and holidays, the theme parks stay open late, usually closing at 10 p.m., 11 p.m. or midnight.

❖ In the winter, the parks close around 6 or 7 p.m.

❖ Last but most important: At Disneyland and other theme parks, advertised opening times are not always the real opening times. If the Disney folks expect crowds, they may open the park 30 to 60 minutes before the scheduled time. There's no way to anticipate this, but you can take advantage of it by being there early. We recommend arriving at least half an hour early at the theme parks.

TICKETS

DISNEYLAND There are several ticket options, called "Park Hoppers": one-, three- or four-day tickets and two different annual passes. If you are a resident of Southern California, you can

GETTING AROUND DISNEYLAND

Disneyland is so built up and spread out that it may seem intimidating at first. Not to worry. The Disney folks are quite practiced at getting visitors where they want to go. Theme-park exits are well marked on all the major roadways. And once you're inside Disneyland, all you have to do is follow the signs. Arriving in the park, you'll be given a detailed map showing the whereabouts of all rides and attractions. Several modes of transportation carry visitors between the different "lands": the Disneyland Railroad and the Monorail. The Monorail also stops at the Disneyland Hotel and the Paradise Pier Hotel, making it easy for families with toddlers to stop off for a mid-afternoon nap before returning to Disneyland for a second round of fun and games.

purchase an annual pass for $99. All tickets include admission and unlimited use of rides and attractions.

	Adults	Children 3–9
		(Under 3 years, free)
One-day Ticket	$45.00	$35.00
Three-day Park Hopper	$114.00	$90.00
Four-day Park Hopper	$141.00	$111.00
Deluxe Annual Passport	$159.00	$159.00
Premium Annual Passport	$219.00	$219.00

KNOTT'S BERRY FARM   You can opt for a day pass or for an annual pass. After 4 p.m. day passes are available at half price. The Premium Resort Passport includes admission to Knott's Soak City U.S.A.

	Adults	Children 3–11
		(Under 3 years, free)
One-day Ticket	$40.00	$30.00
Annual Passport	$109.95	$49.95
Premium Resort Passport	$159.90	$99.90

UNIVERSAL STUDIOS HOLLYWOOD   There are two ticket options: a one-day pass or an annual pass. There is also the Southern California Value Pass, a two-week dual park pass that allows multiple visits to Universal Studios and SeaWorld.

	Adults	Children 3–9
		(Under 3 years, free)
One-day Pass	$45.00	$35.00
Annual Pass	$54.00	$44.00
Two-week Pass	$79.00	$59.00

SEAWORLD   Admission options include a one- or two-day ticket and several different "passports" with various benefits attached.

	Adults	Children 3–11
		(Under 2 years, free)
One-day Ticket	$42.95	$32.95
Two-day Ticket	$46.95	$36.95
One-year Silver Passport	$74.95	$59.95
One-year Platinum Passport	$109.95	$89.95
Two-year Gold Passport	$124.95	$99.95

SAN DIEGO ZOO   There are two ticket options: a one-day ticket or an annual membership allowing unlimited visits to both the

San Diego Zoo and the San Diego Wild Animal Park. Annual membership is $84 for two adults in the same household, $66 for single adults, $25 for children 12 to 17 and $21 for children 3 to 11. Be forewarned: the website offers only a deluxe one-day ticket option that includes admission, the guided bus tour and a round-trip ride on the Aerial Tram. However, a simple entrance fee is payable at the gate.

	Adults	Children
		(Under 2 years, free)
One-day Ticket	$19.50	$11.75
Deluxe One-day Ticket	$32.00	$19.75

SAN DIEGO WILD ANIMAL PARK   Two ticket options are available: a one-day ticket or an annual membership allowing unlimited visits to both the San Diego Wild Animal Park and the San Diego Zoo. Annual membership is $66 for single adults, $84 for adult couples, $21 for children ages 3 to 11, and $25 for children ages 12 to 17.

	Adults	Children
		(Under 3 years, free)
One-day Ticket	$26.50	$19.50

SIX FLAGS MAGIC MOUNTAIN   Six Flags Magic Mountain offers visitors one-day and season passes. However, during most of the year they offer a "Twicket," which allows the bearer a second day of admission for a nominal fee.

	Adults	Kids under 48"
		(Under 2 years, free)
One-day Ticket	$42.99	$26.99
Two-park combo Ticket	$52.99	$52.99
Season Pass	$90.00	$90.00

SIX FLAGS HURRICANE HARBOR   You can purchase a ticket just for Hurricane Harbor, a combination ticket for Hurricane Harbor and Magic Mountain, or a season pass.

	Adults	Kids under 48"
		(Under 2 years, free)
One-day Ticket	$21.99	$14.99
Two-park combo Ticket	$52.99	$52.99
Season Pass	$70.00	$70.00

No matter which theme park you're visiting, the single most important ticket tip is to *buy ahead of time!* If you arrive with ticket in hand, you can avoid standing in long lines. Really, who wants to start their day with a 20-minute wait?

Some area hotels offer theme-park packages and will even help plan your itinerary; ask when you are making room reservations. Or you can order tickets before you leave home by mail, by telephone or online:

Disneyland Resort ~ 714-781-4043; www.disneyland.com

You must order *Knott's Berry Farm* tickets by mail. ~ Department 226, Knott's Berry Farm, 8039 Beach Boulevard, Buena Park, CA 90620; 714-220-5220.

Universal Studios Hollywood ~ 800-864-8377; www.universalstudioshollywood.com

SeaWorld ~ 619-222-6363; www.seaworld.com

San Diego Zoo ~ www.sandiegozoo.org

San Diego Wild Animal Park ~ www.sandiegozoo.org

Six Flags California ~ through Ticket Master, 213-480-3232; www.sixflags.com

Finally, remember that all ticket prices are subject to increase.

DISCOUNTS

Everyone who goes to Disneyland can get bargains. If you know where to look and whom to ask, you'll find discounts galore for restaurants, hotels, nightclubs and rental cars. Disneyland itself offers only minimal discounts for:

❖ Members of the Disney Club. Family membership costs $39.95 a year and includes parents and all children living at the same address. A variety of savings on lodging, dining, shopping and vacation packages are featured on a rotating monthly basis. Discounts change frequently; contact the club headquarters at 800-654-6347 or www.disneyclub.com.

❖ Southern California residents. During certain months residents receive up to 30 percent off Disneyland admission. Residents can also purchase a discounted annual pass. A Southern California driver's license is required for proof of residency.

❖ Those 60 or older. Seniors are granted a hefty discount all year long. A driver's license or passport is required for proof of age.

Universal Studios Hollywood and SeaWorld have similar discounts for Southern California residents and/or senior citizens. Check with each park for specifics of the discounts.

The best discounts are outside the theme parks. Remember that rates will always be the lowest during the off-season; during the summer you'll pay top dollar everywhere. Look for motel and hotel bargains advertised in the Sunday travel sections of major newspapers. Many are good deals, but some are not. Beware of cheap accommodations that say "close to Disney" but are really out in the boondocks. If the place is more than five miles away, forget it. You'll waste half your day getting to and from the parks. There are dozens of budget hotels in the blocks surrounding

Disneyland. Should you find accommodations here, you'll be able to walk to the park, saving yourself the cost and aggravation of parking. As a general rule, you're better off paying a few extra dollars for convenience and peace of mind.

VACATION PACKAGES

There are dozens of packages available for the Disneyland traveler. Whether to buy one depends on your individual needs. If you're flying into Orange County and staying at a Disney hotel, a package can probably save you money. Check for packages that combine airfare, accommodations, car rental and theme-park tickets; they often save up to 20 percent. Packages also clue you in on what your vacation is going to cost since you pay for much of it up-front. And they can eliminate a lot of "what are we going to do?" decisions.

On the downside, many packages come with extras you'll never use. Super-deluxe accommodation fees and meals in fancy restaurants represent lost dollars if you don't use them. Some of the Disneyland Hotel's packages, for instance, include everything from unnecessary in-room amenities and meals to access to the concierge lounge. For some families, these are useless, plus they take away the flexibility of being able to enjoy non-Disney restaurants and sights. The Walt Disney Travel Company does, however, offer packages that utilize a variety of Anaheim hotels and motels.

Above all, shop around. Travel agents can help compare package prices and options. Considering the intense competition among area hotels and attractions, you can't help but find a bargain.

LOCKERS & KENNELS

A locker can be a lifesaver. Great for stowing extra items such as jackets, packages and diaper bags, they're available for a small fee at all the big theme parks.

Disneyland kennels offer convenient, inexpensive day lodging for pets. Besides Fido and Fluffy, the kennels also accept many unusual boarders such as snakes, birds, hamsters, rabbits and goldfish. If your pet falls into the "unusual" category, bring its cage. Kennels are located just outside the main entrance and cost $10 per pet, per day.

There are complimentary kennel facilities for dogs and cats at Universal Studios and Six Flags California.

CREDIT CARDS

Don't leave home without your plastic; at Disneyland, you're gonna need it. The major cards—Visa, MasterCard, American Express, Diners Club and Discover—are accepted throughout Disneyland and surrounding attractions. However, some theme-park vendors and fast-food restaurants do not take credit cards. There are ATMs located inside every park.

CAMERAS

What would a trip to Disneyland be without photographs? Whether you take your camera or camcorder (or both), you will have plenty of opportunities to get those classic Disney shots. Bring your own film and video tapes; you can buy them inside the theme parks—but at premium prices. If you forgot your equipment, you can buy disposable cameras at Disneyland's Main Street Photo Supply Co., which also offers two-hour and overnight film developing. Disposable cameras can also be found at Snoopy's Boutique in Knott's Berry Farm, and at photo and gift shops throughout the other parks.

Flash photography is not allowed in most theme-park theaters and in many indoor rides, but other than these few restrictions, there's hardly a bad place to take pictures inside the area's theme parks. Here are some extra-choice spots for great shots of the kids:

❖ On the bridge in front of Sleeping Beauty Castle (Disneyland)

❖ On Dumbo, before takeoff (Disneyland)

❖ In front of the Mickey Mouse floral portrait located just inside the main entrance (Disneyland)

❖ With Mickey Mouse inside his Toontown house (Disneyland)

❖ With the Doo Wop singers in front of Mel's Diner (Universal Studios)

❖ With Jaws, in the Amity town square (Universal Studios)

❖ Feeding the dolphins, at the Rocky Point Preserve (SeaWorld)

STAR SYSTEM

One of the primary goals of this book is to help you sort through the overwhelming number of theme-park attractions, so we have judged them by originality, imagination, design and *overall* family appeal. Obviously, family members aren't always going to agree on the "best" rides, so we've geared our ratings toward the people in charge: the parents. For instance, some rides popular with young children received low ratings because they don't appeal to adults or even older children. In the "Tips" section for each ride, however, we'll point out if it's particularly popular with toddlers or other age groups.

◆◆◆

DISNEY DOLLARS

Leave it to Disney to come up with its own money. As if your own greenbacks aren't good enough, Disneyland offers visitors "Disney dollars." Here's how they work: When visitors enter the theme parks, they can exchange their own U.S. currency for Disney bills, dollar for dollar. Disney dollars are good at restaurants and stores throughout Disneyland. Of course, there's no logical reason to buy Disney dollars. They're not more convenient than real money, and they don't provide any discounts. They can, however, tempt you to spend more. Says one mother: "Disney dollars seemed like play money. I could spend them with wild abandon—something I'd never think of doing with my own money."

One Star signifies "one to be missed," a dullsville attraction that's a waste of time. *Two Stars* means below average, but with some redeeming entertainment value. *Three Stars* indicates an average attraction, one that shows at least a little imagination but may not appeal to the majority of visitors. *Four Stars* signifies above average, offering ingenuity, fantasy and top-notch design. *Five Stars* is "not to be missed," a very popular, state-of-the-art attraction that makes you want to ride over and over and over.

LODGING

The Anaheim area, especially the few blocks surrounding Disneyland, offers a smorgasbord of lodging possibilities. In keeping with the Disneyland fantasy, most of the budget-priced motels and inns are built around some kind of theme, much to the delight of children. You'll find cowboy-style lodges, motels named after storybook characters and curious futuristic inns designed for an atomic age. Most sprung up during the Disney boom of the '50s and '60s and could use some renovation. Many offer bland facilities at low prices and are fine if you're economizing and don't plan to spend much time in your room.

No matter where you stay, you should book well in advance, as these budget rooms go fast. During high season, we recommend making your reservation several months ahead of time.

In *Hidden Disneyland and Beyond*, we have chosen the best family-oriented accommodations that each area has to offer. You'll find detailed hotel descriptions toward the end of each chapter.

To help suit your budget, we've organized the accommodations according to price. Rates referred to are high-season, so if you are looking for low-season bargains, it's good to inquire.

Budget hotels are generally less than $60 per night for two adults and two children; the rooms are clean and comfortable but lack luxury. The *moderate* hotels run $60 to $120 and provide larger rooms, plusher furniture and more attractive surroundings. At a *deluxe* hotel you can expect to spend between $120 and $175 for two adults with children. You'll check into a spacious, well-appointed room with all modern facilities; downstairs, the lobby will be a fashionable affair, and you'll usually see a restaurant, lounge and a cluster of shops. If you want to spend your time in the finest hotels, try an *ultra-deluxe* facility, which will include all the amenities and cost over $175.

CAMPING

For families, camping is a great way to stay in the Orange County area. First and foremost, it saves money. Not only is camping much less expensive than staying in a hotel, but it also saves on food bills. By cooking some of your own meals, you avoid falling into the trap of eating overpriced theme-park food three times a day. Camping also provides a physical and mental break from the rigors of theme-park touring. Best of all, most campgrounds are family oriented, providing plenty of outdoor activities for all ages.

Campers will need basic cooking equipment and, except in the winter, can make out fine with only a lightweight sleeping bag and a tent with good screens and a ground cloth. A canteen, first-aid kit, flashlight, mosquito repellent and other routine camping gear should also be brought along.

For campground information see "Camping" in the Disneyland chapter and "Beaches & Parks" in Chapters Seven and Eight.

DINING

It seems as if Southern California has as many restaurants as people. To help you decide on this army of eateries, we've organized them according to family appeal and cost with price ratings of budget, moderate, deluxe or ultra-deluxe. Lunch and dinner are served unless otherwise noted.

Dinner entrées at *budget* restaurants usually cost $9 or less. The ambience is informal, service usually speedy and the crowd often a local one. *Moderate*-priced restaurants range between $9 and $18 at dinner; surroundings are casual but pleasant, the menu offers more variety, and the pace is usually slower. *Deluxe* establishments tab their entrées from $18 to $25; cuisines may be simple or sophisticated, depending on the location, but the decor is plusher and the service more personal. *Ultra-deluxe* dining rooms, where entrées begin at $25, are often the gourmet places; here, cooking has become a fine art, and the service should be impeccable.

On a diet? All the major theme parks offer light, low-calorie fare. Check with Guest Relations at each park.

Some restaurants change hands often and are occasionally closed in low seasons. In every instance, we've endeavored to include places with established reputations. Breakfast and lunch menus vary less in price from restaurant to restaurant than evening meals.

TRAVELING WITH CHILDREN

Strollers A stroller is a must inside a theme park. If you don't bring your own, you can rent one at any theme park. We recommend using a stroller for children younger than three. At Disneyland, it's nice to start the day without one, then pick one up later as little legs start to give out. Keep the paperwork; stolen rental strollers are replaced free of charge with a receipt.

Babysitters Guests of the Disneyland Hotel and the Paradise Pier Hotel who need a sitter are given a list of recommended licensed sitters upon arrival. The sitters, who will watch your child right in your own room, charge about $8 to $10 per hour, with an additional fee for additional children. Reservations should be made a day in advance. Call the hotels for more information. ~ 714-778-6600 (Disneyland Hotel); 714-999-0990 (Paradise Pier Hotel). The Grand Californian Hotel offers a nightly children's activities center, open from 5 p.m. to midnight, for children 5 to 12. There is a charge of $9 per hour per child; dinner is $5 extra. Call ahead for reservations. ~ 714-956-6755.

Baby Services   Available in Disneyland, Baby Services offers quiet, dimly lit rooms with changing tables and comfortable rock-ers for nursing. High chairs, bibs, pacifiers, for-mula, cereal and jars of food are also on hand for a fee. Disposable diapers are available here and in restrooms. Most other theme parks offer changing tables in the restrooms, but other services and supplies are limited, so be prepared.

> To make traveling time go faster, take along audio tapes of classic Disney stories.

Nursing Nooks   Disneyland's relaxed family atmosphere and abundance of cool, dark attractions make it a good place to discreetly nurse an infant. In the Magic Kingdom, try the theaters at the Disneyland Opera House and Fantasyland. For those apprehensive about these locations, there are comfort-able rocking chairs at the Baby Services area. Knott's Berry Farm offers three nursing rooms throughout the park. Other theme parks generally provide changing tables.

DISABLED TRAVELERS   For the most part, Disneyland and the surrounding theme parks are easily accessible to travelers with disabilities. Attractions fea-ture wide, gently sloped ramps, and restrooms and restaurants are designed with persons with disabilities in mind. Wheelchairs and motorized three-wheel vehicles are available for rent at the en-trance to every theme park. For hearing-impaired guests, Disney-land offers written descriptions of most attractions. For a small deposit, sight-impaired guests can borrow portable tape recorders and cassette tapes with narrative on each attraction. Check at the Guest Relations desk.

The California Department of Motor Vehicles provides spe-cial parking permits for the disabled (check the phone book for the nearest location). Many bus lines and other public-transit fa-cilities are wheelchair accessible.

There are also agencies in Southern California assisting dis-abled persons. For tips and information about the Orange County and Los Angeles area, contact the **Westside Center for Independent Living**. ~ 12901 Venice Boulevard, Los Angeles; 310-390-3611; www.wcil.org. In the San Diego area, try the **Access Center**. ~ 1295 University Avenue, Suite 10, San Diego; 619-293-3500; www.accesscentersd.org.

There are numerous national organizations offering general information. Among these are the **Society for Accessible Travel & Hospitality** ~ 347 5th Avenue, Suite 610, New York, NY 10016, 212-447-7284, fax 212-725-8253, www.sath.org; and **Flying Wheels Travel** ~ 143 West Bridge Street, Owatonna, MN 55060, 507-451-5005. **Travelin' Talk** is a networking organization that also provides assistance. ~ P.O. Box 1796, Wheat Ridge, CO 80034;

303-232-2979; www.travelintalk.net. They also run **Access-Able Travel Service,** which has worldwide information online. ~ www.access-able.com.

Or consult the comprehensive guidebook, *Travel for the Disabled: A Handbook of Travel Resources and 500 World Wide Access Guides,* by Helen Hecker (Twin Peaks Press).

Be sure to check in advance when making room reservations. Many hotels and motels feature facilities for those in wheelchairs.

SENIOR TRAVELERS

As millions have discovered, Southern California is an ideal place for older vacationers, many of whom turn into part-time or full-time residents to take in the mild climate. Many destinations offer significant discounts, and off-season rates make the area exceedingly attractive for travelers on limited incomes. Throughout much of the year, visitors 60 and older enjoy discounts at most theme parks and attractions. The Golden Age Passport, which must be applied for in person, allows free admission to national parks and monuments for anyone 62 and older.

The **American Association of Retired Persons** (AARP) offers membership to anyone over 50. AARP's benefits include travel discounts and escorted tours. ~ 3200 East Carson Street, Lakewood, CA 90712; 562-496-2277; www.aarp.org.

Elderhostel offers reasonably priced, all-inclusive educational programs in a variety of Southern California locations throughout the year. ~ 11 Avenue de Lafayette, Boston, MA 02111; 617-426-8056; www.elderhostel.org.

Be extra careful about health matters. In addition to the medications you ordinarily use, it's a good idea to bring along the prescriptions for obtaining more. Consider carrying a medical record with you—including your medical history and current medical status as well as your doctor's name, phone number and address. Make sure your insurance covers you while away from home.

FOREIGN TRAVELERS

Passports and Visas Most foreign visitors are required to obtain a passport and tourist visa to enter the United States. Contact your nearest United States Embassy or Consulate well in advance to obtain a visa and to check on any other entry requirements.

Customs Requirements Foreign travelers are allowed to carry in the following: 200 cigarettes (1 carton), 50 cigars, or 2 kilograms (4.4 pounds) of smoking tobacco; one liter of alcohol for personal use only (you must be 21 years of age to bring in the alcohol); and US$100 worth of duty-free gifts that can include an additional quantity of 100 cigars. You may bring in any amount of currency but must fill out a from if you bring in over US$10,000. Carry any prescription drugs in clearly marked containers. (You may have to produce a written prescription or doctor's statement for the customs officer.) Meat or meat products, seeds, plants, fruit and narcotics cannot be brought into the United States. Contact the

U.S. Customs Service for further information. ~ 1300 Constitution Avenue Northwest, Washington, DC 20229; 202-927-6724;
www.customs.treas.gov.

Driving   If you plan to rent a car, an international driver's license should be obtained *before* arriving in California. Some rental
companies require both a foreign license and an international driver's license. Many car-rental agencies require a lessee to be 25
years of age; all require a major credit card. Remember: Seat belts
are mandatory for the driver and all passengers. Children under
the age of five or under 40 pounds should be in the back seat in
approved child-safety restraints.

Currency   United States money is based on the dollar. Bills
come in denominations of $1, $5, $10, $20, $50 and $100. Every
dollar is divided into 100 cents. Coins are the penny (1 cent),
nickel (5 cents), dime (10 cents) and quarter (25 cents). Half-dollar
and dollar coins are rarely used. You may not use foreign currency
to purchase goods and services in the United States. You may,
however, exchange your currency at the Starcade, City Hall or
Bank of Main Street (all inside Disneyland on Main Street) or at
the Disneyland Hotel or Paradise Pier Hotel front desks. All other
theme parks have limited exchange facilities, so you should arrive
at the parks already armed with credit cards and U.S. dollars.

Language Assistance   Disneyland provides translated guides and
maps for many attractions. Check with Guest Services inside
each park; most have foreign-language maps.

Electricity and Electronics   Electric outlets use currents of 110
volts, 60 cycles. For appliances made for other electrical systems,
you need a transformer or other adapter. Travelers who use lap-
top computers for telecommunication should be aware that modem
configurations for U.S. telephone systems may be different from
their European counterparts. Similarly, the U.S. format for video-
tapes is different from that in Europe; U.S. Park Service visitors
centers and other stores that sell souvenir videos often have them
available in European format on request.

Weights and Measures   The United States uses the English system of weights and measures. American units and their metric
equivalents are: 1 inch = 2.5 centimeters; 1 foot (12 inches) = 0.3
meter; 1 yard (3 feet) = 0.9 meter; 1 mile (5280 feet) = 1.6 kilometers; 1 ounce = 28 grams; 1 pound (16 ounces) = 0.45 kilogram;
1 quart (liquid) = 0.9 liter.

▼▼▼▼▼▼▼▼▼▼▼▼▼

Transportation

CAR

Route 5 will be the main transit corridor during your
Disney vacation. Connecting Los Angeles with San
Diego, it passes right through Anaheim near the outskirts of Disneyland—you can even spot the famous Matterhorn
from the freeway. Farther south, Route 5 passes through Santa
Ana, Dana Point and San Clemente, and though it travels inland
at times, feeder highways to the beach towns are clearly marked

and easy to follow. Several other major highways crisscross Orange County. **Route 1,** known in this area as Pacific Coast Highway, ends its long journey down the California coast in Capistrano Beach. A few miles farther inland, **Route 405** runs from Long Beach to Irvine, with feeder roads leading to the main coastal towns.

AIR

John Wayne International Airport, located in Santa Ana, is the main gateway to Disneyland and Orange County. Major carriers presently serving it include Alaska Airlines, Aloha Airlines, America West, American Airlines, Continental Airlines, Delta Air Lines, Northwest Airlines, Southwest Airlines, United Airlines and USAirways. ~ www.ocair.com.

BUS

Greyhound Bus Lines (800-231-2222; www.greyhound.com) serves Southern California, stopping in Anaheim, Santa Ana, San Juan Capistrano, San Clemente, Oceanside, San Diego and Los Angeles. Most stops are flag stops; depots are located in Anaheim (100 West Winston Road; 714-999-1256), Santa Ana (1000 East Santa Ana Boulevard; 714-542-2215), San Clemente (2421 South El Camino Real; 949-366-2646), San Diego (120 West Broadway; 619-239-3266) and Los Angeles (1716 East 7th Street; 213-629-8401).

The **Los Angeles County Metropolitan Transit Authority,** or MTA, serves some areas of Orange County and stops at Disneyland and Knott's Berry Farm. ~ 213-626-4455; www.mta.net.

TRAIN

Amtrak's "San Diegan" travels between Los Angeles and San Diego, with Orange County stops at Fullerton, Anaheim Stadium, Santa Ana, San Juan Capistrano and San Clemente. ~ 800-872-7245; www.amtrak.com.

CAR RENTALS

Arriving at John Wayne International Airport, you'll find the following car-rental agencies: **Alamo Rent A Car** (800-327-9633), **Avis Rent A Car** (800-331-1212), **Budget Rent A Car** (800-527-0700), **Enterprise Car Rentals** (800-736-8222), **Hertz Rent A Car** (800-654-3131) and **National Car Rental** (800-227-7368).

Remember: the closer you are to Disneyland, the more expensive the gas will be. Fill up before you get there.

CAR TROUBLE?

If your car breaks down at Disneyland, Universal Studios or SeaWorld, a security officer will come to the rescue. Security vehicles patrol the parking lots, making rounds every five to ten minutes. Simply hail one of the vehicles, which resemble police cruisers. The officers will either start your car or call someone who can.

TWO

Disneyland

It bills itself as "the happiest place on earth," and over 15 million annual visitors will cheerfully agree that Disneyland is without question the most magical 85 acres they know of. On a hot summer day the park often plays host to as many as 60,000 people enchanted by the fairy-tale architecture, whimsical artistry, flourishing gardens and state-of-the-art attractions. Whether you are 6 or 60, Walt Disney's personal stamp of ingenuity will suite you to the letter. The brilliant cartoonist pushed make-believe to its limit, devising a fictional kingdom woven with cartoon characters, simulated towns and jungles, lighthearted music, squeaky clean streets, shimmering lakes and thrilling rides all spun into one colorful, jubilant experience.

Disneyland is fashioned with 63 major attractions, 33 restaurants and 55 shops spread across eight imaginative and vastly different "lands." The most popular is Fantasyland, a dreamy web of storybook architecture, boat rides, carousels and merry music. Adventureland, with its thatch-roofed buildings, jungle journey and stand of huge natural bamboo, offers a tame trek through the wilds of Africa, the South Pacific and the Caribbean and a thrilling expedition through the Temple of the Forbidden Eye.

Frontierland presents a rocky, desert profile in the exciting realm of pioneers and the Old West. Critter Country is as down-home and backwoods as the Brer beings that live there. In contrast, Tomorrowland evokes a completely different era, albeit an imaginary one, with geometric buildings and "Buck Rogers" design and feel. It's home to Star Tours, one of the park's most popular rides. New Orleans Square, filled with ghosts, pirates and quaint shops, is yet another contrast with its intricate wrought-iron trim and turn-of-the-20th-century atmosphere.

Then there's Main Street U.S.A., the key to the Magic Kingdom and the first sight that greets visitors. Brick streets, old-fashioned lampposts and intricate building facades create a wonderful facsimile of an idealized American town. There's also the colorful depot for the Disneyland Railroad, an old-fashioned steam train that chugs around the perimeter of the park. Just beyond is a small circular park called Central Plaza with shady benches and beds of colorful flowers. Each evening at dusk the American flag that flies in the Town Square is taken down in an unabashedly patriotic ceremony. No matter where they're hurrying to, guests inevitably take a moment to join in The Star-Spangled Banner. The magnificent Sleeping Beauty Castle rises ahead, a constant photo spot as guests pose with the castle's fairy-tale spires and turrets in the background.

The Mickey Mouse flower "portrait" at the park's main entrance is planted nine times a year.

Each area's remarkable attention to detail, from the decorated trash cans to employee costumes and clever restaurant menus, continues to inspire admiration in even frequent visitors. There is unbridled pleasure in immersing yourself in the mood of one land, then being transformed by the aura of a thoroughly different realm. Even on the worst days, when the park is crushed with people and heat threatens to suffocate, it is impossible to elude the spirit of Disneyland.

Nighttime brings more illusions to the kingdom, as beads of light trace intricate rooflines and the Matterhorn glows high in the sky. Summer evening are the most festive: spirited music pulsates from parades, costumed singers pour through the streets and fireworks spray the sky.

There are other theme parks in Southern California. But Disneyland remains the ultimate reality escape for children and provides a spot where adults can think like kids. It's a place that tugs at the hearts of dreamers and even impresses those skeptics who chide its corny humor, conservative overtones and idealistic approach.

Anyone who has experienced the fascination of Sleeping Beauty Castle, the adrenaline rush of Star Tours or the happy vibes of It's a Small World knows the Magic Kingdom has no parallel.

Nuts & Bolts

ARRIVAL

Getting to Disneyland is not a problem, except on summer weekends when lines waiting at the entrance can back up at the park's entrance. The parking lot opens an hour before the park does. Call 714-781-4565 or visit www.disney land.com to verify.

From Area Hotels: Most offer complimentary shuttle service.

From the Disney hotels: The Disneyland Monorail entrance is located in Downtown Disney, a short walk from the Disneyland Hotel and the Paradise Pier Hotel. The Grand Californian Hotel is just steps away from both Disneyland and California Adventure.

By Car: The park is approximately 27 miles south of downtown Los Angeles on Route 5. Follow the signs to the Disneyland main entrance.

At the parking lot you'll pay a fee and enter a six-story parking structure. Be sure to note your parking space because it's easy to lose your car in this giant place. A tram will take you to the main entrance where you'll purchase your ticket.

TICKETS

Disneyland offers several ticket options: one-day, single-park tickets; three-day or four-day dual-park tickets; and two different annual passes. Southern California residents can purchase discounted annual passes for $99 (proof of residency required), though black-out dates eliminate more than a third of the year. All tickets include admission and unlimited use of rides and attractions. Annual passes allow entry to both parks and provide a variety of discounts and special perks.

	Adults	Children 3–9
		(Under 3 years, free)
One-day Ticket	$45.00	$35.00
Three-day Park Hopper	$114.00	$90.00
Four-day Park Hopper	$141.00	$111.00
Deluxe Annual Passport	$159.00	$159.00
Premium Annual Passport	$219.00	$219.00

GAME PLAN If at all possible, avoid Disneyland like the plague on a Saturday. Crowds are huge, and between 10 a.m. and 3 p.m. expect up to an hour-and-a-half wait at popular rides such as Indiana Jones Adventure, Star Tours and Space Mountain. Even a Sunday is better, and during the week many rides have more bearable wait times. The most crowded days of the year, according to park officials, are the 4th of July, Christmas week and New Year's.

Regardless of the day of the week it is advisable to arrive well before opening and head for Main Street, which opens 30 minutes before the rest of the park on days when the park opens after 8 a.m. Call ahead: 714-781-7290; www.disneyland.com. Here you can rent a stroller or locker, obtain maps and reservations, see "Great Moments with Mr. Lincoln" and get your game plan in order. As soon as the rope is dropped, angle to your right to Tomorrowland and you will be one of the first on either Space Mountain or Star Tours.

As soon as you're off one, speed to the other (which will be 30 seconds away). Having polished off those two, you can now dash across the park to the Haunted Mansion and Pirates of the Caribbean, two other attractions that develop lines quickly. This puts you in a perfect position to ride the Indiana Jones Adventure. If you do it right, you will have ridden five major attractions within the first two hours of opening time, and you can see the rest of the park at a more relaxed pace. Don't feel silly doing the "Tomorrowland Dash." You'll find yourself competing with sprinting kids, galloping teens and even grandparents bent on being among the first in line.

Other strategies to consider are the following:

❖ After you've hit the major rides for the day, try to see all of one "land" before moving to another. Otherwise you'll miss something, and it's time-consuming to move backward.

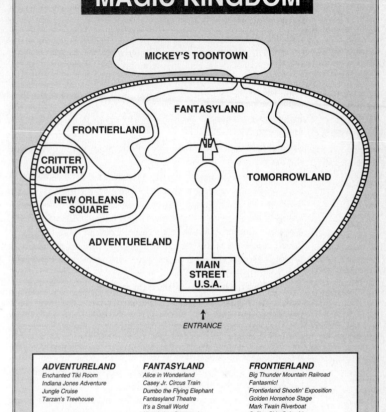

MAGIC KINGDOM

MICKEY'S TOONTOWN

FANTASYLAND

FRONTIERLAND

CRITTER COUNTRY

TOMORROWLAND

NEW ORLEANS SQUARE

ADVENTURELAND

MAIN STREET U.S.A.

↑
ENTRANCE

ADVENTURELAND
Enchanted Tiki Room
Indiana Jones Adventure
Jungle Cruise
Tarzan's Treehouse

MAIN STREET U.S.A.
City Hall
Disneyland Railroad
Main Street Cinema
Penny Arcade
The Walt Disney Story Featuring
  "Great Moments with Mr. Lincoln"

TOMORROWLAND
Astro Orbitor
Autopia
Disneyland Monorail
Honey, I Shrunk the Audience
Innoventions
Space Mountain
Star Tours

FANTASYLAND
Alice in Wonderland
Casey Jr. Circus Train
Dumbo the Flying Elephant
Fantasyland Theatre
It's a Small World
King Arthur Carrousel
Mad Tea Party
Matterhorn Bobsleds
Mr. Toad's Wild Ride
Peter Pan's Flight
Pinocchio's Daring Journey
Sleeping Beauty Castle
Snow White's Scary Adventures
Storybook Land Canal Boats

MICKEY'S TOONTOWN
Chip 'n Dale Treehouse
Donald Duck's Boat
Gadget's Go Coaster
Goofy's Bounce House
Jolly Trolley
Mickey's House
Minnie's House
Roger Rabbit's Car Toon Spin

FRONTIERLAND
Big Thunder Mountain Railroad
Fantasmic!
Frontierland Shootin' Exposition
Golden Horsehoe Stage
Mark Twain Riverboat
Sailing Ship Columbia
Tom Sawyer Island River Rafts

CRITTER COUNTRY
Splash Mountain
Teddi Barra's Swingin' Arcade

NEW ORLEANS SQUARE
The Disney Gallery
Haunted Mansion
Pirates of the Caribbean

❖ Don't expect to see all of Disneyland in one day. Plan at least two days or you'll become frustrated with lines and the sheer enormity of the park.

❖ Unless you're towing toddlers, leave Mickey's Toontown until later in the day, when the youngest children have exhausted themselves and are on their way back to their hotel.

❖ Reservations for dining at Blue Bayou can be made at the restaurant's entrance. Balcony seating (in the Disney Gallery) for Fantasmic! can be made at the Guest Relations window at the main entrance.

GUEST SERVICES

General Information   Disneyland Admissions Department, 1313 Harbor Boulevard, Anaheim, CA 92803; 714-781-7290.

Stroller and Wheelchair Rentals   Both are available just inside the main entrance on the right.

Baby Services   Located at the end of Main Street closest to Sleeping Beauty Castle. Services include preparing formulas, warming bottles and changing infants. Diapers and other baby needs are available. Some park restrooms also have changing tables.

Lockers   Located next to Main Street Cone Shop and Fantasyland Theater on Main Street. Lockers large enough for suitcases are near the Parking Lot Tram Stop, west of the main entrance ticket booths.

Pets   The Kennel Club is to the right of the main entrance. Food and water are provided upon request, but you can't leave your pet overnight.

Lost Children   Facilities for the care of lost children are next to the First Aid Center at the end of Main Street. Messages for lost persons over 12 may be left at City Hall in Town Square.

Lost & Found   Located on Main Street near the lockers between the Market House and Disney Clothiers; 714-781-7290.

First Aid   The First Aid Center is at the end of East Plaza Street just off Main Street. Registered nurses are always on duty.

Banking   There are ATMs located inside the park and checks up to $100 can be cashed at the Bank of Main Street.

Package Express   Serious shoppers should consider this free service, which lets you pick up all your Disneyland purchases at the end of the day at the Newsstand, which is outside the main gate on your right as you exit. Expect a wait if you pick up packages within an hour of closing. Guests of the Disneyland and Disneyland Pacific hotels can have their packages sent directly to their rooms.

GETTING AROUND

To get a feel for the place, think of Disneyland as a giant wheel whose spokes lead to each of the eight themed areas. At the base of the wheel is Main Street U.S.A., which serves as the park's entrance and the place to get oriented. The Disneyland Railroad travels the rim of the wheel.

At the wheel's hub sits Central Plaza, a pleasant park in front of Sleeping Beauty Castle. The plaza is a good meeting place if your party decides to split up during the day or if someone gets lost. From the hub, bridges and walkways lead to each land. Traveling clockwise, you'll encounter Adventureland, New Orleans Square, Critter Country, then Frontierland, Toontown, Fantasyland and Tomorrowland.

On a map the transitions between lands look fairly easy, though in reality there's plenty to foul you up. The entire kingdom is riddled with sinuous waterways and curving lanes that don't always take you along the most direct route. Anyone who's just ridden Space Mountain and attempts a dash to Big Thunder Mountain with kids in tow will find they have embarked on a demanding trek. Translation: Use a map to plot your course, taking it slow until you get your bearings. If you get lost, a Disney employee can always help.

Main Street U.S.A.

What finer introduction to an enchanted kingdom than a postcard-perfect street? This replica of a beautiful American town affords a visually exciting collage of wrought-iron balconies, ornate balustrades, gingerbread designs, old-fashioned lampposts, painted benches, shade trees, merry music, popcorn and pretzel carts and hanging pots brimming with flowers. Bright-red fire engines clang, horseless carriages putt along and muscled horses haul trolleys packed with visitors.

Much of Main Street is lined with clever shops and businesses whose task seems to be to entertain as well as sell. Disney Clothiers Ltd. sells everything with a Disney logo or character embroidered, painted, sewn or otherwise integrated into its design. Not bad are men's dress socks with tiny Mickeys woven into the pattern. As for The Emporium, if it's not there you probably don't need it. It's the largest store in Disneyland, purveying

GO TO THE HEAD OF THE LINE

No doubt about it, waiting in line is one Disney tradition guests would rather do without. The nifty FastPass lets you skirt some of those long queues. Insert your park pass into the turnstile, come back during your designated window of time and walk right in. The system currently operates on some of the most notoriously long-lined attractions—Space Mountain, Splash Mountain, Indiana Jones Adventure, Big Thunder Mountain Railroad, Pirates of the Caribbean, Haunted Mansion, Autopia, Star Tours and Roger Rabbit's Car Toon Spin.

buttons, books, tapes and CDs, pens and plush toys as well as fashions and gifts featuring your favorite Disney characters.

Interspersed among the shops are nifty sights and eateries that funnel heady aromas out their open doors. The Blue Ribbon Bakery has chocolate chip cookies baked on the premises daily. Next door at Gibson Girl Ice Cream you'll find truly yummy frozen yogurt. Chocolate, vanilla and strawberry ice cream plus the special flavor of the day come in sugar cones at Main Street Cone Shop. Each shop has its own ambience, some busy and bright, others formal and Victorian, and still others rustic and woody.

There is so much to keep the eye (and mind) busy here that it takes awhile to absorb everything. Fortunately this area is rarely clogged with people and can be visited anytime. Plan to come between mid-morning and mid-afternoon, when more popular attractions are crowded.

Main Street generally stays open a half hour later than the rest of the park, so visiting at the end of the day is another good strategy. While everyone else is funneling out, you can shop and play at leisure. And buying souvenirs just before closing means you won't have to rent a storage locker or lug the bags around all day. If you do shop during the day and you're a guest at any of the Disneyland Resort hotels, you can ask to have your packages sent directly to your room.

Main Street is also a good place for one parent to take the kids while the other goes solo on Space Mountain or Star Tours or any other ride closed to small children.

WHAT TO SEE & DO
To explore Main Street, begin by stopping at **City Hall** for maps, entertainment and dining schedules, lost and found and general information. One of Main Street's best spots is the **Penny Arcade**, where a cent will buy you time on an old-fashioned reel machine. There are also mechanical nickel and dime machines and a few modern video games.

Vintage Disney flicks including some great silent cartoons run continuously at the **Main Street Cinema**. Though there are no seats and you have to stand, the octagonal room with six screens is cool, dark and a welcome respite from lines and summer heat. The center circular platform with railing is exclusively for children. Kids are often fascinated by these unfamiliar, black-and-white cartoons, but it's the adults who can while away half an hour or more watching such classics as *Steamboat Willie*. The first cartoon with sound, it has a particularly nostalgic story line: A clever mouse named Mickey falls in love with a rosy-cheeked beauty named Minnie. Main Street is also home to two larger attractions:

The Walt Disney Story, Featuring "Great Moments with Mr. Lincoln" ******** The idea of a historic attraction might start your kids whining about this being a vacation from school, but recent updates to this stalwart attraction give it that hi-tech edge that will likely appeal to everyone in the family. The animatronic Mr. Lincoln is back and more lifelike than ever. In addition to movements that make audience members wonder if there's really a person in there, the former president has gotten a makeover to reflect the man's less-than-tidy appearance on the day of the Gettysburg Address. In addition, the Civil War is vividly illustrated in a dramatic presentation that uses actual photographs and a state-of-the-art sound system (delivered via headphones) that will leave you certain you're in the middle of the battlefield.

> Main Street stays spotless because it has four employees who do nothing but pick up every scrap dropped by guests.

TIPS: Despite the improvements, the attraction has still not achieved huge popularity and is rarely crowded. Come mid-day when you need a cool respite from the rest of the park.

Disneyland Railroad ★★★ With their striped awnings, brightly painted bench seats and thunderous engines, these old-fashioned steam trains offer loads of fun. You can hop on one of four turn-of-the-20th-century trains at the Main Street station for an 18-minute circuit of the park with stops at New Orleans Square (for Frontierland), Toontown (for Fantasyland) and Tomorrowland. Between the Tomorrowland and Main Street stations the train enters a cave to treat riders to a diorama of the Grand Canyon. To the clopping strains of Ferde Grofe's "Grand Canyon Suite" the train moves slowly through the canyon, close to deer and wolves, as the seasons change from a summer thunderstorm to winter snow. The scene shifts to how the canyon looked centuries before when pterodactyls, apatosarus and other beasts inhabited its depths. Kids love the theatrics, and for adults it's a great way to rest tired bones while getting a splendid introduction to each land.

TIPS: Trains run every five minutes. Lines can form at all four stations; seats open faster when you're leaving an area that's drawing more people, as New Orleans Square/Frontierland in the evenings, when Fantasmic! is presented.

Adventureland

The crude wooden gate between Central Plaza and Adventureland marks a decided metamorphosis: on one side are brick lanes, cropped lawns and the bright orderliness of the plaza; on the other are dim, watery passages, tangles of vines and croaks of toads. Here in Adventureland, Disney's interpretation of exotica thrives with totem poles, carved spears and bright blossoms that poke across footpaths. The jungly scheme is peppered with the flavors of Africa, the South Pacific and the Caribbean. Even the air is heavy with the musty scent of the tropics (enhanced, no doubt, by the millions of gallons of water that support the Jungle Cruise).

The "faraway place" theme is emphasized by the architecture, a fusion of thatched huts, wrought-iron balconies and Spanish tile roofs. The breezy network of shops across from the Jungle Cruise offers straw Indiana Jones hats, camouflage clothes, whimsical jewelry, treasure chests and other "loot," sold by helpers in tropical-print shirts. A supply raft bringing coconuts "floats" near the ceiling, and a cageful of skulls bears the warning "Past Due Accounts."

Perhaps of all the lands, Adventureland most appeals to all ages. Families, singles, couples, seniors—they all savor Adventureland. From the mammoth Tarzan's Treehouse to the adventure-packed Jungle Cruise, each ride features something for every person. No rides here can be classified as "just for kids," and only the Indiana Jones Adventure has a height restriction.

WHAT TO SEE & DO

Indiana Jones Adventure ★★★★★ This ride is one of the park's hottest attractions. And why not? Those of us who'd been thrilled by Indy's big-screen adventures now have the chance to go along for the ride. The "adventure" begins as soon as you enter the lush, tropical grounds of the Temple of the Forbidden Eye, an excavation site somewhere on the "Lost Delta of India." A generator housed in a wooden shed whirs away, while in a tent, presumably Indy's, an old wooden radio is playing 1940s swing music. After climbing several stone steps, you enter the temple and follow a long, cool, twisting passage carved out of rock and earth. Even on a long wait, there's plenty to keep you and the kids entertained. As you descend into the underground excavation, be sure to pull the rope at the well (you can't miss it), and look for a skeleton hidden in a rocky niche. In the "spike room," where skulls are hung atop spiked bamboo poles, *don't* heed the "Don't Touch" warning signs, and see what happens. The real adventure begins when you board a "troop transport" for the final, fast and furiously harrowing leg of the journey. There's nothing terrifying about the ride (unless you cringe at the sight of a wall-full of bugs

UP CLOSE AND PERSONAL WITH WALT DISNEY

Fans of the original Disney won't want to miss **A Walk in Walt's Footsteps**. The two-and-a-half-hour guided excursion wends through all the park landmarks where Walt made his mark. There are also lots of neat tidbits of lore, such as the legendary opening-day fiasco wherein a mushy Main Street U.S.A. (the asphalt had been laid just the night before) snatched high-heel shoes right off of women's feet. The tour runs daily at 10:30 a.m. Cost is $16 for adults and $14 for children ages 3 to 11. Theme park admission is required but not included in the tour price.

or rats), and there are plenty of thrills: a collapsing rope bridge and the giant rolling boulder from *Raiders of the Lost Ark*, for example. But most of the excitement comes from sharp stomach-churning twists and turns, and the jerking starts and stops the transport makes. Of course, Indy in robotic form shows up a few times (in the dim light, he almost looks real!). Although it would be hard to discern the difference, the transports are programmed by computer so the ride in each car is a bit different.

TIPS: The usual warnings for this type of fast-action ride apply: it's not recommended for pregnant women or people with back or neck problems. Kids must be 46 inches high to ride. Waits can get up to an hour pretty quickly, especially on weekends, so plan accordingly. The actual ride lasts just over three minutes.

Tarzan's Treehouse ★★★ Disney purists may well scoff at this new attraction, a redesign of the stalwart (and ill-attended) Swiss Family Treehouse. Still, even the most loyal Disney-philes can't help but notice the liveliness of the revamped attraction based on the loin-clothed one. It's a vast improvement to the heretofore stale arbor abode.

Fans of the movie will recognize the trappings instantly. Bongos and Tarzan yells echo throughout, and story scenes range from Tarzan's discovery by his gorilla mother Kala to the ape-man's re-discovery of his human roots. Acrophobes beware—the tree top is high, high enough to see out over all the roofs of New Orleans Square.

For kids, the best part of the trip may well be at the bottom, where a vine allows for a gentle swing, and a string of pots and pans is the perfect place to reenact the "Crashing the Camp" scene; look for some of the film's characters here as well. If you really want to get back to nature, check out the selection of creepy crawlies—cockroaches, millipedes, snakes and such (live ones)—available for your inspection.

TIPS: A new attraction, this tree draws a line, something rarely seen during its days as the Swiss Family abode. Still, as it is a self-guided walking tour, the line always moves. The slow pace is actually a blessing. Steep stairs (particularly on the way back down) require care—be sure to hold little ones' hands.

Jungle Cruise ★★★★ One of Disney's most famous and best-loved rides is this fun-filled, crazy cruise through a skillfully simulated jungle. Visitors sit elbow-to-elbow on bench seats in canopied riverboats with names such as *Amazon Queen* and *Nile Princess*. A captain, smartly outfitted in safari hat and belted jacket, urges his charges to "Wave goodbye to the people on the dock, you may not see them again," then guides the group on what he warns is a "perilous" subtropical trek. It's one of the few rides narrated by "real" people—a refreshing feature—and these narrators are amusing, with their corny jokes and wisecracks. ("It's okay to take photos of the elephants. They've worn their trunks today.") During the ten-minute, action-packed voyage, explorers elude elephants, hippopotamuses, zebras, wildebeests, giraffes and pythons (which threaten to "get a crush on you"). They also dodge waterfalls, escape from headhunters and squeak through the ruins of an ancient city. In one shore scene, apes have plundered a camp, leaving a jeep on its back with its wheels still turning and radio blasting. In another scenario that includes a stack of skulls, the "head" salesman is selling arts and crafts. "The one on top is Art," quips the guide. None of the stuff is real, of course, though some scenes are authentic enough to frighten preschool children. Most kids are easily calmed, however, and by the end of the ride don't want to get off despite warnings by the guide to "leave all your jewelry and other valuables but make sure you take your children."

There are hidden Mickeys on each ride at Disneyland. See if you can spot them.

TIPS: An excellent steel-drum band often plays on the elevated stage atop the Jungle Cruise boathouse. Besides getting into the irresistible sounds yourself, take the time to watch how children respond to the dynamic rhythms and you'll no doubt see some impromptu choreography.

Enchanted Tiki Room ★★ An air-conditioned Polynesian Island hut is the venue for this tropical serenade by 225 loquacious, robot-like parrots, flowers and tiki gods. You'll either think this is the funniest, silliest thing going, or you'll be bored to distraction. There seems to be no middle ground. You sit on benches while the sound system blasts "In the Tiki, Tiki, Tiki, Tiki Rooooom," which becomes repetitive and eventually borders on the obnoxious. The totem poles that blink and sing are proof that Disney can be overly fatuous.

TIPS: If the idea of listening to faux birds and flowers sing for 17 minutes sounds dull, skip this one. Otherwise consider it a chance for a good giggle and to get off your feet.

New Orleans Square

One of the park's most enchanting areas, New Orleans Square has pirates, a haunted mansion, a restaurant that overlooks a bayou alight with fireflies, and a section of very, very French shops that can distract you for more than an hour if you're in the mood. This representation of New Orleans a hundred years ago, when she was the unchallenged Queen City of the Mississippi, includes iron-trellised balconies, winding streets, sidewalk cafés and wandering Dixieland jazz minstrels. Many consider it the prettiest theme area, and indeed with its view of Rivers of the Americas and the majestic *Mark Twain* and *Columbia* making their circuits, it may well be.

Restaurants here offer jambalaya, seafood creole and other creative dishes indigenous to the area.

Pirates of the Caribbean ★★★★★ Arguably one of Disney's greatest feats, this attraction combines the best of the best rides: realistic scenery, spirited music, nonstop action and a couple of short but stomach-lurching drops. Unlike the bright outdoor scenery of Jungle Cruise, this boat trip takes you through the dark and clammy hollows of pirates' dens. In early scenes peg-legged men are chained to stone floors, and buzzards pick at skeletons strewn on a deserted beach while haunts cling to the mast of a ghost ship. For most of the ride, the swashbucklers are plundering, frolicking and raising hell in general. During a chaotic sea battle, the pirate galleon aims across the bows of guests' rafts. Elsewhere pirates carelessly fire pistols, pursue screeching ladies and set the town ablaze. Chickens cluck, dogs bark and drunken pigs twitch their legs in strangely realistic ways. Several sights border on the raucous, including the auctioning of women, though Disney manages to make it all seem good fun. The attention to detail is masterful, down to the mole on one pirate's chin.

TIPS: Small children may be frightened by some of the ride's scenes. The wait here can be up to an hour during the middle of a busy day, but by 7 or 8 p.m. there is rarely more than a 15-minute line. Not to be missed.

Haunted Mansion ★★★★★ This creepy edifice is home to 999 frighteningly funny ghosts, ghouls and goblins who carry on an incessant search for Occupant No. 1000. "Here lies old Fred. A great big rock fell on his head." So reads one of the wacky graveyard epitaphs outside the Mansion, a vast, ominous house in the far corner of New Orleans Square. It's a fitting introduction to one of Disney's best-ever attractions, an ingenious design with so many special effects and illusions that you find yourself saying, "I know this isn't real, but . . . ."

A gloomy butler greets visitors at the front doors and ushers them into an eight-sided gallery with portraits of "former guests," cobwebbed chandeliers and a ceiling that rises . . . or is the floor sinking? After a sepulchral introduction, he leads everyone to their "doom buggies" for a spirited ride through rooms with phantoms, ghoulies and various netherworld inhabitants. There's a piano player who's nothing more than a shadow, a spooked cemetery and its petrified watchman, a teapot pouring tea and a screeching raven that won't go away. Voices howl, figures skate across ceilings, and ghosts become more vivid as the darkness gets thicker.

All the special effects are great, but the show-stoppers are the "holograms." Using advanced technology and imagination, Disney pushed 3-D projection to its limits. Life-size human images, dressed in everyday attire, float around and mimic the manner-

WHAT TO SEE & DO

isms of their living counterparts. In one party scene, holograms whirl around the floor in sync with the music while hologram "humans" at a banquet fade in and out. Perhaps the most fascinating (and talked-about) hologram is the woman's head in the crystal ball: Her lifelike image chatters nonstop. The kicker, though, is at the ride's end, when you gaze into a mirror and find you have your own spook (read hologram) nestled beside you.

TIPS: Despite the attraction's expert effects, it's not really scary for most people. Small children, however, will likely be frightened by what to them is most certainly "real."

The Disney Gallery ★★ Practically above Pirates of the Caribbean, this pleasant gallery is done in the style of a New Orleans mansion with parquet floors and white gingerbread trim. It features a fascinating display of original sketches and artists' renderings done during the park's planning stages. It's interesting to see how concepts for various rides and attractions evolved. Included are limited-edition lithographs, animation cells plus posters and books that are for sale.

TIPS: Just off the gallery is a small, cool patio with a fountain plus tables and chairs. Because it's hidden away it's rarely crowded and is a wonderful place to spend a few quiet minutes.

Critter Country

This four-acre backwoods area, Disneyland's rugged Northwest territory, is the setting for Splash Mountain, an enormously popular ride. One of the least-crowded eateries, the Hungry Bear Restaurant, offers "the bear necessities." At Brer Bar food stand you can get a Mickey-shaped soft pretzel.

WHAT TO SEE & DO

Splash Mountain ★★★★ Considering that the wait here is sometimes over an hour, the ride itself is somewhat anticlimactic. You sit in hollowed-out logs that float on a rushing stream for a long uphill pull past old milling gear and machines, then meander outdoors past the homes of Brer Fox, Brer Bear and Brer Rabbit. After a few little drops the logs float inside the mountain where you're almost Zip-A-Dee-Doo-Daahed to death by what has become the Disney National Anthem. More than a hundred animated *Song of the South* characters are out in force, with Brer Rabbit trying to get honey from a hive swarming with bees and Brer Fox narrowly escaping an alligator.

You're pulled up another hill for a brief drop, then up again, to be plunged over a steep, 47-degree flume drop, screeching five stories into the briar patch of Splash Mountain, spraying spectators as you "watch your life splash before your eyes." From there it's a mellow float past the Swimmin' Hole and the *Zip-A-Dee Lady* steamboat, where the characters are gathered for the ride's final musical tour de force.

TIPS: If you're really averse to getting damp, don't sit in the front seat. And if you don't want to participate at all, the best vantage point for seeing the ride's steep, speedy final descent is just across from the ride's entrance. There is a height restriction of 40 inches and children must be at least 3 years old to ride.

ANOTHER TIP: As you exit Splash Mountain you'll see yourself in freeze-frame on a video screen. All your delight, exhilaration or perhaps terror has been captured by the camera on the infamous flume drop and is yours on a souvenir photo for a price, of course. Sit in front for the best shot.

Teddi Barra's Swingin' Arcade ★★ If anyone in your group is drawn to old-fashioned shooting galleries, this is the place. You can challenge animated figures to a quick-draw contest and shoot down mechanical bears as they scamper up trees and through the woods. You need quarters for this frontier-themed fun-and-games emporium.

Frontierland

Back through New Orleans Square and around the corner from Critter Country, Frontierland places you in the realm of the pioneers. Flags of the original Thirteen Colonies fly proudly over the log-walled stockade entrance. Reminiscent of an 1800s mining town, Frontierland presents a rugged face of cactus, rust-colored rock, adobe buildings and trading posts. River Belle Terrace, which overlooks the route of the *Mark Twain* sternwheeler, serves up yummy pancake and waffle breakfasts. At the Pioneer Mercantile you'll find American Indian crafts. The main draw is Big Thunder Mountain Railroad, which simulates the thrills and spills of a runaway mine train. Appealing to all ages, the area recalls early America during the days when the West was still as wild as its reputation.

WHAT TO SEE & DO

Big Thunder Mountain Railroad ★★★★★ This roller coaster–like ride has much more to it than curves and drops. It's a perilous journey aboard a roaring mine train. Boarding open-air ore cars, you embark on a harrowing excursion through the dark caverns of Big Thunder Mountain and some of Disney's most creative

THE WONDERS OF AUDIO-ANIMATRONICS

The Audio-Animatronics system used at Disneyland to bring humans, animals, birds and flowers to life is accomplished by recording audible and inaudible sound impulses, music and dialogue on digital laser discs that have up to 32 tracks controlling as many as 438 separate actions. Playback relays music and voice to speakers, while inaudible impulses control lighting and activate the figures.

scenery. A hint of things to come is evident when the 30-passenger train chugs out of the station with no one at the controls. Within moments, you're engulfed by darkness and become the center of attention for a swarm of bats.

As the train climbs high into the mountain, you pass brilliantly colored phosphorescent pools, and a raging waterfall narrowly misses the tracks. In Coyote Canyon, furry residents howl as the train throttles into the black depths of a chasm. At the top of a natural-arch bridge you get a momentary view of desert landscape, then re-enter the mountain as the train rumbles like a full-force earthquake. Shoring columns shake and ten-foot rocks tumble toward your teetering train. Miraculously the train finds a way out and returns to the boom town of Big Thunder.

> The *Mark Twain* is the first paddle-wheeler built in the United States in half a century.

TIPS: A very popular ride, even though the wait can be from 30 minutes to one and one-half hours. Children shorter than 40 inches are not allowed to ride.

Mark Twain Riverboat ★★★ One of the original Disneyland attractions, this sternwheeler with white gingerbread railings is still as beautiful to look at as it is to explore. The ship lazily paddles past plantation docks on the Rivers of America as it circumnavigates Tom Sawyer Island. Keep an eye open for moose, deer and other wild animals in the dense forest of Frontierland.

TIPS: Although kids will want to explore the multidecked sternwheeler, adults can find this ride a good opportunity to corral a seat for a 15-minute respite.

Tom Sawyer Island River Rafts ★★ Guests are transported to a cleverly designed island in the center of the Rivers of America. Steamboats, rafts and a giant sailing ship ply these waters, tossing blue-green ripples against the island shore. Visitors crowd onto timber rafts (it's standing only) for fun, motorized transportation to the island. Cool and woodsy, Tom Sawyer Island offers a retreat from lines and plenty of places where children can romp. Guests of all ages can relive childhood escapades, exploring a baffling maze of tunnels inside Injun Joe's Cave, swaying across the precarious suspension bridge and scaling Castle Rock. While children burn off energy, adults can stroll leisurely or rest on one of the island's many benches.

TIPS: Unless you want a shady place to sit, adults without kids may want to save this for their second day at Disneyland. There's usually no line, so visit when other attractions are packed. The island closes just before dusk.

Sailing Ship Columbia ★ Among the ships and boats sharing the Rivers of America is the square-masted sailing schooner *Columbia*. Adults can appreciate the authentic rigging of this 1790-model ship, but kids become a bit bored after they've made their circuit of the deck. It follows basically the same route as the *Mark Twain* with the highlight of the trip occurring when the ship unleashes a cannonade at Fort Wilderness.

TIPS: The beauty of the *Columbia* may be better appreciated from a distance than aboard. Skip it if you're pressed for time.

Fantasmic! ★★★★★ First-time visitors to this nightly show on the River of America can often be heard postulating about what kind of experience they suppose they're in for. But imaginative inventors of this crowd pleaser, the crown jewel of Disneyland entertainment, have come up with a live musical performance that simply defies exact description: a 22-minute spectacle with songs, film clips and special effects that leave the uninitiated and even repeat visitors glued to the action.

The show, performed on Tom Sawyer Island but visible from New Orleans Square, weaves the tale of Mickey Mouse's dream battle between good and evil (read: Disney heroes and villains). In addition to toe-tapping original music and myriad special effects, there's a rope-swinging Captain Hook/Peter Pan battle aboard the sailing ship *Columbia*, as well as live appearances by some classic villains (Maleficent and the Wicked Queen from *Snow White*, to name two) and virtually every animated prince and princess ever drawn. Most amazing is the precision interplay between live performers, movie clips and special effects (a feat carried off by nearly two dozen computers). Live characters seem to appear and vanish from nowhere, and film clips, projected off cascading water "screens," create the impression of animated images dancing in midair.

As the show draws to a close, climactic bursts of water and pyrotechnics draw plenty of "oohs" and "ahs" from the crowd, and the grand finale leaves everyone cheering for more. Takes place nightly during the summer, on weekends the rest of the year, and is visible from New Orleans Square. Check the map at the Magic Kingdom entrance for show times. An absolute don't-miss!

TIPS: To really appreciate Fantasmic!, you'll have to be able to see it. Unfortunately, the folks at Disneyland didn't seem to anticipate the magnitude of the event and there are only a few really good viewing areas to be found. Two of the best: the grassy area at the River's edge, or the bridge in front of Pirates of the Caribbean. To secure a spot in either, you'll have to come early—we're talking hours early as crowds for the 8 p.m. shows tend to start gathering as early as 6 (some devotees get there as early as 4 p.m.). If you're late, you'll find cast members extremely vigilant about shooing people out of no-standing lanes. Your best bet: Assign a designated spot-saver while the rest of your party ventures elsewhere.

Frontierland Shootin' Exposition ★ At 20 shots for a quarter, peerless marksmen can sharpen their aim at the infrared-beam targets. They are interactive and reward you with a stunt whenever you make a bull's-eye. It's a good place to visit when other parts of the park are crowded.

TIPS: When there's a line at every other restroom in the park, the ones in Frontierland will be less crowded.

Golden Horseshoe Stage ★★★ Near the *Mark Twain* dock, this old-fashioned, brass-railed saloon is home to several musical shows that change throughout the day. They generally consist of knee-slapping humor and eye-rolling cornpone. Campy? Sure. Song, dance and slapstick permeate the various 30-minute acts. In the spirit of Saturday matinees, a snack bar provides eats so you can munch while you watch.

TIPS: Chairs for the show are on a flat surface, meaning little kids may well end up studying the back of someone's head. Arriving really early (that means getting in line about 45 minutes ahead) may net you a front-row seat. If you're a latecomer: before taking a seat in the back row (a particularly horrible vantage point), see if the upstairs balcony is about to open (the second level opens when the floor is full); you may end up with a much better view.

▼▼▼▼▼▼▼▼▼▼▼▼▼▼
Mickey's Toontown

Ever wonder what it would be like to visit the set of an animated Disney movie? Toontown is as close as you are likely to get. From the moment you wander under the tracks from Fantasyland or arrive at the Toontown train station, you find yourself in a whimsical land where the pastel-colored buildings slant every which way and cartoons seem to come alive. Round one corner and you'll discover a talking mailbox; round another, you're likely to run head-on into Goofy or Roger Rabbit.

Toontown, you see, is where Disney's animated characters are said to make their homes. You won't find any Do Not Touch signs here. Ring the bell at the camera shop, and a flash goes off. Push the button outside the power house, and the steam spews out. Lift the lid on a crate outside the warehouse, and animal sounds come back at you. Stop by the insurance agency, and you can check on coverage for "Smashing into brick walls disguised as tunnels."

It doesn't take long to walk from the commercial center of Toontown to Mickey's Neighborhood. But for those sore of foot, the *Jolly Trolley* carries up to eight passengers at a time on a wacky, weaving track through town. You can buy cartoon gags at the Toontown Five & Dime or the Gag Factory, or grab a bite to eat at Daisy's Diner, Pluto's Dog House or Clarabelle's Frozen Yogurt.

There's lots to appeal to small youngsters. Donald Duck's Boat, *Miss Daisy*, moored in tiny Toon Lake, features a rope-net ladder, a pipe slide, a rope-pull whistle and bell and a periscope that offers a panoramic view across Toontown. Goofy's Bounce House, set amidst a garden of popcorn stalks and squashed squashes, provides inflated trampoline-like furniture for the over-3, under 4-foot-6 set. The Chip 'n Dale Treehouse, built into the branches of a manmade oak, has a spiral staircase to the top of the slide and a bin of plastic roll-in-and-crawl-through "acorns" near its foot. And for the true toddlers, Toon Park has a play area for kids . . . with seats for parents.

Mickey's House ★★★★ This delightful "home" of Disney's first and favorite character should appeal to everyone who visits Toontown, from toddlers to grandparents. Guests enter through the living room and wander through the den, viewing mementoes of the life and career of Mickey Mouse, from photos of Mickey with Walt Disney himself to a replica of Steamboat Willie's boat in a bottle. There's a giant telephone, a smiling radio, a player piano that continually cranks out the Mickey Mouse Club theme, a *Random Mouse Dictionary* on a shelf. Pluto Pup's bed is located inside the house, but his doghouse is through the laundry room in the garden, where a frisky gopher pulls giant carrots back into the ground. The path leads past a small warehouse of cartoon movie props to the screening barn, where you can watch film trailers of *The Sorcerer's Apprentice*, *The Band Concert* and other Mouse classics while waiting to meet Mickey himself, shake his hand, get his autograph, pose for a photo.

WHAT TO SEE & DO

TIPS: There's often a deceptively long line here. It moves fast and is rarely longer than 15 minutes.

Minnie's House ★★ This is a much smaller version of Mickey's house next door, with a distinctly feminine touch. Minnie herself often greets guests, who enter through her bedroom and boudoir. There are fruit scents, a computerized makeup mirror on her dressing table, and a phone with answering-machine messages from Mickey nearby. The kitchen tempts with holographic chocolate-

EXPLOSION OF ENTERTAINMENT

Disneyland entertainment isn't limited to what's on the ground. Stick around during the nighttime hours and check out one of Disney's renowned displays of skyward magic. **Believe, There's Magic in the Stars** features a little bit of everything: Tinkerbell flying around the castle, fireworks in the shape of hearts and even a trio of atmospheric bursts that resemble a certain pair of ears. During the day, the **Parade of Stars** is the place to see dozens of Disney characters. The fireworks display is meant to be seen over the castle; the entrance end of Main Street will give the best views.

chip cookies on the table, a fallen cake (complete with candle) in the oven, a variety of cheeses in the refrigerator, and a working dishwasher with a balancing act of smiling cups. In the garden beyond the back door there is a talking wishing well.

TIPS: If time is tight, consider skipping Minnie's House in favor of Mickey's. The spirit of both houses is similar, but Mickey's has more to it.

Gadget's Go Coaster ★★ This very short roller coaster often has a very long wait. Once you're on, it's fun, but it's over all too quickly. Credited as the invention of one of the stars of the *Rescue Rangers* cartoon, it looks like a screwed-up junior-high science project built of giant recycled wooden block toys, pencils, straws, toothbrushes, combs, scissors and miscellaneous "stuff." Guests ride in hollowed-out acorns over a red track that weaves over and around a pond from which frogs squirt a stream of water. A fish bowl mounted upon a deflated soccer ball provides an unlikely source for a steam engine that ostensibly lifts the acorn train up its first and highest hill.

TIPS: Fifty seconds of fun may not be worth waiting 50 minutes or longer in line. Also, it's likely to be frightening to younger children. If time is short, admire the wacky ingenuity of the construction, then move on.

Roger Rabbit's Car Toon Spin ★★★ A taxicab whirls its passengers through the wacky world of Roger Rabbit, his sexy wife Jessica, and the villainous weasels who are plotting to eradicate the residents of Toontown with their toxic "Dip." With black lighting and plywood cutouts, this ride is akin to Fantasyland's popular Snow White and Pinocchio rides, with two major pluses: It's considerably longer and, though your cab follows a track, you have some control over your spin with your steering wheel. In that way, it's rather like putting the Mad Hatter's Tea Party on a track through Mr. Toad's Wild Ride. Adults and older kids may find the waiting line more interesting than the ride itself: It winds through Toontown's back alleys and into the Toontown Cab Co. garage, where you're challenged to decipher such Toon license plates as "ZPD2DA" (Zip-A-Dee-Doo-Dah).

TIPS: Lines are shortest in the evening, when many visitors are watching the Fantasmic! show.

▼▼▼▼▼▼▼▼▼▼▼

Fantasyland

Truly a colorful, whimsical place, Fantasyland is a combination of circus-style canopies, gleaming turrets and gingerbread houses. Dominated by the majestic Sleeping Beauty Castle, it is filled with fanciful lanes that lead you along like the chapters of a fairy tale. Fantasyland has more attractions than any other land (14, more than twice that of most lands). Obviously, children are the biggest fans of these rides, which feature happy lyrics and themes from many of Disney's best-loved films and characters. There are flying Dumbos, whirling Mad Hatter tea-cups, King Arthur's carousel horses and Snow White's forest. Most adults enjoy the rides, too, and those who don't still delight in the imaginative setting and remarkable attention to detail (in true Disney style, even the garbage cans are splashed with glowing color).

Not surprisingly, Fantasyland is usually the most crowded area of Disneyland. Perhaps that's because this make-believe land epitomizes what Disney does best: bring out the kid in everyone.

WHAT TO SEE & DO

Sleeping Beauty Castle ★★★★ This majestic structure gets four stars not for what it contains, but because it is *the* frame of reference for all of Disneyland. Towering above Main Street and encircled by a rock-rimmed moat, the castle is a masterful facsimile of Mad King Ludwig's famous Neuschwanstein castle in Germany. Its royal-blue turrets and gold spires glisten in the sun, providing the ultimate in visual fantasy. You cross the medieval palace's drawbridge into a world of magic and wonder.

The Sleeping Beauty tale is told in colorful, three-dimensional miniature sets, complete with the Prince's tender kiss that brings the fair maiden back to wakefulness. This attraction won't thrill any but the very young, although adults may appreciate the detail in the lilliputian dioramas.

> The 11 million gallons of river water in Disneyland are dyed to maintain a clean "muddy" look.

TIPS: Because this is a walk-through attraction there is rarely a line. During peak periods, however, the movement of the crowd will prevent you from lingering at any tableau that might be a favorite.

Matterhorn Bobsleds ★★★★★ This thriller, down "icy" slopes and through "frozen" caverns, is a unique roller-coaster ride that zooms in and out of Matterhorn Mountain. You'll hold onto your lederhosen while sleek, four-passenger bobsleds climb to an eight-story height inside the mountain, then take a major plunge past waterfalls and a glacier grotto. Sharp, steep turns and gut-wrenching drops elicit the screams of riders that are amplified as they echo through the mountain's hollow interior. Finally, sleds splash into a sparkling alpine lake, usually dampening the riders in the front seat. There's more than ice to chill you while careening down the slopes. The Abominable Snowman may lurch from the shadows to add a frigid tingle to the experience. This is one of the park's most visual rides. From almost every angle spectators can watch the sleds whiz in and out of the mountain and decide whether or not to brave the ride.

TIPS: Enormously popular, so expect a wait at almost any time. To ride, children must be at least 3 years old.

Peter Pan's Flight ★★★ Small children love this air cruise in colorful pirate galleons. The setting is Never-Never Land, from Sir James Matthew Barrie's 1904 fairy tale about a half-elfin boy who "wouldn't grow up." You glide around brightly lit indoor scenes for rendezvous with Tinkerbell, Captain Hook, Mr. Smee and other favorite Peter Pan characters.

Because of its popularity with families, the short (two-and-a-half-minute) ride typically has long lines. Although adults may not find the wait worth it, children in your party may insist on queuing up for the ride, based on reports from friends who have done it.

TIPS: Can be frightening to very small children who don't like the feeling of being off the ground in the dark.

It's a Small World ★★★★ The dazzling, colorful facade of this popular attraction is embellished with stylized versions of European landmarks and adorned with a daffy clock that comes to life with a trumpeting fanfare every 15 minutes. The ride itself is a leisurely cruise in sherbet-colored boats that take you through glittery scenes of more than 600 Audio-Animatronic singing-and-dancing dolls, all attired in their distinctive native costumes. There are Canadian Mounties, hip-swaying hula girls, leprechauns, kings and queens, snake charmers, flying carpets, pyramids, sphinxes, giraffes and hippos, volcanoes, sombreros and even an "underwater" scene representing Hawaii. The theme of world unity shines through in the detailed costumes and settings from countries around the globe. A favorite (if not *the* favorite) Disney ride of small children, it is a feel-good experience with lighthearted lyrics. But be prepared to have the Small World theme jingling in your brain for the rest of the day.

TIPS: Though a very popular ride, it has fast-moving lines and rarely more than a half-hour wait.

Dumbo the Flying Elephant ★★ Disney's version of a carnival midway ride is based on the endearing elephant with oversized ears. The mouse who befriended Dumbo perches jauntily in the center. Super tame but fun, it features a squadron of Dumbos that glides in a circle and lifts up when riders press a button inside. Kids plead to go on this attraction over and over again.

TIPS: Popular mainly with small children and (believe it or not) has one of the slowest lines in the park.

Alice in Wonderland ★★ This one is as cute to watch as it is to ride. You get into an improbably hued caterpillar that crawls through the queen's castle, taking you down the rabbit hole for Alice's very important date with the White Rabbit. The croquet game, Tweedledum and Tweedledee, the Cheshire Cat, the playing-card guards and the mad tea party are all there. From the outside, the caterpillars present a pastel panorama as they worm their way around oversized flowers and leaves, in and out of the castle.

TIPS: Very popular ride with constant lines. Although the ride is slow moving, small children may be apprehensive about the initial downhill trip into darkness.

Snow White's Scary Adventure ★★★ This Disney-style spook-house ride features wooden cars that bump and twist their way around boiling cauldrons, screaming witches, ghoulish trees and other creepies. The idea, of course, is that you accompany Snow White on her perilous journey through the forest. Some of the cardboard cutouts and other set work seem hokey, but the rock that nearly lands on your head at the end is a hoot. Though it's not really scary, small children are often uneasy.

TIPS: Not popular with seniors and adults without children.

Mr. Toad's Wild Ride ★★★ Like Snow White's Adventures, this spookhouse jaunt jostles you along a track through various calamities. Following the escapades of Mr. J. Thaddeus Toad from the classic fantasy *The Wind in the Willows*, you joyride down the cobblestone streets of Merry Old England, plowing through cardboard barn doors and haystacks, meeting up with an oncoming locomotive in a dark tunnel.

TIPS: Popular with older kids, the ride is often too wild for young children.

Mad Tea Party ★★ The faster you turn the center wheel the faster you spin in this 90-second whirl. Sixteen giant pastel teacups turn in one direction while the platform they're on turns in another, practically guaranteeing the dizzies when it stops. But the midway-style ride can be a blast. Indeed, some teenagers head straight here after Space Mountain, waiting in line for consecutive rides, challenging one another to see whose cup spins the fastest. The ride's fanciful theme is taken from an Alice in Wonderland scene where the Mad Hatter throws a tea party for his unbirthday.

TIPS: The center wheel can be a chore to turn. If the kids in your group want a real twirl, be sure an adult is with them.

SNOW-CAPPED MATTERHORN MOUNTAIN

The highest point at Disneyland, Matterhorn Mountain is a 147-foot replica of the famous Swiss peak near Zermatt. It's the first visible sign of Disneyland to those arriving via Harbor Boulevard. It's built to 1/100th scale and was inspired by the Disney feature film *The Third Man on the Mountain*. Although hollow, it contains enough wood to build more than 300 homes.

Pinocchio's Daring Journey ★★ Pinocchio, that young chip off the old block, finds out that Pleasure Island isn't so pleasurable in this ride. It's the classic tale run through at warp speed. You enter Stromboli's Puppet Theatre through the first of what seem like endless cardboard doors that pop open just in time to let your wood cart through. Along the way Pinocchio's nose grows, he is threatened in the evil amusement park, swallowed by a whale and finally emerges as a real boy back in his own bed, safe with Geppetto. If you don't know the Pinocchio tale, this ride won't tell it, but children enjoy the action and constant movement even if they don't understand it all.

TIPS: There's a repetitiveness to this, Snow White's Scary Adventure and Mr. Toad's Wild Ride. If time is short, see just one.

King Arthur Carrousel ★★★ A true showpiece of a carousel with 72 graceful, white steeds in a perpetual gallop. One of the original Disneyland attractions, the trusty mounts are decorated with whimsical hearts and flowers on their bridles and martingales. Notice that although all the horses are white, no two are identical. Also, instead of traditional merry-go-round music, the carousel organ renders such Disney song classics as "Chim-Chim-Cheree" and "When You Wish Upon a Star." Together with the melodies, the glittering lights, mirrors and almost constant motion make this a singular experience for all ages.

TIPS: Lines are rarely longer than 15 minutes.

Casey Jr. Circus Train ★★ The little train "who knew he could" (actually there are two of them) winds around Storybook Land for good views of the canal boats and the Dumbo ride. "Let's get this show on the road," says the disembodied conductor's voice that, with a clang of the train's brass bell, sends passengers on their way. Cars are circus wagon cages complete with bars, carrying a cargo of "wild animals." If crawling into a cage isn't your style, there are two open sleigh-like seats just behind the engine. The mini-choochoo chugs up a hill, goes through a tunnel, and at one point gets moving at a pretty good clip. It stops just above the canal boat waterway for a view of its home station across the lake and a close-up look at a "patchwork quilt" garden with 50 types of cacti and succulents.

TIPS: Nice, tame ride outdoors that seldom has long lines.

Storybook Land Canal Boats ★★★ Miniature canal boats are piloted through a land where everything is built in detailed miniature. Passing through the mouth of Monstro, the giant whale, you encounter the straw, wood and brick homes of the Three Pigs, then the village where Alice in Wonderland lives. You see London Park, where Peter Pan taught Wendy how to fly, and the home of Ratty, who takes care of the Toad Hole. The Black Forest, home to Snow White and the Seven Dwarfs, Cinderella's cottage

Everybody
Loves a Parade

Armchair performers, now's your chance to experience a parade from the other side of the barricade.

Designed as a tribute to Disneyland's 45th birthday, the current **Parade of the Stars** procession features dozens of favorite characters (just about every Disney princess makes an appearance somewhere, as do Mickey, Minnie et al.) some rarely seen personalities (the trio of Sleeping Beauty fairies and the Blue Fairy, to name a couple), not to mention a number of dancing mushrooms and hippos.

Still, it's the crowd that provides the highlights. Guest stars are recruited from the audience to dance alongside the pros. Adorned in animal hats and tutus (guys, this means you, too), the unabashed stars for a day flit down Main Street attempting split leaps, pirouettes and the occasional pas de deux. Even if the resulting family photo becomes fodder for blackmail, there is a saving grace: you get to keep the hat.

Being in this parade is a blast. If you want a chance to participate, be on the parade route about an hour ahead, act enthusiastic and look for the cast members in blue cloud overalls and animal hats.

and the château where she went to live with her prince, Geppetto's village where he carved Pinocchio, and Mr. Mole's home in the river bank all are represented. The cave at the end? It's the underwater kingdom of *The Little Mermaid*'s King Triton. Nearby is Prince Eric's castle, also from *The Little Mermaid*. Aladdin's palace of Agrabah and Cave of Wonders are also depicted.

TIPS: The amazing details, right down to miniaturized trees, make this attraction fascinating to anyone who takes the time to appreciate its features.

> Disneyland's wardrobe department has more than half a million articles of clothing.

Fantasyland Theatre ★★★ A beautiful dame, a private eye and an unsolved kidnapping. Disney's newest Fantasyland Theater production is hardly a film noir. But *"Mickey's Detective School"—a Musical Toondunit* is a whole lot of fun. Follow Mickey (the aforementioned detective) and Minnie (the aforementioned dame) as they search for Mickey's missing dog, Pluto. Expect appearances from some Disney personalities of questionable character (Cruella De Vil, for one). And try not to look too shifty, or you might just be questioned yourself.

TIPS: Graduated seating is helpful, but tall folks can still get in the way of the wee ones behind them. If you don't mind sitting back a ways, try the seats in front of the light box; from there, your kids can stand without blocking anyone's view (just be sure you're not in the way of the lights themselves).

ANOTHER TIP: Since you'll want to come a little early to get a good seat, why not make it a picnic? The snack bar inside the gate sells hot dogs, pizza and other snacks so you can have lunch—killing two birds while you wait.

Tomorrowland

Walt Disney's original vision for Tomorrowland was as a showcase for the technology of the future. Amid ultramodern buildings with sleek designs, Walt's imagination catapulted visitors into another era; there was the innovative House of the Future (which, as early as the 1950s, predicted gizmos such as electric toothbrushes and large-screen televisions), the Rocket to the Moon and even a "Bathroom of Tomorrow."

Alas, over time, Walt's tomorrow became dated. As the future became the present, the average earth citizen was neither hurdling through space in a flying saucer nor sporting Day-Glo polyester (the 1970s not withstanding) on the job in a plastic office building. Tomorrowland began looking like yesterdayland, more like a 1950s sci-fi flick than a visionary's gaze at the future.

Today Tomorrowland seems to embrace the fantasy of science fiction rather than the realities of science fact. Much about it is fantastical, from the twirling planets and spaceships of the Astro Orbitor ride, to the area's "Buck Rogers" landscaping and rock designs. Here you'll encounter all-time favorite rides such as Space

Mountain (with updated sound system), Star Tours and Astro Orbitor.

Still, not everything at today's Tomorrowland comes strictly from the minds of Imagineers. Inspired by the attraction at Epcot in Orlando, Disneyland offers its own brand of Innoventions. Interestingly, this addition seems to take the Land back to Walt's original concept, with corporate sponsors showcasing prototype gizmos and gadgetry of the future in the areas of home, entertainment, workplace/education, recreation/health and transportation. (Who knows, maybe there'll be another Bathroom of the Future.) Housed in the old rotating Carousel of Progress theater, Disneyland offers a unique turn (if you'll pardon the expression) on the Innoventions concept, with the entire building slowly revolving to provide varied points of entry. Fans of Epcot will be happy to find other touches of the Orlando park, from the leaping interactive fountains to the "Honey, I Shrunk the Audience" attraction.

Star Tours ***** A product of the imagination of George Lucas and the Disney Imagineers, this ride welcomes you to the Tomorrowland Spaceport, complete with R2D2 repairing a battle-scarred StarSpeeder. Mercifully, while you wait in the sometimes-interminable lines, you're entertained with a sales pitch for the latest intergalactic travel packages now being offered.

WHAT TO SEE & DO

The action really begins as you approach a set of steel doors, where an orange-suited flight attendant ushers you aboard a 40-passenger StarSpeeder. Safety instructions include the usual routine: "Stow your carry-on luggage under your seat and fasten your seat belts." This is no idle advice—the visual sensations and motions here are very, very, VERY real. The technology, which is borrowed from the world of *Star Wars*, is similar to the flight simulators the military uses to train pilots.

It's easy to believe you're aboard a StarSpeeder as it takes off for the Moon of Endor. You actually feel what you see on the screen in front of you as you encounter a galaxy full of misadventures. The action is virtually out of control from the word go, as the flight's rookie pilot proves that Murphy's Law applies to the entire universe. You're flung from side to side as the ship takes a wrong turn through a maintenance area, then blasts through the ice crystals in the center of a comet, dodges asteroids and finally plays tag with laser cannons and enemy starships on the *Death Star*. It's an amazing experience, not to be missed.

TIPS: Very realistic; way too intense for small kids. Children must be at least 3 years old and at least 40 inches tall. Do not ride if you get motion sickness or have a bad back. Avoid after a meal.

Space Mountain ***** Next to Star Tours, this roller coaster in the dark is the wildest, most imaginative mind trip in the theme-park lineup. Looming 118 feet above the area, the gleaming, concrete-and-steel structure resembles a ribbed, bronze cone spiked with icicles. After a two-story escalator ride, you begin a two-and-a-half-minute journey through worlds unknown. Meteor showers, whirling galaxies and a gaseous nebula created by three-dimensional aerial projections turn Space Mountain's massive, black interior into a tingling sight-and-sound experience.

Much of the thrill comes from not being able to see where you're going. By roller-coaster standards the ride is quite civilized—no upside-down loops, no gut-wrenching drops, and top speed is less than 30 miles per hour. But Disney's packaged the experience along with a in-vehicle stereo sound system (those are actually speakers on either side of your head) that provides adrenaline-inspiring notes perfectly in time to the heart-pounding climbs and climactic drops. Add the effects of darkness and the ever-moving celestial bodies, and the result is disorientation and an unparalleled rush.

TIPS: Children shorter than 40 inches are not allowed to ride. Not recommended for pregnant women and those with weak stomachs or bad backs. The dark surroundings and squeals of riders will either scare you off or draw you in. Not to be missed if you like life on the edge.

Astro Orbitor ★★★ Kids adore this colorful, carnival-style ride, an updated and faster version of the old Rocket Jets, which puts them airborne for 90 seconds in futuristic aircraft. The open-cockpit vehicles twirl amid a structure flanked by wildly spinning planets. The trip can be tame or mildly exciting, depending on how often you raise and lower your jet. Fans of the old Rocket Jets will find the Astro Orbitor a bit faster, the feeling of speed created by the ride's lower stance, and the effect of the counter-rotating planets. On the down side, you don't get quite the view you did in the jets. The attraction is an exact replica of the Orbi-tron featured in Disneyland Paris.

TIPS: Astro Orbitor is a good place for one parent to take young children while the other rides nearby Space Mountain with the older kids. Like the Rocket Jets, the Astro Orbitor can accommodate only about 22 passengers per ride, but the wait may not be as long now that you can board the ride without waiting for an elevator.

Honey, I Shrunk the Audience ★★★★★ Welcome to the world of professor Wayne Szalinski, the antihero in Disney's *Honey, I Shrunk the Kids*. After numerous misadventures, Szalinski is tapped to receive the Inventor of the Year Award, and you're invited to the ceremony. In a flash of anticipated mayhem, the entire audience becomes pint-sized, menaced by giant snakes, slobbering dogs and stomping, oversized shoes. Like its counterpart in Epcot at Disney World, this 3-D attraction has brilliantly timed its film and live-action effects for action that literally jumps from the screen (and makes most people literally jump from their seats). The 3-D effects are staggeringly realistic, and there are some startling surprises that I won't ruin by revealing here (suffice it to say that if you don't howl, you're one of the few!). If you're into some scary fun with some good laughs, this attraction is an absolute don't-miss.

TIPS: As much as it's based on a kids' movie, this is no kids' attraction, and actually sets many little ones (my daughter included) to sobbing. Heed the "Young Children May Become Frightened" warning carefully. I wish I had.

Innoventions ★★★ Disney history buffs will recall Walt's original plan for Tomorrowland as a showcase for gizmos of tomorrow. Here's where the park gets back to business.

A concept borrowed from Disneyland's sibling park in Orlando, Innoventions offers a glimpse at some newfangled wares. Unlike the self-milking cows and plastic houses of Walt's original Tomorrowland displays, Innoventions touts more practical gadgetry—newer, faster computers and "smart houses" that can be programmed by phone—that have roots in reality; even the most far-out products are generally in development and just a couple of years away from store shelves. Constantly updated exhibits keep it fresh. The fact that its housed in the old Carousel of Progress building (the structure actually rotates, changing your point of entry each time you come) adds some nostalgia. The old "Great Big Beautiful Tomorrow" tune (the theme song from Carousel of Progress) has even been incorporated.

Still, the hallmark is the chance to tinker. Visitors can actually get their hands on most of the stuff here. The corporate sponsors —Compaq, AT&T and General Motors, to name a few—make it feel unmercifully commercial, much like a trade show. But you won't mind as you poke your way through the funky toys. But beware: technophiles could lose an afternoon before you can say "megabyte."

TIPS: Rarely crowded so browse anytime.

◆◆◆◆◆◆◆◆◆ ◆◆◆ ◆◆◆ ◆◆◆◆◆◆ ◆◆◆◆◆◆◆◆◆◆◆◆◆◆◆◆◆◆◆◆◆◆◆◆◆◆◆◆◆◆◆◆

DRIVERS, START YOUR ENGINES

Wannabe roadsters have a new option for getting behind the wheel.

Autopia combines two old driving courses (one in Fantasyland and one in Tomorrowland) for one giant lap around the park. Your reward for successfully navigating your sports car, SUV or compact? Why, a driver's license, of course. All that and no traffic. In Southern California, who could ask for more?

Disneyland Monorail **★★★★** The Mark V Monorail System adds immeasurably to Tomorrowland's aura of urban futurism. Though considered an attraction, the Monorail also provides speedy transportation for two and one half miles around the edge of Tomorrowland and off the property to Downtown Disney. Leaving Tomorrowland, the route runs through Disney's California Adventure theme park. On the return trip you'll get a good overview of the south side of the park and the backside of Tomorrowland.

TIPS: The best view is in the first car with the engineer where there's room for four passengers. Most people don't think of this, so even if you're one of the last to board, don't hesitate to approach the engineer with your request.

Disneyland Lodging

When Disneyland opened on July 17, 1955, Anaheim had five hotels and two motels, with a total of 87 rooms. There were 34 restaurants in the city. Since Mickey Mouse came to town the totals have increased to more than 150 hotels and motels comprising more than 17,000 rooms, and well over 450 restaurants. This, of course, makes for a marvelously varied selection, with accommodations ranging from bare-bones budget motels to super-deluxe mega-resorts.

Yet the sheer number of hostelries can be confusing. Along Harbor Boulevard, Anaheim's main strip, dozens of hotels lie within ten minutes of Disneyland's main gate. If you're visiting Knott's Berry Farm as well, see Chapter Four for hotels in that area. Because the two parks are about ten miles apart, one hotel can serve as convenient headquarters for both attractions.

When checking hotels, in addition to price and availability, be sure to ask about packages. Some places have excellent money-saving offers that can include room, breakfast, park admittance plus tax and gratuities. Many are priced per day, some are three-day, two-night affairs. Some even have multi-attraction packages that include Disneyland, Knott's and Universal Studios.

Be sure to inquire about discounts. Especially during winter months hotels and motels are eager to fill their rooms and will

ALL WET

Only an enchantress could create a maze that changes form as you go—that, or a diabolical Disney Imagineer. The latter has fashioned the **Cosmic Wave**, a labyrinth of spurting fountains that constantly changes configuration. Wind your way in and find yourself faced with a wall of water that blocks the way you came. Even those with an expert sense of direction can't deter a good dousing. How wet will you get? Let's just say nearby kiosks selling dry t-shirts are making a killing. Think twice if your label reads "Dry Clean Only."

gladly extend discounts to AAA members, senior citizens and some airline frequent-flyer members. Don't overlook the corporate discount many hotels extend for the asking. The **Walt Disney Travel Company** offers help with family travel arrangements and packages. ~ P.O. Box 4180, Anaheim, CA 92803; 714-765-8888, 800-854-3104. If you'd like to make your own arrangements, the **Anaheim Area Visitor & Convention Bureau** will send you an excellent Travel Planner listing hotels and tours. ~ 800 West Katella Avenue; 714-765-8888, 888-598-3200; www.anaheimoc.org.

Unless otherwise noted, the following price categories include two adults and two children under 18 staying in a room. Budget hotels are generally less than $60 per night; moderate-priced hotels run $60 to $120; deluxe hotels are between $125 and $175; and ultra-deluxe facilities cost above $175.

Unless you plan to sightsee or drive to dinner, you can easily settle in at a hotel (many offer shuttle service to both Disneyland and Knott's) and not have to go near a car for several days. Even if you're at a hotel that charges for shuttle service, it's bound to be less than rental-car fees plus parking.

The original hotel in the Disneyland family, appropriately named the **Disneyland Hotel**, remains a family favorite. True, the square-box design (explained by the fact that the hotel was not built by Disney) may underwhelm Disney enthusiasts. But grown-ups who spent their youth padding tiredly through the halls after a day at the park can't help feeling nostalgic. Though changes have occurred all around it, the hotel remains much the same—so much so, you could imagine some sort of 1950s automobile exiting the parking lot. Within its 60-acre property, the 1000-plus-room resort has beautifully landscaped paths that wind among waterfalls, streams and ponds willed with brightly colored koi. The Neverland Pool has added more whimsy, with volcanoes, the Mermaid Pool and a slide through Skull Rock. In total, the hotel has three swimming pools, a tropical "beach," a fitness center, a jacuzzi, several restaurants and lounges and four shops. Rooms, in three highrise towers, are spacious and accommodating. ~ 1150 West Cerritos Avenue, Anaheim; 714-778-6600; www.disneyland.com. ULTRA-DELUXE.

Like the Disneyland Hotel, the **Paradise Pier** (formerly the Disneyland Pacific) was not born as a Disney property, but has been spiffed up to join the family. Fitted with colorful awnings and Disney art, the building is a complement to the Paradise Pier section of the California Adventure park that it overlooks. Staying here is the most economical way to get the full Disney treatment, but the Pacific is also the most lacking in the frills department. Rooms are big enough, but contemporary decor might strike some as spartan. Still, you're within shouting distance of all that the resort has to offer, and there's a character breakfast right downstairs in the on-site restaurant. ~ 1717 Disneyland Drive, Anaheim; 714-999-0990, fax 714-956-6582; www.disneyland.com. ULTRA-DELUXE.

The Anaheim Marriott offers an outstanding luxury-hotel experience. Two towers, 19 and 17 stories in height, are centered on 15 acres of flower-filled grounds. The lobby reflects a soft, contemporary feel with a sunken sitting area. Just two blocks from Disneyland, it's an easy walk or a short ride on a local shuttle. The hotel has a connecting indoor/outdoor pool, an outdoor pool, two whirlpools plus saunas and a Nautilus-equipped fitness center. There's also an arcade. Children under 18 stay free. Its 1032 rooms are medium size with small balconies, some with Disneyland views. The hotel's well-trained, obliging staff seems to feel personally responsible for your good time. ~ 700 West Convention Way, Anaheim; 714-750-8000, 800-228-9290, fax 714-748-2449; www.marriotthotels.com/laxah. ULTRA-DELUXE.

Two blocks from Disneyland stands the cavernous, 1576-room **Hilton Anaheim**, a glass-enclosed monolith. The airy atrium lobby holds four restaurants, two lounges, an arcade and assorted shops, along with a pond and fountain. A 25,000-square-foot fitness center, a basketball court, an indoor pool, an outdoor pool and a netted driving range are also among the amenities. The modern guest rooms are individually decorated. The Vacation Station, which takes place from Memorial Day until Labor Day, lets kids check in at their own counter and receive a free gift; a lending library allows them to borrow books, toys and games during their stay. The Hilton provides complimentary shuttle service to Disneyland. ~ 777 Convention Way, Anaheim; 714-750-4321, 800-222-9923, fax 714-740-4460; www.hilton.com. ULTRA-DELUXE.

The snow-covered roof at **The Alpine Motel** next door to Disneyland will no doubt please the little ones in your family. You won't find five-star luxury here (this is, after all, a budget motel), but the rooms are clean, the service is friendly, the price is reasonable and you won't have far to walk to get to Mickey's front door. ~ 715 West Katella Avenue, Anaheim; 714-535-2186, 800-772-4422, fax 714-535-2186. MODERATE.

Families who want some room to spread out might like the **Anaheim Desert Palm Inn and Suites**. One-bedroom accommodations sleep up to six people and the hotel even throws in a continental breakfast (although don't expect it to get too illustrious —we're talking toast, danish and coffee here). Those who want more elaborate morning munchies can make their own; all rooms come with refrigerators and microwaves. An outdoor pool and a game room round out the amenities. ~ 631 West Katella Avenue, Anaheim; 714-535-1133, 800-635-5423, fax 714-491-7409; www.anaheimdesertpalm.com. MODERATE TO ULTRA-DELUXE.

Folks at the family-owned **Candy Cane Inn** work hard to make you feel right at home. So named because it was established on Christmas Eve, the Candy Cane is superbly tended, with large (though simply furnished) rooms, lots of gardens and a daily continental breakfast served around a nice pool and jacuzzi. Everyone here is extra helpful; you can either walk to the park or take the shuttle. All rooms have refrigerators and coffee makers. ~ 1747 South Harbor Boulevard, Anaheim; 714-774-5284, 800-345-7057, fax 714-772-5462. MODERATE.

> It takes more than 100,000 lightbulbs of 260 types to keep Disneyland bright and glowing.

Little princes and princesses won't be able to resist the ultra-cute **Castle Inn and Suites**. The medieval decor features castle towers with faux-stone trim and shield emblems. There's a nice pool to kick back at, and the staff at this family-run property is friendly. All rooms feature refrigerators and microwaves. ~ 1734 South Harbor Boulevard, Anaheim; 714-774-8111, 800-227-8530, fax 714-956-4736; www.castleinn.com. MODERATE TO DELUXE.

Kids can feel like little cowpokes at the **Holiday Inn & Suites Anaheim**, a place where "Gunsmoke" decor creates a Western theme. Amenities include an outdoor pool, a hot tub and two restaurants. ~ 1240 South Walnut Street, Anaheim; 714-535-0300, 800-824-5459, fax 714-491-8953. MODERATE TO ULTRA-DELUXE.

The large rooms at the **Anaheim Fairfield Inn by Marriott** are brightly decorated and feature refrigerators. Service here is extra friendly, providing one kid-pleasing extra: A nearby McDonald's will deliver Happy Meals via room service! ~ 1460 South Harbor Boulevard, Anaheim; 714-772-6777, 800-228-2800, fax 714-999-1727. MODERATE.

One of the nicest of the hundreds of hotels and motels encircling the perimeter of Disneyland is the 199-room **Best Western Park Place Inn and Mini-Suites**, where children stay free. Crisp, contemporary styling sets it apart from many of its neighbors; accommodations are fresh and colorful. On the premises are a restaurant (kids eat free at certain hours) and gift shop, as well as a pool, a sauna and a jacuzzi. A complimentary continental breakfast in provided. You can walk to Disneyland, right across the street, or hop on the free shuttle. ~ 1544 South Harbor Boulevard, Anaheim; 714-776-4800, 800-854-8175, fax 714-758-1396; www.bestwestern.com. MODERATE TO DELUXE.

Best Western Raffles Inn, situated two blocks from Disneyland, offers a compromise between the huge highrise hotels and roadside motels in central Orange County. Just three stories high and sensibly sized (122 rooms), it actually conveys a bit of the "inn" feeling. It looks like one, too, with its tree-shrouded manor-house facade. Rooms feature Early American furnishings and some contain kitchenettes. Bonuses include in-room movies and an outdoor pool and jacuzzi. Rates include complimentary breakfast and shuttle service to Disneyland. Kids under 18 stay free. ~ 2040 South Harbor Boulevard, Anaheim; 714-750-6100, 800-654-0196, fax 714-740-0639. MODERATE TO DELUXE.

Camping

In Southern California, camping usually means parking your RV somewhere pleasant. In this highly urbanized area, a spot to pitch a tent is almost impossible to find unless you're willing to wander half an hour or more from Disneyland. Most facilities that bill themselves as campgrounds actually focus on recreational vehicles; some, however, do provide facilities for tent campers.

Situated in the heart of Santa Ana Canyon, **Canyon RV Park and Campground** covers 66 acres, a fraction of which has been developed for campgrounds. The balance is a natural streamside wilderness that includes a nature trail flanked by cottonwood, oak and willow trees. There are restrooms, showers, a pool, nature and bike trails, and a visitors center. ~ 24001 Santa Ana Canyon Road, Anaheim; 714-637-0210, fax 714-637-9317; www.canyonrvpark.com. BUDGET.

Five miles from Disneyland and a block and a half from Knott's Berry Farm, **Destiny Anaheim Vacation Park** has 222 spaces with RV hookups in a quiet, friendly, family-oriented park. It has phone and cable hookups, hot showers and laundry facilities, and also permits pets. Children will no doubt gravitate to the rec room, which has a large-screen TV and an assortment of games, and the pool. ~ 311 North Beach Boulevard, Anaheim; 714-821-4311, fax 714-761-1743; www.destinyrv.com. BUDGET.

Offering 300 sites, including a special area for tents, **Travelers World** is half a mile from Disneyland. Shaded by palms, this RV park features full hookups, a pool, gameroom, laundry and minimarket. Kids will enjoy the playground, and there's a small car wash on the premises. Pets are permitted. ~ 333 West Ball Road, Anaheim; 714-991-0100, fax 714-991-4939. BUDGET.

CC Camperland is a small, family-type RV park nine blocks from Disneyland with 70 hookups, showers and laundry facilities. It's pleasant and shady with a pool and pool table, and allows small pets. The area for tents is dirt, not grass, but is close to picnic tables. The public bus stops at the property to take you to Disneyland. ~ 12262 Harbor Boulevard, Garden Grove; 714-750-6747. BUDGET.

Disneyland Dining

The park gets high marks for recognizing that modern-day guests may want lighter, healthier fare that is low in the calorie and cholesterol departments. However, most of the eateries are still of the fast-food variety, with dishes that suffer from time spent on steam tables or inside plastic wrappings. The small brochure you receive when entering the park lists restaurants by area.

For the convenience of eating on Mickey's turf you may have to contend with long lines, crowded dining areas and a feeling that you'd better hurry because the people standing nearby holding food-laden trays with hungry kids in tow need your table. One solution is to eat anytime other than between 11:30 a.m. and 2 p.m., and between 4:30 and 8 p.m. Two meals a day, a late breakfast and early dinner, might work for your group. Or you can simply eat from vendor carts whenever you feel the urge. Soft pretzels, popcorn, frozen-juice bars, soft drinks, corn dogs and ice cream are readily available.

> Each guest leaves an average of a pound of trash in the park every day. That adds up to about 12 million pounds per year.

On the other hand you'll have a first-class, table-service meal if you're brave enough to handle the inevitable lines at Blue Bayou in New Orleans Square, one of the park's few full-service restaurants.

On the plus side, you have more than 30 restaurants and refreshment centers to choose from in the park. The hosts and hostesses are usually attentive and helpful and are always dressed in costumes reflecting the era and setting of the area where they work.

It's all part of the experience, unless you want to leave the park by taking the Monorail to Downtown Disney, where several more options are available. Be sure to make reservations at your chosen destination, though, since crowds here can get fierce.

Disneyland food services are grouped by the "land" in which they are located, and all are moderately priced (about $10 for a dinner entrée) except for Blue Bayou.

MAIN STREET   This has one of the park's most interesting collections of eateries, with its facilities among the most popular in the park. A sit-down breakfast option is **Carnation Café**, which specializes in sandwiches and also has a children's menu that includes macaroni and cheese. BUDGET. The largest restaurant is the spiffy **Plaza Inn**. Freshly decorated with marble and stained glass, this eatery is comfort-food heaven with fried chicken, pot roast, stews, pasta and an endless selection of deserts. Buffet-style breakfast is served daily alongside Pooh and other favorite characters. MODERATE.

Follow your nose to the **Blue Ribbon Bakery**, where oven-warmed goodies such as cookies and scones are served alongside gourmet sandwiches made with fresh-baked breads. BUDGET.

ADVENTURELAND   In keeping with the Adventureland theme, **Bengal Barbecue** purveys portable snacks including skewered meats and vegetables, Mickey Mouse pretzels and iced cappuccinos. BUDGET.

NEW ORLEANS SQUARE This area contains the park's premier restaurant, the **Blue Bayou**. Since the restaurant sits next to Pirates of the Caribbean, you can gaze out on a bayou scene complete with flickering fireflies, chirping crickets and an old-timer who rocks on the front porch of his shanty. The food is quite good, especially the Monte Cristo sandwich (served at lunch only) and the ever-changing fish dishes. Long lines are to be expected, but the restaurant does take same-day reservations. MODERATE TO DELUXE.

You can dine to the sounds of jazz at lunch or dinner at the **French Market Restaurant**. This buffeteria features Southern-style entrées including fried chicken, seafood jambalaya and pasta. MODERATE. Located close by, **Café Orleans** has a good selection of sandwiches and salads. MODERATE. Directly across from Café Orleans, **Royal Street Veranda** serves clam chowder in a bowl of French bread. BUDGET. Other gastronomic opportunities include **La Petite Patisserie**, which purveys sweet French pastries, and the **Mint Julep Bar**, where the delectable aroma of fritters, espresso and cappuccino (especially in the morning) is irresistible. BUDGET.

CRITTER COUNTRY For a "honey of a treat," and "the bear necessities," **Hungry Bear Restaurant** will satisfy your appetite with burgers, chicken nuggets, onion rings and other kid favorites. When all other food facilities are jammed, you may have better luck here because it's tucked away in a corner of the park that doesn't get much through-traffic. The rustic patio is roofed, so it's a good rainy-day destination.

FRONTIERLAND **River Belle Terrace**, with a view of Rivers of America, serves Mickey-shaped pancakes, eggs and bacon in generous, brunch-size helpings. The expected salads and sandwiches are there for lunch and dinner, but a standout is the vegetable stew served in a bread basket. MODERATE. Don't wear your best finery to **Rancho del Zocalo**—the barbecue fare may get a

HAM AND CHEESE AND MICKEY

Kids love to eat alongside Mickey Mouse, Donald Duck and the rest of the Disney gang. These galas, called **Character Meals**, feature colorful balloons, favorite Disney tunes and autographs by the animated personalities. Goofy's Kitchen at the Disneyland Hotel offers daily lunch and dinner character buffets, as well as lunch buffets on weekends (ask about special birthday celebrations, too!). At the Storyteller's Cafe in the Grand Californian you'll find daily character breakfasts. The Paradise Pier Hotel has daily character breakfasts in the PCH Grill; weekends in the upstairs parlor, the Pier also hosts the Practically Perfect Tea with Mary Poppins. Call 714-778-6600 and ask for dining reservations. BUDGET TO DELUXE.

little messy. The food-court eatery also sports Mexican, with burritos and tacos to go along with your chicken and ribs. Just make sure to get lots of napkins. Those who prefer the neater knife-and-fork approach can opt for prime rib. MODERATE.

Chili in a bread bowl, chips and cookies are served at the **Golden Horseshoe Stage** during show times, and you can pick up a burger or hot dog at the **Stage Door Café** next door to enjoy during the performance. BUDGET.

FANTASYLAND The **Village Haus**, which re-creates the atmosphere of the film *Pinocchio*, is the primary dining facility in Fantasyland. Intricate turrets, gables and weather vanes adorn the exterior; colorful murals decorate the inside. On the menu are hamburgers, pizza, and Mickey-shaped chicken nuggets for kids. MODERATE. There's the **Fantasyland Fruit Cart**, located near Fantasia Gardens, that provides a place to stop for quick snacks and fresh fruit. BUDGET.

TOMORROWLAND Food takes a back seat to entertainment at Tomorrowland's **Club Buzz**. The fare is vintage Disney—burgers, fried chicken, salads. But, come during show time and see Buzz tear up the universe alongside such characters as Space Cadet Starla and those adorable Little Green Men. The food's served all day, but the shows are at designated times only. If the floorshow is part of your preferred menu, check at Guest Services for the schedule. MODERATE. **Redd Rockett's Pizza Port** serves salads, pizza, and pasta dishes. A child-sized "space"ghetti meal is available for those under 8. MODERATE.

DOWNTOWN DISNEY Come here for a nearly endless number of dining experiences. It's a good idea to make reservations because the area tends to become crowded with guests (not to mention locals) and waits for tables can stretch to hours long. Relax upstairs or downstairs over Mediterranean dishes at **Catal Restaurant & Uva Bar**. DELUXE. Revel in Southern Italian specialties at **Naples Risorante e Pizzeria**. DELUXE. For music and food of New Orleans, try out **Ralph Brennan's Jazz Kitchen**. MODERATE TO DELUXE. Chain eateries **House of Blues**, **Rainforest Café** and the **ESPN Zone** (all MODERATE) have all set up shop with their familiar brands of food and entertainment. Snacks and desserts are on the menu at **Häagen-Dazs**, **La Brea Bakery Café**, **Marceline's Confectionery** and **Wetzel's Pretzels** (all MODERATE).

Restaurants of every description surround Disneyland, and most offer moderately priced food. At **Goofy's Kitchen**, Disney Character Meals are wildly popular. Presented for breakfast and dinner every day and lunch Monday through Friday, the meals are attended by Goofy and other Disney char-

Dining Outside Disneyland

acters who interact with the kids and pose for photos. The all-you-can-eat buffet includes muffins, waffles, cereal and fruit at breakfast, and hot dogs, hamburgers, chicken and roast beef at dinner. Character attendance occurs during summer only. ~ Disneyland Hotel, 1150 West Cerritos Avenue, Anaheim; 714-778-6600, reservations 714-956-6755. MODERATE.

If it's steak you're after, try **Hook's Pointe & Wine Cellar** at the Disneyland Hotel. The menu also features delicious mesquite-grilled dishes like cognac-marinated rib-eye steak and Pacific salmon; the well-stocked wine cellar helps you recover from the day's events. ~ Disneyland Hotel, 1150 West Cerritos Avenue, Anaheim; 714-778-6600. DELUXE TO ULTRA-DELUXE.

Grownups and kids can both get their favorites at **Disney's PCH Grill**. This restaurant at the Paradise Pier Hotel is a trendy-looking place where adults can enjoy tasty fusion cuisine (check out the grilled sea bass and baked panko salmon) while kids get a supply of their own favorites (macaroni and cheese, pizza, etc.). The kids' pizza is make-your-own; toss the fixings together at the table (on a Mickey-shaped tray, of course) and then bring it to the chef to watch it bake. Mornings, the restaurant hosts a charming character breakfast. ~ Paradise Pier Hotel, 1717 Disneyland Drive, Anaheim; 714-999-0990, fax 714-956-6582. DELUXE TO ULTRA-DELUXE.

A full sushi bar in Disneyland? That's exactly what **Yamabuki** has to offer, as well as stir-fry dishes, tempura and teriyaki. Laid out in a Japanese-style fashion, the dining area includes a traditional *tatami* room where guests are invited to take off their shoes, sit on cushion-covered straw mats and indulge in the culinary delights of authentic Japanese cuisine. No lunch Saturday and Sunday. ~ Paradise Pier Hotel, 1717 Disneyland Drive, Anaheim; 714-239-5683, reservations 714-956-6755. DELUXE TO ULTRA-DELUXE.

LUNCHTIME STRATEGY

Between 11:30 a.m. and 2 p.m., and 4:30 p.m. and 8 p.m., park food services are jammed. It's impossible to get near the Blue Bayou, one of the few table-service restaurants. An alternative is to catch the Monorail from Tomorrowland to Downtown Disney. Have your hand stamped and your ticket stubs with you when you disembark, then walk a block to **Goofy's Kitchen**, an all-you-can-eat buffet at the Disney Hotel. Dine with Goofy and company for breakfast, lunch or dinner; there's also a children's buffet. Another option is to check out the action at Downtown Disney.

One of the area's best values for atmosphere and satisfying dining is **Mr. Stox**, which boasts a versatile menu of steak, rack of lamb, veal, pasta and mesquite-broiled fresh seafood. Special touches include savory herbs and spices grown in a garden out back, plus homemade breads and desserts and an award-winning wine cellar with over 900 selections. No lunch on Saturday and Sunday. ~ 1105 East Katella Avenue, Anaheim; 714-634-2994; www.mrstox.com, e-mail mrstox@mrstox.com. DELUXE.

For steak and seafood, try **JW's Steakhouse** at the Anaheim Marriott. Of special interest to those from out of state is the extensive California wine list that includes some of the area's best, but not necessarily most expensive, vintages. Dinner only. ~ 700 West Convention Way, Anaheim; 714-748-3187, fax 714-750-9100. DELUXE TO ULTRA-DELUXE.

Ming Delight Restaurant offers a completely different Asian dining experience. The Mandarin and Szechuan cuisine is served in a sophisticated setting complete with elegantly carved Chinese chairs and red-and-gold wallhangings. The extensive menu has intriguing fare like Four Delights in a Bird Nest (shrimp, chicken, beef and pork) and Happy Family (shrimp, scallops, chicken and beef). Kids seem to like the grown-up atmosphere and can't keep their hands off the Lazy Susan that adorns the center of each table. ~ 409 West Katella Avenue, Anaheim; 714-758-0978. MODERATE.

Tiffy's Family Restaurant & Ice Cream Parlor is a winner with kids from the moment they walk in the door and spot the stuffed animals and candy counter. Motherly waitresses make recommendations and help with ordering. The kids' menu includes corn dogs, tacos, hamburgers and hot dogs, but the big hit is the homemade ice cream in flavors like pineapple coconut and chocolate peanut butter. Adults can choose from boneless barbecued chicken, fish and chips, chicken fingers and more. The pseudo stained-glass skylights and etched-glass partitions give the place a vaguely saloon-type atmosphere, but it's a plain old coffee shop that does its job well. ~ 1060 West Katella Avenue, Anaheim; 714-635-1801, fax 714-635-1802. MODERATE.

Flaky Jake's is cavernous and informal with ceiling fans and a white gazebo in the center and legions of people lined up to place their orders. Hamburgers and sandwiches come ready to embellish with any of the 20 items from the toppings bar. Other items are ribs, fish and chips, steak and chicken. Kids love the noisy atmosphere and the mini-arcade in the corner. ~ 101 East Katella Avenue, Anaheim; 714-535-1446, fax 714-991-3663. BUDGET TO MODERATE.

As buffets go, **Hansa House** is unimaginative but reliable. The Swedish-American food is fresh and varied. Captain's chairs are clustered at light hardwood tables, and the walls are papered in a vaguely Scandinavian blue print. Kids are charged according to their age. Breakfast, lunch and dinner are served. ~ 1840 South Harbor Boulevard, Anaheim; 714-750-2411. BUDGET TO MODERATE.

It's impossible to miss the **Spaghetti Station Restaurant,** a funky building surrounded with wagon wheels and antique mining paraphernalia. Inside, the Western mini-museum keeps you entertained while you wait. Adult fare includes the Geronimo (spaghetti with marinara sauce) and Sitting Bull (New York steak and spaghetti). The kids can fuel up with Billy the Kid (spaghetti with meat sauce), Sugarfoot Sal (spaghetti with tomato sauce), Pony Pizza (pepperoni pizza) and Little Bighorn ravioli. ~ 999 West Ball Road, Anaheim; 714-956-3250; www.spaghetti-station.com, e-mail webmaster@spaghetti-station.com. BUDGET TO MODERATE.

Disneyland Shopping

Inside Disneyland, Main Street is the prime shopping area. Because it's open earlier and later than the park itself, you have good opportunities to shop when there's nothing else to do. This is also where rental lockers are located, so you can stash your purchases instantly if you don't want to send them to package pickup to collect later. Guests at any of the Disney hotels can have packages send directly to their rooms.

Watches and clocks featuring Mickey Mouse and other Disney characters can be found at **New Century Timepieces,** along with traditional watches. Glass-domed anniversary clocks and wall cuckoos are among the myriad ways to determine the time of day in this interesting shop. At the **20th Century Music Company,** you can purchase Disney soundtracks, or make your own CD with "sounds from Disneyland." The **Market House** is an old-fashioned general store with candies and natural-food snacks, coffee and cider. You're even welcome to sit down to a game of checkers. Expertly crafted glassware and crystal at **Crystal Arts** can be engraved and monogrammed to take home as personalized gifts. Chances are those mouse ears you see on kids all over the park have come from the **Mad Hatter Shop**. It also has Easter bonnets, Tyrolean headgear and Donald Duck hats. Names are embroidered free on mouse ears.

In Adventureland there are shops to remind guests of this area's harrowing adventures, plus camouflage clothing and Indiana Jones hats. At the **Indiana Jones Adventure Outpost,** there's the full range of logo items: T-shirts, sweatshirts, mugs and even licorice strips. **South Seas Traders** sells shell jewelry and Polynesian beachwear and swimwear, and you'll find shells, snakes and shrunken skulls at **Tropical Imports**.

One of the favorite shopping areas is in New Orleans Square, where unique cooking and serving accessories, gadgets and recipe books tempt the connoisseur at **Crystal d'Orleans**. In the spirit of Mardi Gras, **Mascarades d'Orleans** carries a glittering selection of masks, costumes and accessories. Collectors of Christmas ornaments should not miss **L'Ornement Magique**, where Yuletide decorations and gifts featuring Disney characters are available year-round. You won't want to use it for a rainstorm, but at the **Parasol Cart** you can have your hand-painted parasol personalized. If you decide to have your portrait done at **Portrait Artists**, watch for a few minutes to decide which artist to choose. Although each has an interesting personal style, you may find one artist's technique more appealing than another's.

> Each day the Disneyland crew polishes 221 automobiles and 205 ships and boats.

Shopping's somewhat limited in Critter Country, but if you liked Splash Mountain you might want to stop at the **Briar Patch**, the ride's official souvenir headquarters. At **Pooh Corner** all the clothing, toys, jewelry and books feature Winnie the Pooh and his friends.

Where else would you expect to find a coonskin cap but in Frontierland? They and other Western-themed items are available at **Western Ho Trading Company**. Browse through the interesting Western and Indian-themed gifts, including well-done turquoise and silver jewelry, at the **Pioneer Mercantile**. The wonderful, earthy smell of leather at **Bonanza Outfitters** may draw you inside, but once there you'll be fascinated by items like fringed leather vests for one-year-olds and tiny moccasins for babies.

Fantasyland is where adults say they most frequently succumb to their tykes' pleas for souvenirs. A quick glance at too-cute-for-words shops like **Tinker Bell Toy Shoppe**, **It's a Small World Toy Shoppe** and **Stromboli's Wagon** confirms why. Cuddly plush dolls, toys and Disney characters beg to be picked up and held.

Shopping takes a back seat to the rides in Tomorrowland, although the sports-oriented **Premiere Shop** offers some possibilities; it's stocked with apparel, golf balls, collectible pins, cards, plaques and autographed balls. If you missed the mouse ears earlier, there's a second chance here at **The Hatmosphere**.

DOWNTOWN DISNEY In addition to being a paradise of food, Downtown Disney is also a shopper's heaven. The flagship store is most certainly the **World of Disney**, stocked with mountains of Disney merchandise. If you can't find that pin, hat, stuffed Pooh, logo jacket or sweatshirt here . . . it doesn't exist. Handbag addicts will be drawn through the doors of **Petals** which features the latest in bags from Kate Spade and others. If you don't already know how to surf, the ultra-hip togs at **Liquid Planet** will make you want to learn. In addition to selling every brand of sunglasses known to man, **Soliton** also sells some nifty accessories such as key chains containing lens cleaners. Dress up your refrigerator at

Tin Pan Alley, which specializes in a multitude of unique and interesting magnets.

▼ ▼ ▼ ▼ ▼ ▼ ▼ ▼ ▼ ▼ ▼ ▼ ▼ ▼

Disneyland Nightlife

If there was any question before, the introduction of **Downtown Disney** proves the point: Disneyland isn't just for children. Big kids can get their fill of entertainment anywhere along this recently created stretch of Disney metropolis. There's live music and dance at **House of Blues, Y Arriba! Y Arriba!** and **Ralph Brennan's Jazz Kitchen.** The action at the **ESPN Zone** is primarily on tape, but you can still enjoy the game and a brew (there's food here, too). For a quiet yet tasty evening, savor the food and wine at **Catal Restaurant & Uva Bar.** DELUXE. For upscale and romantic, nothing beats the gourmet cuisine at the spectacular **Napa Rose** restaurant at Disney's Grand Californian Hotel. (See "California Adventure Dining" for further details.) If all of that seems too formal, check out the California Adventure itself. With rides and its own boardwalk, it rates as a first-class date park.

Be sure to check the Disneyland schedule for evening events inside the park. See "Nightlife" in Knott's Berry Farm (Chapter Four) for information on the best nighttime shows for kids outside the parks.

THREE

California Adventure

Given California's image as a kind of real world Neverland (perpetual sunshine, sparkling sand, a population that seems to never grow old) a theme park based on the Golden State might seem redundant.

But then, what better next-door neighbor for Fantasyland?

After nearly a half-century as an only child, Disneyland at last got itself a sibling, namely the ode to all things Golden State: Disney's California Adventure. That a slab of asphalt begot an amusement park would have to be the work of Disney magic. The resort's citified locale left designers with a challenge: The Anaheim site had only a finite space—55 acres of parking lot, to be precise. It was no small amount of masterful Imagineering that metamorphosed 15,000 parking spaces into a sparkling ocean bay complete with seaside amusements and waves lapping up against the pilings of a boardwalk.

In all there are three lands here—four if you count the Sunshine Plaza, the park's entryway equivalent of Main Street U.S.A. in Disneyland. The Hollywood Pictures Backlot immerses you in Tinseltown with shows, an inventive animation tour, and even a restaurant that makes you feel as if you've entered an ABC soap. Paradise Pier, with its upscale carnival-style rides, so accurately recalls bygone seaside amusement parks you'll be looking for the tilt-a-whirl (thankfully, there isn't one). The Golden State, the most sprawling section of the park, takes you from the High Sierras to the Pacific Wharf, San Francisco and Monterey.

Purists have scoffed that taking inspiration from reel (as opposed to real) life lacks imagination. And that the simplified landscape does an injustice to the actual place. True, walking from the Golden Gate Bridge to, say, Hollywood does feel a little like touring the Golden State CliffsNotes style. On the other hand, that Disney's adventures in California are a mite tidier than the average Angeleno's has got to be a good thing. Who, after all, would want to visit a park in which rides include a trip to plastic surgery-land?

But all of the pontificating aside, the real question is, will you like it? The answer is a qualified yes. Disney has done a good job celebrating what's best about the Golden State, and this reel-life version is quaint and entertaining. That's not to say coming here is a substitute for, say, hiking Yosemite (one would hope not, anyway). It is, after all, just a theme park.

In truth, enjoying the California Adventure has less to do with content than expectation. Those who anticipate a whiz-bang ride emporium are destined to be disappointed. True, there are some bonafide doozies here (see "Soarin' Over California"), but they share equal billing with an atmosphere that's designed to be leisurely soaked up.

Much like the Animal Kingdom down in Orlando, DCA (as its acronym goes) courts a slower pace. Designers seem to want you to stroll rather than dash from place to place. Novelties—such as old-fashioned ice cream cones, a glass of wine (in a nod to one of the state's famed industries, the park unapologetically serves alcohol) and those love-'em or hate-'em boardwalk games where you toss a ball to win a lovably homely stuffed toy—encourage a comfortable pace.

Not that that's a bad thing. In theme park terms, it can be a relief—in a way, this is the perfect neighbor for Disneyland. Parents who've witnessed their children's over-stimulated meltdowns might just be grateful for the chance to take their time. Furthermore, issues regarding value—early complaints centered around the fact that California Adventure charged the same as Disneyland but for noticeably fewer rides—will be addressed in the coming months with the introduction of several new attractions. Young children, who were considered underserved when the park opened in 2001, will have myriad new options when DCA opens Flik's Fun Fair in fall 2002 (the new themed area will include five kids' attractions). Thrill riders will get an added attraction when Tower of Terror arrives in 2004.

With expectations in order, the park makes for an enjoyable day. Still, you'll have to make your own call. For whatever it's worth, my own daughters—albeit rollercoaster-phobic, ice cream–adoring, show-loving preteens—called it an absolute California dream.

▼▼▼▼▼▼▼▼▼▼▼▼

Nuts & Bolts

ARRIVAL

New off-ramps from I-5 that head directly into Disneyland have simplified driving enormously, as has the addition of a new, 10,000-vehicle, six-story parking garage. Nevertheless, traffic, particularly on holidays and summer weekends, is often snarled. Peak times are also known for long lines at the ticket window. Buying tickets in advance (either online or at your hotel) can speed the entry process enormously. Off-site hotels occasionally have promotions that make buying in advance even more advantageous.

From Area Hotels: Most offer complimentary shuttle service.

From Disney Resort Hotels: Guests of the Disneyland Hotel and the Paradise Pier Hotel can take the monorail into both parks for no charge. Those staying at the Grand Californian have an easy walk to Disneyland and Downtown Disney and have a special entrance from the hotel to the middle of the California Adventure. The parking-lot trams also stop at the Disneyland Hotel and will take you to the park's main gate, or you can make it with a five-minute walk.

CALIFORNIA ADVENTURE

PARADISE PIER

California Screamin'
Golden Zephyr
Jumpin' Jellyfish
King Triton's Carousel
Maliboomer
Mulholland Madness
Orange Stinger
Sun Wheel
S.S. rustworthy

GOLDEN STATE

The Boudin Bakery
Golden Dreams
Grizzly River Run
"It's Tough to be a Bug"
Mission Tortilla Factory
Redwood Creek Challenge Trail
Seasons of the Vine
Soarin' Over California

HOLLYWOOD PICTURES BACKLOT

Disney Animation
Hyperion Theater
Jim Henson's Muppet*Vision 3D
Superstar Limo
Who Wants to Be a Millionaire—Play It!

SUNSHINE PLAZA

↑
ENTRANCE

By Car: The park is approximately 27 miles south of Downtown Los Angeles on Route 5. Follow the signs to the Disneyland Resort.

At press time, the cost of parking was $7. Be sure to note your parking row (and the color and license of your rental car) because it's easy to lose your car in this giant place. A tram will take you to the main entrance. Reduced-rate parking is available on Disney Way east of Harbor Boulevard, but you'll have to walk to the park as the lot *is not* serviced by the tram. Guests can be dropped off at the special 15-minute drop-off zone south of the Esplanade traffic signal.

TICKETS

The Disneyland Resort offers several ticket options, called "passports." One-day tickets are good for one park, one day. Multiday "hopper" passes come in three- and four-day denominations and cover entrance to both parks. Annual two-park passports include the *Premium*, good for every day of the year, and the less-expensive *Deluxe*, which is blacked out on roughly 45 dates occurring on holidays and peak-season weekends. At $99, the *Southern California Annual Passport* (for Southern California residents only) is ultra-economical, but is blacked out for roughly 160 days including holiday weeks, peak weekends and Saturdays throughout the year.

	Adults	Children 3–9
		(Under 3 years, free)
One-day Ticket	$45.00	$35.00
Three-day Park Hopper	$114.00	$90.00
Four-day Park Hopper	$141.00	$111.00
Deluxe Annual Passport	$159.00	$159.00
Premium Annual Passport	$219.00	$219.00

GAME PLAN

For the most part, the California Adventure seems to be less crowded than Disneyland, a condition that's no doubt better for visitors than for park management. That's not to say you won't hit any lines—summer afternoons during the week, for example, can be popular for groups to visit, which can increase the crowd factor significantly. Still, overall, lines are manageable, particularly if you make use of FastPasses where available.

If you're starting your day early, turn right inside the main park entrance and head straight to Soarin' Over California. Like It's a Small World at Disneyland, Soarin' has become this park's flagship ride; it's often the attraction guests choose to begin and end their park visits, leading to a queue that's usually full. A good strategy is to grab a FastPass as you get in line, thereby ensuring yourself two trips in quick succession (most everybody wants to ride it more than once). If you're sweltering under the summer sun, consider making your second stop Grizzly River Run, a water ride that will leave you, shall we say, refreshed. The upside of this approach is proximity because Grizzly is right next door. The downside is that you'll spend at least part of your visit in squishy clothes. Alternatively, you could save Grizzly for the end of your stay (not too late, as the ride can be a lot less fun in the cooler hours after the sun has gone down), which will leave you and your soggy clothes just a short walk from the park exit.

As the midday hours start to bring more visitors, a good refuge can be found in the Hollywood Pictures Backlot. Large-capacity rides (such as MuppetVision) and walk-throughs (such as Animation) make lines move quickly. And since most of Holly-wood's features are indoors, you'll have the great good benefit of being in air conditioning just as the California sun starts to bear down. As your stomach screams for lunch (and the later you eat the shorter your wait for food), head down through the Golden State and nosh your way through some particularly tasty food stops (the Lucky Fortune Cookery and the Pacific Wharf Café, to name two). This also might be a good time for a "Vineyard" break, when you can actually partake of a little wine tasting. When you're done eating (and walking), you'll find yourself on the ap-proach to Paradise Pier—but save the area's stomach-churning rides (Maliboomer and, particularly, the Orange Stinger) for *well* after you've fully digested.

A couple of other strategies to consider:

❖ **Stop and smell the roses:** At 55 acres with roughly two dozen attractions (and some of those short enough to defy the term "attraction"), the park is absolutely do-able in one day. That's not to say you should attempt to race through it. On the contrary, the ambience seems to inspire a surprisingly unfrenetic and relaxed pace. To boot, the park has a nice collection of non-theme-park-like fare. Take time to enjoy it.

❖ **Group your destinations:** Sure, compared to the behe-moths, this park seems small. But there's still a lot of ground to cover. You'll save yourself a lot of headaches (not to mention aches and pains in parts southward) if you plan your day so as not to be traipsing back and forth from one end of the park to the other.

STREET SHOW

Entertainment isn't limited to what you find on the inside of attractions. The streets of California are teeming with starlets, characters and lively bands. There's even storytelling along the Redwood Creek Challenge Trail. Most performances operate on a schedule. Check at the board on the way in.

Guests of the regal Grand Californian Hotel can save some additional stress on the dogs by hoofing it to the special hotel entrance located in the Grizzly Recreation Area.

GUEST SERVICES

General Information Disneyland Resort Guest Services: 1313 Harbor Boulevard, Anaheim, CA 92803; 714-781-4565.

Stroller and Wheelchair Rentals Stroller and wheelchair rentals (as well as some electric convenience vehicles) are available just inside of the park's Golden Gateway to the right.

Baby Services Located next to the Mission Tortilla Factory in Pacific Wharf. You'll find facilities for preparing formulas, warming bottles and changing infants. Diapers and other baby needs are available for purchase. Changing tables as well as diaper machines are featured in most park restrooms.

Lockers Located outside the park to the left of Guest Relations and inside the park, just inside the gate to the right.

Pets The kennel is located to the right of the Disneyland Park main entrance.

Lost Children Children under ten will be taken to the Baby Care Center next to the Mission Tortilla Factory in Pacific Wharf.

Lost & Found Located in the Golden Gateway Guest Relations Lobby.

First Aid The First Aid Center is located near Baby Services next to the Mission Tortilla Factory in Pacific Wharf. Registered nurses are always on duty.

Banking An ATM is located outside the park to the left of Guest Relations. Numerous ATMs are also located inside the park, and checks up to $100 can be cashed at the Guest Relations Lobby in the Golden Gateway.

Packing Express Serious shoppers should consider this free service, which lets you pick up all your California Adventure purchases at the end of the day at the Main Entry Plaza (allow at least two hours before pickup). Guests staying onsite can have their packages sent back to their hotels.

Shows and Attractions Get details about attraction wait-times at the Information Board located right past the Golden Gate Bridge on your right.

IT'S NOT A SMALL WORLD, AFTER ALL

Veteran Disney visitors will be challenged by the new geography (two parks, three hotels *and* Downtown Disney). You're best off approaching the resort as an entirely new entity. Those who try to navigate based on their recollections of old are doomed to become hopelessly disoriented.

Though designers strove for authenticity, this California is devoid of the unwieldy thoroughfares for which California is famous. In fact, ease of navigation is a particular standout here. Speaking as one of the directionally challenged, I found it difficult to get lost. The landscape is literally a level playing field, with attractions sprawled out and clearly visible before you. You don't have to walk far from the entrance before you see glimpses of Paradise Pier (as marked by the towering Sun Wheel) at the other end of the park.

GETTING AROUND

The layout is less traditional than Disneyland in that the main hub (in this case, the Sunshine Plaza) isn't actually dead center of the park. Instead, it's midway between Hollywood and Grizzly Peak, with the rest spreading out to the northeast behind it. Nevertheless, "lands" are clearly marked by distinct character differences from one to the next (in other words, there's no mistaking it when you've left Pacific Wharf and entered Paradise Pier).

Enter through the Golden Gateway. Turn left into the Hollywood Pictures Backlot. Go right or straight ahead to cover all points of the Golden State, and a straight shot back to Paradise Pier. The Pacific Wharf Bridge will help you navigate around the Eureka! street parade by taking you straight from the Golden State on to Paradise Pier.

Walk into the park, cross under the Golden Gate Bridge and find yourself in the Sunshine Plaza, the "Main Street" of California Adventure. Though small compared to its relative at Disneyland (there are only two stores and two counter-service eateries here), the park's central point is nevertheless designed to attract your attention. The towering 50-foot sun for which the gateway is named reflects off of a fountain below it, and makes for an excellent central meeting place in the event your party gets separated. In addition, the plaza is a prime viewing spot for the Eureka! and Electrical parades, since the procession routes loop around the fountain. Perhaps, most importantly, this is where you'll be able to start your day with the park's strongest cup of coffee. The Baker's Field Bakery, located in the middle of the California Zephyr (a replica of a famous post–World War II train) roasts fresh beans throughout the day, and serves some tasty baked goods as well. Just follow your nose.

Sunshine Plaza

Golden elephants stand guard on either side of the entrance, and you can practically hear Ethel Merman's intonations about show business (and there being nothing like it).

Hollywood Pictures Backlot

This Southern California portion of the park pays homage to California's real-life fantasyland otherwise known as Hollywood. All along Hollywood Boulevard are sound stages, klieg lights and movie props (there's even a theater in the style of an old-fashioned movie palace) designed to replicate the feel of old-time Tinseltown.

WHAT TO SEE & DO

Disney Animation ★★★★ What kids (or adults, for that matter) haven't wished themselves into the landscape of a Disney animated feature? Though this engaging attraction won't exactly launch you into the air via pixie dust, it is the next best thing.

Housed in a cavernous structure midway down Hollywood Boulevard, Disney Animation does its best to fully immerse you in the fine art of drawing classics. Eight themed areas span the animation world. Enter through the Courtyard Gallery, a giant room where similarly giant-sized clips of Disney films play overhead. In an adjoining theater, veteran Disney World visitors will recognize the *Back to Neverland* film from Disney/MGM down in Florida. For those unfamiliar with the primer, it's not to be missed: a hysterical look at the art of animation, featuring Robin Williams as a wannabe Lost Boy and Walter Cronkite as his straight man. Down the hall and also played for much deserved laughs, the new and equally entertaining Drawn to Animation show (featuring the funny dragon Mushu from *Mulan* fame teamed up with a living, breathing animator) details the process of character development. Exit the Drawn theater and find yourself in the Art of Animation Gallery, a museum that showcases how familiar characters have evolved.

For kids, the most spellbinding portions of the attraction by far are the entrancing rooms of the Sorcerer's Workshop. Prepare to stay awhile in each of the three galleries. Collectively, these rooms are imagination heaven, with magic mirrors, slightly spooky Disney music, and walls that magically change decor. Experiment with early animation tools (zoetropes, whirling drums and others) in the Magic Mirror Realm. Let Lumiere and Cogsworth (of *Beauty and the Beast* fame) assess your inner character in the Enchanted Books room. Lend your voice to characters

HOLLYWOOD'S GOLDEN AGE

What else to do in Hollywood but take in a show? With its classic marquees and ornate interior, the **Hyperion Theater** harks back to bygone movie palaces. Though it looks old-fashioned, this theater is post-millennium state-of-the-art, with a high-tech sound system and ultra-modern stage designed to accommodate Broadway caliber shows. In fact, one of its first offerings was *The Power of Blast*, excerpts from the Tony–award winning Broadway show, *Blast*. Be sure to check the schedule at the start of your visit for the latest offerings and a list of show times.

from *The Little Mermaid* and other animated films in Ursula's Grotto.

TIPS: Large-capacity theaters make for quick entry into Back to Neverland and Drawn to Animation. The interactive nature of the Sorcerer's Workshop, however, can make for some lengthy waits. If the line is short for the Workshop when you arrive, visit it first since the queue will fill up when the theaters let out.

ANOTHER TIP: Though the workshop is great fun, dark rooms and spooky music can be intimidating. Those with little ones might want to be prepared to make a quick exit.

Jim Henson's Muppet*Vision 3D ★★★★★ You'd have to be a real grouch not to laugh at this lively performance starring Kermit, Miss Piggy and friends. One of the best family shows in all of the Disney empire, this transplant from Disney/MGM in Florida—combining a 3-D film with special effects and live action—is completely and unapologetically silly, with plots ranging from a disenfranchised bunny to a lovelorn pig in her underwear. Bubbles fly, fireworks soar, and an irascible chef launches unintelligible barbs—not to mention a cannon blast. There's even an in-the-fuzz appearance by a life-size Muppet. The pièce de résistance: a mischievous 'toon escapes from the 3-D FX lab and wreaks havoc on the timely but completely unconventional patriotic finale, "Salute to All Nations But Mostly America." A don't-miss all around.

TIPS: The large-capacity theater seats nearly 600 people, enabling even long lines to move quickly. But this is one attraction you won't mind waiting for because the pre-show is every bit as funny as the main event.

ANOTHER TIP: Unlike other 3-D shows such as "It's Tough to be a Bug" and "Honey I Shrunk the Audience," Muppet-Vision is quite child-friendly. Even so, the glasses take some getting used to, and some of the effects (such as a balloon burst and fireworks explosions) might be startling. Because of a large-size surprise about halfway through the show, skittish children might do better at least a few rows back from the front.

Superstar Limo ★ Silly is the best (and perhaps kindest) word to describe this weird limo trip through Hollywood (so weird it may be a memory by the time this makes it to print!). Ostensibly an adventure in which you're headed to an important "biz" meeting, travelers arrive on queue at LAX, where a sultry voice dispenses wisdom about luggage and no-parking zones. "Limos" then escort you through the black-lit worlds of Bel Air, Hollywood and Beverly Hills pool parties, all the while the announcer narrating in his best Don Pardo impersonation. Along the way, look for animatron celebrities including Drew Carey, Tim Allen, Melanie Griffith and Antonio Banderas. The adventure ends at your movie premiere, where Whoopie Goldberg introduces you as Hollywood's newest star.

It's hard to know exactly what to make of the adventure, which is neither a thrill ride nor particularly imaginative (though the appearance of an animatronic Joan Rivers at the end may have the effect of making some folks think it's a fright show). Ride attendants do their best to play up the attitude by referring to all guests as "stars." But despite their best efforts, the adventure falls flat. The exit photo usually captures guests looking more confused than entertained. Nevertheless, you'll want to at least make an effort to look stately as the ride misses no opportunity to temporarily affix your kisser onto billboard-sized posters.

TIPS: Definitely not one of Disney's best. Unless your trip to SoCal requires that you star-gaze (albeit in animatron form), skip it.

Who Wants To Be a Millionaire—Play It! ★★★★★ It looks the same, sounds the same and feels the same as the one on TV . . . but there's no Regis and you can't actually win a million dollars (congenial stand-in hosts do quite nicely, however, and you'll have to settle for a million points instead). Still, everyone has a ball at this interactive version where contestants take the hot seat and vie for such prizes as hats and collectible pins.

The dramatic set is a twin of the original, "Hot Seat" and all. The "Fastest Finger" seats are here, but don't fret if you don't snag one for the game. They may look cool, but every seat in the audience is armed for play, meaning each and every guest has the same opportunity to land in the chair of honor. Two of the "Lifelines" are familiar: "Ask the Audience" and "50/50." Since odds are you haven't stationed some knowledgeable person at a nearby phone for the "Phone a Friend" option, the last Lifeline is the less-encouraging "Phone a Complete Stranger," where another Disney guest picks up your call from elsewhere in the park. Don't think the upper-award-level questions are any easier than those posed by Regis. During one foray, the Fastest Finger question listed four actresses and challenged players to put them in order of their conversion to Judaism. Wannabe Hot-Seat inhabitants will have to move fast (hit your answer as soon as you see the green light) because the winners seem to punch in at the speed of light. Even if you don't answer a single question correctly, you'll have an absolute ball.

TIPS: Typically, shows are every hour on the hour. But check the schedule on the way in to ensure you don't miss out. During peak season, this is a FastPass must since shows often fill to capacity.

ANOTHER TIP: The 12 Fastest Finger seats don't have any benefits over the rest of the stage—except that they're really cool to sit in. If you want to snag one, be sure to arrive plenty early—even if you're holding a FastPass for the show—and put on your most colorful behavior.

Coming
Attractions

Like the Golden State itself, the landscape of the California Adventure is a constantly growing universe. The park's coming attractions encompass both ends of the spectrum—low-key kiddie entertainment and all-out terror.

TERROR ON HOLLYWOOD PICTURES BACKLOT

Thrill seekers, be prepared to get that sinking feeling in 2004 when the **Twilight Zone Tower of Terror** goes up in the Hollywood Pictures Backlot. Imagineers pay homage to Rod Serling's spooky TV spectacle with a lift up (and, more importantly, back down) in the haunted elevator shaft of the Hollywood Tower.

COMING SOON TO AN ANT HILL NEAR YOU

Once a low-key emporium of exhibits and coloring stations, the area known as Bountiful Valley Farm will get an overhaul in fall 2002 when the park introduces **A Bug's Land**. The new area will fold "It's Tough to be a Bug" and what was Bountiful Valley farm into a self-contained themed area akin to Toon Town in Disneyland.

Once inside the new area, the universe becomes oversize, and visitors will feel bug-sized amid enormous garden tools and greenery. Look for **Flik's Fun Fair**, a new attraction section with five kiddy rides including **Flik's Flyers, Tuck & Roll's Drive 'Em Buggies, Heimlich's Chew Chew Train, Francis's Ladybug Boogie** and **Princess Dot's Puddle Park**.

▼▼▼▼▼▼▼▼▼▼
Golden State

With scenic vistas as diverse as San Francisco, Monterey and the High Sierras, this sprawling section of the California Adventure could qualify for statehood all by itself.

Six districts cut a wide swath through the center of the California Adventure. There are plenty of attractions here (particularly over towards Condor Flats and Grizzly Peak). But you'll want to take your time strolling them thar hills—especially in Pacific Wharf, in which numerous tasty food stops will feed more than just your imagination.

WHAT TO SEE & DO

PACIFIC WHARF Cross over the Pacific Wharf Bridge and there's no mistaking your arrival in Cannery Row. The seaside town charm makes it one of the coziest—and most artfully re-created—spots in the park. And don't miss out on the area's main event: food, food and more food.

The Boudin Bakery ★★ One of the park's educational features, this short trip through the origins of a loaf of sourdough bread challenges the notion of what makes an attraction. Nevertheless, the film, starring the ubiquitous Rosie O'Donnell and Colin Mockery of "Who's Line Is It Anyway?" fame is amusing enough to elicit a few chuckles. And wannabe bakers might learn a few things about the bread trade, such as that sourdough doesn't use yeast as a leavening agent. The fishbowl view into the actual kitchen (the facility actually does produce—and, of course, sell—bread) lets you watch the bakers in action. The smell is absolutely heavenly—the primary reason for the second star in the rating. Odds are you won't be able to resist picking up a loaf of bread on the way out.

TIPS: Do not visit this attraction on an empty stomach lest your nose leads you to invest your entire stash of pocket money in multiple loaves of bread, available for sale at the tour's end.

Mission Tortilla Factory ★ Like the Boudin Bakery, this educational food tour significantly stretches the definition of an attraction. A short walk-though details the history of the tortilla. You probably won't be bowled over the experience, but the history is kind of interesting. And the video presentation, which will have little ones thinking they're watching tiny people, is kind of fun. The fact that the place is a working tortilla factory will either impress the kids or just make them hungry. If it's the latter, Disney has (naturally) ensured that the finished products can be purchased. They're available at the Cocina Cucamonga Mexican Grill next door.

TIPS: Never crowded so browse any time.

THE BAY AREA Sure, in this Land it's only a few steps from the Sierras. But the patch of land occupying the space between Grizzly

Peak and Paradise Pier feels every bit the San Francisco landscape it purports to be.

Golden Dreams ★★ This elaborately produced film about notable events in California history is interesting in terms of the reactions it elicits. There are those who absolutely love it, those who absolutely hate it, and very few who fall somewhere in between.

Unquestionably visually beautiful, the film stars Whoopi Goldberg as Calafia, a fictional queen who, as detailed in a 16th-century novel, ruled the island of California. The Queen, whose first appearance is delivered via a wonderful special effect, traverses time, spanning 500 years of California history starting with American Indian days. The film tackles the lofty task of depicting the state's entire history—the good, the bad and the ugly—in the space of about 25 minutes. Though overall quite appealing, it leaves large holes where you might scratch your head and wonder how exactly we got from point A to point B—perhaps fodder for some post-park internet research. Most baffling to those non-Californians among us is the end montage that features images of notable Californians. Few are immediately identifiable, and all would have benefited from on-screen identification.

TIPS: The large-capacity theater seats 350 people, making wait times palatable. Save this one for the middle of the day when you need a rest.

GOLDEN VINE WINERY Though it might come as a surprise, the very land that Disneyland now occupies (in *Orange* County, no less) was once prime territory for grapes (a plague in the late 1800s wiped out the vineyards). So the introduction of grapevines to the Golden State section of the park would seem to bring the property around full circle.

The famed California wine country comes to the Disneyland resort via Robert Mondavi. More than 300 grapevines surround a mission-style building that could have been plucked right out of

I LOVE A PARADE

A couple of years after the lights supposedly went out forever (they even sold off the bulbs for charity), the **Electrical Parade** is back. The time-honored favorite is a welcome addition to DCA's nighttime entertainment roster, with thousands of bulbs lighting up the street from Paradise Pier to the Sunshine Plaza. Electricity isn't the only show in town. During the day, look for **Eureka! A California Parade.** This new procession celebrates the best of California, from its diversity to its extreme sports. Times and days of operation vary for both shows. Call ahead or check online for details.

Napa Valley. Ask about daily wine tastings; better yet, grab a cheese platter or a good meal at one of the two Vineyard restaurants and enjoy.

Seasons of the Vine ★★★ You don't have to be a wine lover to appreciate this short film on wine making. But even non-oenophile's might exit longing for a good Chardonnay (guests under drinking age notwithstanding).

The seven-minute film—a "Window into Wine Country," according to the PR—takes place inside a simulated cave. Despite its remarkably authentic look, the magic of Disney's faux version is that it's mercifully temperate (warm and dry—or at least air-conditioned) instead of characteristically cold and dank. The film uses a neat special effect that makes you feel as if you're actually watching out of a window. That, and the fact that the winemaking explanations are less long-winded than in real vineyard-speak make the attraction, if not completely interesting, at least entertaining for the kids. Exit stage left into the Mondavi gift shop, complete with the kind of knick-knacks you'd find in Napa Valley.

TIPS: Save this one for when the kids are tired and need a rest.

CONDOR FLATS Home of the California Adventure's airport hangar. Touch down here for one of the best attractions the Disney empire has ever created.

Soarin' Over California ★★★★★ All of the advance praise heaped upon this novel attraction made me wonder if it could possibly live up to its billing. But even a stellar review (as I'm about to give here) doesn't do justice to this unexpected treasure.

Passengers check in at the airport hangar, where aviator music intones and walls are adorned with photos of classic planes and their pilots. What follows is the closest thing you're likely to feel to flying without a plane.

Housed in an enormous theater, three rows of vehicles vaguely simulate hang gliders, with feet dangling below and a metal canopy above. Seats rise up and move forward into the bowled screen

A GLASS OF WINE, A LOAF OF BREAD, AND . . .

Sometimes show times conflict with meal times. Now, Disney allows you to do both at the same time. Electrical Parade picnic baskets, available for purchase in several places around the park, feature sandwiches, drinks and snacks. Separate offerings are available for adults and kids. Order by 4 p.m. and then pick up your food between 5 and 8. Another option: Ask about Mondavi packages that offer a prime parade-viewing spot along with your meal. Inquire at guest relations for details.

ahead. Breezes blow and aromas waft as you seem to soar over projected images of mountains, rivers and even golf greens. Hot-air balloons fly ahead. Surfers hang ten below. Vehicle movements so finely match those on film you'll swear you're moving more than just in place. You'll flinch at the sight of an oncoming golf ball, and be challenged not to lift your feet as the ride skims down over the water.

Magnificent effects aside, one of the best things about Soarin' is its wide appeal. Even non-ride lovers feel comfortable in its gentle grasp. It took much talk to convince my eldest daughter, who generally disdains rides, that this was one she would love. She subsequently returned four times. If you're traveling with a nervous rider (or if you're nervous yourself), ask for a seat in the back row, which doesn't get elevated as high into the air.

Tips: Lines are admittedly long, and FastPasses are a good idea. If you do end up on the standby line (FastPasses for the ride are often "sold out" by midday) take heart: it might not be as bad as it looks. Soarin' theaters are large and typically move even long lines along at a good clip.

Another tip: Loose shoes are notorious for falling off during the ride. Store flip-flops and other unreliable footwear, along with the rest of your personal belongings, in the bins below your seat.

GRIZZLY PEAK RECREATION AREA   Go back to nature in Disney's own wilderness. Hike through the redwoods, careen down a rushing river, or just appreciate the unusual Southern California scenery.

Grizzly River Run ★★★★ Southern California summers are notorious for the blazing-hot sunshine. So a ride down this rushing river of twists and turns will leave you, shall we say, refreshed.

Billed as the world's longest and highest manmade river raft (a title that, in this world of instantly obsolescent superlatives, could be history by the time this makes it to print), the ride snakes down the side of California Adventure's Grizzly Peak, a mountain topped by the image of a roaring bear. Eight passenger rafts careen and spin through caves, down inclines and past waterfalls, threatening all on board with a good dousing as they go. Two drops are steep enough to be exciting, but not so steep as to be unappealing to those averse to thrill rides.

In the spirit of such attractions, the underlying goal is to get you wet—soaked in some cases—and it's a good bet that the plan will succeed. That cars spin arbitrarily means there's no way to predict which seat might end up the dry one, although those sitting next to the doors (where water often rushes up and over on to the floor) seem to fare the worst. No matter—even if you don't get the outright splashes, you're sure to get sprayed by the mist fountains on the way out. Bottom line: nobody emerges completely dry. On the other hand, you'll be having way too much fun to care.

TIPS: Unlike some raft rides, this one has no plastic-covered storage bin to stash your stuff. If you want to save your valuables, not to mention keep a few things dry (a good idea, particularly if it's a cool day), use the lockers on the other side of the bear, just a few steps from the entrance to the ride. The first two hours are free.

Redwood Creek Challenge Trail ★★★★

In fairness to those for whom this attraction was created, I have to give it four stars. Though adults won't likely be careening along the zip line (then again, some might), kids will find it a perfectly heavenly place to blow off some steam.

Trails meander along the area's "natural" wonders, including a giant slice of ancient redwood tree that lived as far back as A.D. 818 (the tree was felled by a windstorm 1937). Piped in sounds are so authentic, it's hard to tell what's real and what's Memorex. Nearby, look for swinging tires and a rock wall. Access the Eagles Ascent via either ropes or stairs. Give your best vocal performance on the Hoot and Holler slides (the written rule states, "The one who makes the most noise wins"). Step over the "crick" at Hibernation Hollow—but look out for the bear (it's just a sound effect inside the cave, but it can sometimes scare little ones).

Storytimes at Ahwahnee Camp Circle (get the schedule from a local Park Ranger) provide a perfect respite.

TIPS: Designers mercifully incorporated a one-door setup, meaning there's only one way to get in and out. Still, it's a veritable maze inside, and parents of little ones will have to follow along behind. Weary parents of older kids, on the other hand, might consider a seat on a bench in the circle at the entrance, where you can watch for your kids to come out (this is a particularly good place to bring those two-way radios you've been dragging around).

BOUNTIFUL VALLEY FARM   With its "acreage" of fields with sprouting vegetables, this agricultural section of the park highlights the mainstay crops of California. Old MacDonald music plays as you get to know a few factoids about the Golden State's farming industry (betcha didn't know that California grows more than 84 percent of the nation's garlic). On a hot day, look for the Irrigation Station, a simulation of how much water flows through an aqueduct that is really just a nifty excuse to get wet.

"It's Tough to be a Bug" ★★★★★

After centuries dodging tennis shoes and being maligned as the planet's greatest nuisances, the creepy crawly critters of the world have united to buzz about their plight. Animated masters of ceremony resembling the folks from *A Bug's Life* (the attraction's movie was actually based on the feature film) detail the atrocities of bug treatment and set out to demonstrate the perils of being the size of a thumbtack.

What follows is pure and silly fun. This 3D/live-action spectacle is an absolute hoot—that is, assuming you don't mind being "flattened" by a giant fly swatter.

Without giving too much away (and that would definitely ruin the fun), brilliant special effects creep out, startle and, thanks to motion mechanisms in the seats, literally shake up all of the audience members who laugh, squirm, squeal, and more than occasionally leap to their feet. It's all in good fun—unless you happen to be a self-confessed creepy-crawly-phobe, in which case you might want to reconsider. On the other hand, you may never swipe at mosquitos the same way again.

TIPS: Loud noises, all-too-real special effects, and larger-than-life "bugs" make this one way too frightening for many children. Some brave little ones (mostly over age 8) do actually enjoy it, but more often the whimpering starts as soon as the first bugs appear.

Paradise Pier

With its freewheeling atmosphere and sun-scorched pavement (seemingly worn down by the salt air, no less), Disney's Paradise Pier is a perfect recreation of seaside amusement areas of the past. Band organ music plays, Ferris wheel riders shriek, and hand-holding couples pad along the boardwalk holding stuffed animals won by throwing a couple of balls through a hoop.

With classic Disney finesse, Paradise Pier pays homage to the original seaside wonderlands such as those at Santa Monica and Santa Cruz. Critics have snipped that this carnival-style emporium was a sellout for the mouse, given that Walt initially created Disneyland as an escape from such establishments. But Paradise Pier is first-rate fun. What could have been cheesy is, in fact, happily nostalgic—the best of what such enterprises had to offer. Mostly the best, anyway. A thorn in the collective side of parents are those aforementioned boardwalk games in which you can part with many dollars en route to claiming a prized stuffed some-

PLAY BALL

Authenticity and attention to details are things for which Disney attractions are known. Unfortunately, in this case, they may have been too authentic. Granted, barker-style games are seaside amusement staples. But their placement along the Disney Boardwalk will likely feel maddening to parents who've already forked over a walletful to get into the park, and will probably pay yet more to take home some sort of Disney-themed plush toy. Games—most are some version of a ball toss—cost $2 a pop. For your best bet, check out the New Haul Fishery; at press time, it guaranteed a prize every time.

thing or other. Personally, I'd rather just buy the toy and skip the aggravation.

Nevertheless, for the most part, parents will find a walk down memory lane—and there are a number of kiddy rides to satisfy the smallest in your party.

WHAT TO SEE & DO

Sun Wheel ★★★ Never before have I ridden a Ferris wheel that could be considered a thrill ride. Surprise! The trip up seems so benign. But once you start swinging, it's a whole different story.

Only the third wheel of its kind in the world (the other two are at Coney Island and in Japan), the Sun Wheel puts a neat spin on what might otherwise have been an ordinary ride. Caged in gondolas, riders travel the 168-foot wheel, getting stellar views of the entire park. While eight red gondolas go the traditional upright path, sixteen purple and orange cars freely swing on contraptions shaped like oversized paper clips. The result is an unsettling (or thrilling, depending on your perspective) feeling of falling as you come over the top. Suffice it to say that such experiences can instantly bridge a communication gap; my fellow passengers and I spoke completely different languages, but we had no trouble expressing the common language of terror. Unfortunately, the ride's short length keeps it from realizing its true potential. In order to accommodate crowds, visitors typically get only one non-stop ride around.

TIPS: While the view is good during the day, it's even more interesting at night when the Pier's bright lights are all aglow.

ANOTHER TIP: Riders generally make three revolutions: two locals for pick up and drop off, and an express once around. The on/off segments can take a while (my ride, from start to finish, topped a half-hour). The moral of the story: don't forego the bathroom break for later.

Mulholland Madness ★★★★ Paying tribute to the chaos that is the Los Angeles road system (specifically Mulholland Drive), Madness careens and dips in small, "woody-wagon" mobiles that feel as if they're going to careen right off the track (don't worry, they won't). Sharp turns and a car nose that extends over the wheels (hence that over-the-cliff sensation) make the front seat particularly thrilling—or frightening. Height requirements (42 inches and up) means its accessible to kids too short for the big guns (California Screamin'—48 inches). But that doesn't mean it's a kiddie ride. If you're traveling with a first-time coaster rider, opt to take the first spin in the back seat.

TIPS: The small capacity of this ride makes lines long! Fast-Passes here are a must—grab one as soon as you enter Paradise Pier before hitting any other rides.

California Screamin' ★★★★★ With its pretty white beams and classic-coaster looks, this entry into the thrill riding department may momentarily fool you into thinking it's an old-time wooden sleeper. But this baby's got metal.

All the planks and struts are just a front for a high-tech, 21st-century ride. True wooden-coaster lovers may be initially disappointed that Screamin's heart is pure steel. But there are benefits —most noticeably a smooth ride. While wooden coasters jangle your teeth, this one takes its high speeds while leaving your fillings intact. The high-tech approach also allowed designers to have some fun. Instead of picking up speed on a downslope, passenger cars peel *up* out of the station—going from zero to 55 in a mere four seconds. Six-thousand-feet of track includes sharp turns, steep drops and an upside-down loop (Disneyland's first), the latter taken inside a familiar-looking silhouette. True daredevils may find it lacking next to some of the panic-inducing contraptions location elsewhere, but those looking for good fun without abject terror are bound to have a blast.

> One can indeed be the loneliest number—but it can also net you a shorter wait for some of the park's flagship rides. In order to prevent operation with empty seats, solo riders are often moved to the front of the line. Ask the attendant before you queue up.

TIPS: With six passenger cars traveling at once, Screamin' is a large-capacity ride. Don't be intimidated by long lines since they tend to move fast. Nevertheless, FastPasses can slow the wait.

ANOTHER TIP: With lights all around, Screamin' is an even more thrilling adventure. Riding late in the day will also result in shorter waits.

Maliboomer ★★★ Three, two, one . . . blast off. Sit down, strap in and be prepared to catapult 180 feet straight up in a mere two seconds. Though the simple thought of being shot up into the sky was enough to cause me waves of nausea (the things I do for my job!), this ride isn't nearly as terrifying as it looks. (Then again, for the woman seated next to me who screamed *hysterically* from start to finish, it was exactly as horrifying as it looked.) The whole experience takes about a minute and a half. The most unnerving portion is the anticipation you feel as you wait for the attendant to hit eject. Cars shoot skyward and then bob softly up and down before depositing you back safely on the ground. Those with their wits about them might notice the sound of a bell (as if you're the ball in the anvil game) or the fact that you get some pretty stellar views of the rest of the park. Skittish riders will be happy to know that multiple safety checks ensure that everyone's seatbelt is fully functional.

TIPS: Gravity is a wonderful thing, so make sure to leave any loose items in the bins attendants provide as you board. Even loose shoes have been known to take flight.

Orange Stinger ★★★ Sure, it looks innocuous: a few dozen swings (48 to be precise) suspended from long chains and configured in a circle, looping around inside a structure quaintly designed to resemble a partially peeled orange. How scary could it be?

While even big kids look like little kids suspended in these baby-style swings, the thrills here are decidedly full-size. Widely arcing spins lean swings dramatically inward and increase your sense of speed (and perhaps dread). The center axis (to which swings are attached) bobs up and down, alternating the pattern in which you move. The sound of buzzing bees (hence the name) adds to the chaotic sensory experience. Those who love this sort of thing can't get enough, pumping their fists in joy as they circle, and exiting only to re-enter in the same breath. But, even some of those with hearty, "I love spinning rides" constitutions have been surprised at their reactions (just ask my Tea Cups–loving daughter who got off positively green-faced). Fortunately, at only about a minute long, the Stinger shows mercy for those with un-expected responses. Either way, a definite before-lunch ride.

TIPS: First-time riders might want to choose swings on the in-side rows; circles are a little less dramatic, and you don't have the sensation of nearly impacting with the walls.

ANOTHER TIP: There's no place to put your stuff, so leave it with a friend before getting on—or strap it on tight. This includes (perhaps especially!) flip-flop footwear.

Golden Zephyr ★★ You go up, you go down, you go around. If you've ridden Astro Orbiter in Tomorrowland or Dumbo in Fan-tasyland, you've done this—except you don't get to control the up/down motions. Long chains allow for some sensation of speed. And there is a nostalgia factor in the design. All that aside, as a first ride for kids, you simply can't beat its smile factor.

TIPS: The track record of this one (it has been notorious for being closed) makes it somewhat undependable. Don't even men-tion it to the kids until you actually see it running.

Jumpin' Jellyfish ★★ Kids who aren't ready for the big guns can defy gravity on this pint-sized attraction. Mini-Maliboomer is designed to look like jellyfish rising up beneath shelters resembling little parachutes. The ride is primarily populated by parents with smallish children (40 inches and up) or unhappy-looking older children who are appeasing their parents' determined mission to get their money's worth by doing every ride in the park. The ride is gentle (don't expect any thrills), rising 50 feet up in the air and bobbing softly back down.

TIPS: Though there doesn't seem to be a weight requirement, there's no mistaking this ride as a replacement for grownups un-prepared for Maliboomer. Strictly for kids.

King Triton's Carousel ★★ It would be a sin to visit an amuse-ment park and not ride the carousel. Colorful sea creatures—sea-horses, otters, flying fish—circle around to the sounds of piped-in beachin' music. Parents will have fun identifying the tunes. Little ones will feel positively royal.

TIPS: Rarely crowded, so enjoy!

S.S. rustworthy ★★ What would an amusement park be without a place to get wet? Strictly for kids, this permanently grounded fireboat (the story goes that it wasn't originally christened the S.S. Trustworthy) comes with bells and whistles (literally) to pull, tug and play with. Standard interactive ship fare—steering wheel, viewfinders and water cannons—are sure to entertain the kids, while giving mom and dad a much-needed chance to sit down.

TIPS: In the fireboat tradition, there's plenty of H_2O for soaking. Watch out for surprise bursts of water. Determined kids can (and often do) get plenty wet. One solution: dry-dock the sweatshirt before they enter so you have something warm to put on them after. Otherwise, plan on shelling out for a dry shirt later on.

California Adventure Lodging

For true Disney treatment, you can't do better than the **Grand Californian Hotel**. The luxury is indeed grand, and has created quite a buzz since its opening in 2001. The nature-inspired architecture looks like it belongs in a glade or tucked beside a California canyon. Furnishings have been carefully designed in the Craftsman style, a mode of decor native to California. No detail has been spared. Many of the pieces were handmade and those that are mass-produced still maintain the feel of their artisan heritage. You don't have to be a fan of the Arts & Crafts movement to be impressed. Rooms (and there are more than 700 of them) are elegant, with nice touches like double vanities in the bathrooms. That's not to say that you won't find standard Disney fare, such as mouse upholstery and hidden Mickeys. This is, after all, Disneyland, a fact that is obvious in the way it accommodates families. The hotel's location inside a theme park allows for lively views from the balcony of your room (not all rooms have such views; those that do charge a premium). Mindful of the potential for noise, designers created a well-sound-proofed property, and rooms are thankfully (perhaps surprisingly) quiet. Order room service around the clock, or dine in one of the two on-site restaurants: the upscale Napa Rose or the family-friendly Storytellers Café. White Water Snacks serves light bites near the pool. At the Hearthstone Lounge, sit and order coffee and baked goods in the morning, or wine and cocktails in the evening. Three pools make relaxing at the Grand Californian a treat. Kids can splash around the Mickey-shaped pool or enjoy the novel slide at the Redwood Pool. For a quieter swim, check out the Fountain Pool, which is devoid of the bells and whistles of the others. ~ 1600 South

> Disney is so proud of the Grand Californian Hotel, it offers tours of the property throughout the day (check at the front desk).

Disneyland Drive, Anaheim; 714-635-2300, fax 714-300-7301; www.disneyland.com. ULTRA-DELUXE.

▼▼▼▼▼▼▼▼▼▼▼▼▼▼▼▼▼▼▼▼▼▼▼▼▼▼
California Adventure Dining

The question is not *what* to eat in the California Adventure. It's *how much*. Visitors used to the hamburger/hot dog routine will be pleasantly surprised by the variety of available eats.

Though park planners had high hopes for the future of a couple of celebrity-chef type places (one by Wolfgang Puck and another by Robert Mondavi), the establishments weren't quite the right fit and have since been replaced. Still, the park has succeeded in adding a significant number of new flavors. Those who prefer those aforementioned hot dogs and hamburgers can still get them. But if your taste is for dim sum, clam chowder or a tortilla, you'll find that, too. Better still—in some establishments, you can even wash it down with a good brew.

That said, no matter what you eat, you'll still have to contend with the staples of Disney dining—namely high prices and long lines. Furthermore, some of the eateries have the irritating habit of closing at odd hours.

If you're one to plan ahead, schedule a priority seating time at one of the park's sit-down restaurants, such as the ABC Soap Opera Bistro or Avalon Cove. Those eating on the fly will do better to grab a snack at one of the myriad counter-service spots and forestall meals until after 2 p.m., when lines begin to shrink (they're usually pretty manageable before 11 a.m. as well). Unless you're planning to eat, avoid the Boudin Bakery at meal times; the heavenly aroma of baking bread will lead you to wait for a sourdough purchase no matter how long the line.

Ease of accessing an out-of-park dining experience makes that choice a viable option as well. Downtown Disney is just a few steps away from the park entrance (although priority seating is a good idea there, too). And there are yet more choices at any of the three Disney hotels.

SUNSHINE PLAZA   Grab a cuppa joe to go at the **Baker's Field Bakery.** Located in the heart of the California Zephyr train, the counter-service joint has all the staples to start your day—potent coffee (straight up or fancy lattes and brews) and a caseload of baked goods that includes croissant sandwiches. MODERATE.

HOLLYWOOD PICTURES BACKLOT   In addition to food, look for a healthy serving of cornpone. Counter-service eateries include: **Award Wieners,** serving "Hollywood's Hippest Hot Dogs"; **Schmoozies,** mixing fruit smoothies; and **Between Takes** for nothing but nachos (all MODERATE). Health-conscious diners can have their pick of to-go produce at the **Fairfax Market.** MODERATE.

The **Hollywood & Dine** food court has a little of everything—from Chinese to pizza to salads. MODERATE.

Soap fans will be in their glory at the **ABC Soap Opera Bistro**. The eatery is unquestionably the park's most creative place to dine, with six themed rooms decked out to look exactly like your favorite ABC soap places, such as the Chandler living room from "All My Children." Costumed waitstaff serve with attitude. And surprise, surprise—the food is really quite good. DELUXE.

GOLDEN STATE The **farmer's market** at the Bountiful Valley Farm has healthy snacks such as fresh fruit. MODERATE. The humorously named **Sam Andreas Shakes** serves milkshakes that are "delicious to a fault." MODERATE.

One of the most food-intensive sections of the park, Pacific Wharf serves a little of everything. Grab a Korean noodle bowl or some dim sum at the **Lucky Fortune Cookery**—and don't forget to try out the delicious and unique selection of fortune cookies. MODERATE. Follow your nose to the **Pacific Wharf Bakery**, where, in addition to sourdough bread, you'll find such light fare as pastries, soups and salads. MODERATE. The **Cocina Cucamonga Mexican Grill** has everything you can fit into a tortilla, from grilled chicken to PB&Js. MODERATE. **Rita's Baja Blenders** is the place for fruit drinks, California style. MODERATE.

In Condor Flats, Disney gets back to standard fare at the **Taste Pilots' Grill**. But kids and the rest of the family are sure to like the enormous burgers and ribs. MODERATE.

Really hungry families (or those about to run a marathon) can load up on pasta at the **Wine Country Trattoria** in the Golden Vine Winery. The cute place has indoor or outdoor tables and features everything from lasagna swimming in cheese to hearty soups and pastas. MODERATE TO DELUXE. Upstairs, situated on the balcony, the **Vineyard Room** is more suited to grownups who

PIN-DEMONIUM

Since its introduction at Disney World to coincide with the millennium celebration, Disney pin trading has reached frenzied proportions. The most enthusiastic collectors have so many they actually have to rent strollers to display their stash. Look for pin stations around the park where you can buy pins, trade with the attending cast member and get information. Cast members around the park wear lanyards sporting pins they're willing to trade for the asking. Most park stores sell pins as well, but there's a different collection everywhere you go. But take heed; it's easy to get carried away.

want to sip wine and sample a changing menu of Italian dishes. DELUXE TO ULTRA-DELUXE.

Get a caffeine boost at **Malibu Mocha,** a coffee shack located near the Bay Area toward Paradise Pier. BUDGET.

PARADISE PIER   Cross over the boardwalk and find park-style fare ad nauseam. **Burger Invasion** (under a pair of familiar golden arches), **Corn Dog Castle, Strips Dips n' Chips, MalibuRitos** and **Pizza Oom Mow Mow** all serve the obvious fare. MODERATE. Hang ten at **Catch a Flave** for a mountain of soft-serve ice cream. MODERATE.

Give the dogs a rest at scenic **Avalon Cove,** either upstairs for drinks and appetizers, or downstairs for a complete character meal. Reservations strongly recommended. DELUXE TO ULTRA-DELUXE.

OUTSIDE THE CALIFORNIA ADVENTURE   Restaurants at the Grand Californian Hotel include the gourmet **Napa Rose,** featuring an extensive wine list and an outstanding menu of California cuisine, from grilled goat cheese–stuffed grape leaves to Colorado porterhouse. ULTRA-DELUXE. Families will feel more comfortable at **Storytellers Cafe,** a lovely, buffet-style eatery featuring character breakfasts and American contemporary cuisine at lunch and dinner. DELUXE. See "Dining" in Disneyland (Chapter Two) for information on Downtown Disney.

▼▼▼▼▼▼▼▼▼▼▼▼▼▼▼▼▼▼▼▼▼▼▼▼
California Adventure Shopping

What would a trip to a theme park be without a souvenir stuffed animal? Thankfully, you'll never have to find out. As at any such establishment, the California Adventure is loaded with places to fix you up with fluffy Mickeys, goofy hats, collectible pins and just about anything else you can think of.

By and large, Disney merchandise varies little from store to store. For the most part, once you've seen one, you've seen 'em all. As veteran visitors, my kids have to really hunt to find that special something upon which to spend their precious souvenir money. Bought in small numbers, pins make wonderful mementos.

The biggest difference among souvenirs will be the logo the item bears—such as California Adventure versus Disneyland. Still, most of the lands stock some items unique to that section. Ask if you're looking for necessities (such as over-the-counter pain relievers or sunscreen) because some of these items are kept behind the desk.

Below are a few of the best stops.

SUNSHINE PLAZA   If your child is still mulling the selection of stuffed animals as you near the end of your visit, a good place to stop is **Engine Ears Toys.** Located near the park entrance in the nose of the California Zephyr train, the place has a hearty sam-

His wife, no slouch herself as an entrepreneur, saw an opportunity to supplement the family income during the Depression by serving chicken dinners on their wedding china. In not too many years, people were flocking to Cordelia's Chicken Dinner Restaurant, often waiting hours in line for her scrumptious meals. By 1940, when the restaurant was serving as many as 4000 Sunday dinners, it was Walter's turn to really crow. As a diversion for the waiting patrons, he began building Ghost Town, and the nation's most popular independently owned family theme park was hatched. Now, doesn't Knott's Berry Farm sound a whole lot better than Knott's Waiting Area for a Delicious Chicken Dinner?

In 1969 Knott opened Fiesta Village, a tribute to California's early Spanish heritage. The five-acre Boardwalk, the third themed area, opened in 1975 as the Roaring 20's and today pays tribute to Southern California's seaside culture. Camp Snoopy joined the park in 1983, with six acres themed to the California High Sierra. It's the official home of the famous Charles Schulz beagle, Snoopy, plus his pals Linus, Lucy and Charlie Brown.

Dolphin and sea lion shows were added when Knott's opened its Pacific Pavilion in 1986. In 1988 the fifth themed area was opened—Wild Water Wilderness, a four-acre, river-wilderness area featuring Bigfoot Rapids, a raft ride down a raging, white-water river. The most recent addition here is Mystery Lodge, an exploration of the traditions of the American Indians who lived on the Pacific Northwest coast.

Indian Trails celebrates the arts, cultures and traditions, old and new, of the people who first populated this continent. It's a one-on-one participatory adventure that gives all ages an opportunity to explore the heritage of American Indians.

The Farm was purchased in 1997 by Cedar Fair L.P., which operates four other amusement parks nationwide. Although owned by a corporation, Knott's does an excellent job of maintaining a down-home feel. Knott's Berry Farm is an amusement site that welcomes more than three million guests each year. Attractions appeal to those of all ages and succeed not only because they amuse but also because they provide a sense of nostalgia and history.

At least a dozen hotels are within a ten-minute walk of the park's entrance. If you're visiting Disneyland and are staying in Anaheim, some hotels offer shuttle service to Knott's for a fee.

▼ ▼ ▼ ▼ ▼ ▼ ▼ ▼ ▼ ▼

Nuts & Bolts

ARRIVAL

By car, exit Route 5 at Beach Boulevard and proceed south. Beach Boulevard literally runs into the park. Freeway signs direct you to the Farm, and there are signs along the boulevard as well, so it's hard to get lost. Independence Hall is on your left as you approach Knott's. Stay to the right and you'll be directed to one of seven lots where you can park all day for a fee. If you're pointed toward a lot on the east side of Beach Boulevard, a tunnel takes you safely under the busy thoroughfare. You'll also use this tunnel to get from the park proper to Independence Hall, which is outside Knott's.

TICKETS   Two ticket options are available: a day pass and an annual pass. The Premium Resort Passport includes admission to Knott's Soak City.

	Adults	Children 3–11
		(Under 3 years, free)
One-day Ticket	$40.00	$30.00
Annual Pass	$109.95	$49.95
Premium Resort Passport	$159.90	$99.90

GAME PLAN   The 150-acre park can easily be visited in a day even when crowds are at their peak. You might want to arrive before it opens, buy tickets and roughly plot your day with the map you're given. Mrs. Knott's Chicken Dinner Restaurant on Grand Avenue serves good, inexpensive breakfasts. From there you're within three minutes of the gate, poised for opening time.

On a cloudy Tuesday in February, five minutes is the longest you'll wait for a ride, but on a summer weekend day you'll have to plan tactics carefully to avoid mammoth lines.

Knott's narrow-gauge steam train hauls more passengers than any steam train in the United States.

If you're a teenager or unencumbered adult, the best time-saving idea on entering the park is to make a sharp right through Camp Snoopy and hop aboard Montezooma's Revenge, which is at the edge of Fiesta Village. From there, head through the Village across the train tracks to The Boardwalk and jump on the Boomerang. If you can do both of these rides before 10 a.m. you have a leg up on the day's schedule. Then, proceed to some of the other high-energy rides like Wave Swinger and Tampico Tumbler, which will be less crowded.

Toddlers and tykes under six will want to spend most of their time in Camp Snoopy, which was designed especially for them. That, and the merry-go-round in Fiesta Village right next door, can comprise a full day for little ones. A sit-down indoor show in the afternoon can provide an opportunity for a nap.

The themed sections of the park flow naturally into one another. After hitting the highlights, you should see one area completely before moving to another to avoid backtracking. Parents with kids of different ages will want to split up. A 12-year-old will not be content with time spent in Camp Snoopy, and a four-year-old won't make the height restriction on many thrill rides.

The park is well supplied with shady, comfortable places to sit. Take advantage of them. You'll be able to see everything even with

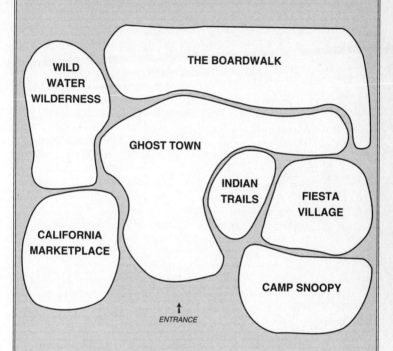

KNOTT'S BERRY FARM

WILD WATER WILDERNESS

THE BOARDWALK

GHOST TOWN

INDIAN TRAILS

FIESTA VILLAGE

CALIFORNIA MARKETPLACE

CAMP SNOOPY

↑
ENTRANCE

WILD WATER WILDERNESS
Bigfoot Rapids
Mystery Lodge
Wilderness Nature Center
Wilderness Scramble

GHOST TOWN
Butterfield Stagecoach
Calico Mine Train
Denver & Rio Grande Railroad
Ghost Rider
Timber Mountain Log Ride
Wild West Stunt Show

THE BOARDWALK
Boomerang
Charles M. Schulz Theatre
HammerHead
Kingdom of the Dinosaurs
Perilous Plunge
SkyCabin
Supreme Scream
Windjammer
Wipeout
Xcelerator

FIESTA VILLAGE
Dragon Swing
Gran Slammer
Hat Dance
Jaguar
Merry-Go-Round
Montezooma's Revenge
Tampico Tumbler
WaveSwinger

CAMP SNOOPY
Beary Tales Playhouse
Camp Bus
Camp Snoopy Theater
Charlie Brown Speedway
Edison's Inventor's Workshop
Flying Ace Balloon Race
Grand Sierra Scenic Railroad
High Sierra Ferris Whell
Huff and Puff
Log Peeler
Petting Zoo
Red Baron
Rocky Road Trucking Company
Snoopy's Bounce
Timberline Twister
Woodstock's Airmail

INDIAN TRAILS
Children's Camp

a number of reconnoitering breaks, and you won't feel frazzled at day's end. The park has 60 food facilities, four full service and the rest buffet, sandwich or fast food. But if you decide to eat in the park on a busy day, try to time it before 11:30 a.m. and after 2 p.m. to avoid long waits. Most weekdays won't be a problem, although you might find yourself checking out several facilities to determine where lines are the shortest.

GUEST SERVICES

General Information   Guest Relations, Knott's Berry Farm, 8039 Beach Boulevard, Buena Park, CA 90620; 714-220-5200; www. knotts.com.

Stroller, Wheelchair and Other Rentals   These as well as power chairs are available just inside the main entrance on the right.

Cameras   Snoopy's Boutique sells disposable cameras.

Baby Services   Baby stations with diaper-changing tables and feeding and nursing facilities are next to the schoolhouse in the Wild Water Wilderness area, in Camp Snoopy near the suspension bridge, and outside the park next to D'vine Home and Candle Shop.

Lockers   Lockers are at the main gate on the left, in Wild Water Wilderness next to the baby station, and just inside the Ghost Town main gate on the left.

Pets   Except seeing-eye dogs, pets are not allowed inside the park.

Lost Children and Lost & Found   Both facilities are located at the main gate in the Information Center.

First Aid   A station is located next to GhostRider.

Banking   An ATM that honors almost all bank cards is at the left of the main gate and next to Cordy's Corner in The Boardwalk.

GETTING AROUND

Knott's Berry Farm is roughly a square, with the entrance and California MarketPlace at lower left. Ghost Town covers the largest

INDEPENDENCE HALL

One of the most visible of Knott's attractions is **Independence Hall**, located across Beach Boulevard outside the main park. The brick-by-brick replica of Philadelphia's historic hall is so exact you can see fingerprints in the bricks just like in the original, and the 2075-pound Liberty Bell here weighs just five pounds less than the original. When the real Independence Hall was to be restored for the nation's bicentennial in 1976, the original blueprints were nowhere to be found, so the reconstruction committee contacted Knott's for the blueprints it had drawn. Memorabilia in the hall includes photos and signatures of the signers of the Declaration of Independence, costumed mannequins of the era, even a harpsichord that was the entertainment center of its day.

area, but Camp Snoopy has the most attractions packed into its six acres. It's a toss-up as to whether to proceed straight ahead into Ghost Town or to make a sharp right into Camp Snoopy. The kids in your party probably will make the decision for you. The highest-energy areas and the ones that pulse with action at night are Fiesta Village where Montezooma's Revenge lives, and The Boardwalk, home to HammerHead and Boomerang. We've arranged our tour in a roughly clockwise fashion, beginning at Ghost Town and ending at Indian Trails. A good meeting place in case your group gets separated is in front of the church beside the lake in Ghost Town. It's the only church in the park, and the shady area in front is a good place to wait.

▼ ▼ ▼ ▼ ▼ ▼ ▼ ▼ ▼ ▼ ▼

Ghost Town

If Ghost Town looks old, that's because it truly is. But this rickety reincarnation of a piece of the Wild West is still very much alive. Walter Knott was fascinated by tales of the West, having grown up with stories of his mother's trek to California in a covered wagon. It was these tales that inspired him to create Ghost Town.

More than just a designer's imagination of how the West might have appeared, Ghost Town consists of historic structures that were relocated to Knott's Berry Farm. The Haunted Shack originally stood in Esmeralda, Nevada, and was reconstructed nail-for-nail. The Old Trails Hotel, now next to Ghost Town's general store, began its life in 1868 as a hostelry in Arizona (it was relocated, board by board, from Prescott in 1940). America's last operating narrow-gauge railroad, the Denver & Rio Grande, was bought in 1952 by Walter Knott, who moved its engines, passenger cars and even rails to his farm. Adhering to authenticity, he brought in other deserted buildings including a Kansas schoolhouse and a jail. The result is a fascinating, realistic 1880s California mining community.

Ghost Town's population consists of townspeople in period costume who are eager to chat about their lives and professions. At the Geode Shop the lapidist will help you select a promising "coconut"—a round, rough, seemingly uninteresting rock that reveals a swirl of colorful agate or a center of sparkling crystal when cut with his diamond-bladed saw. He'll explain how these 65 million-year-old rocks were formed and sometimes turned up by miners who crowded into California during the Gold Rush. Don't miss the dinosaur egg inside the shop.

You can watch high-kicking can-can girls at the Calico Saloon, pan for gold, or watch Dr. I. Will Skinem set up his Medicine Show and banter with a sheriff trying to run him and his questionable cures out of town. Spinners, weavers and prospectors will spin yarns for anyone who cares to listen. And watch out for the gunfights that break out at any time along village streets.

Butterfield Stagecoach ★★★ For a genuinely historic circuit of Camp Snoopy and Fiesta Village, climb aboard this 100-year-old stagecoach. It's so far off the ground (to allow for the rocks and ruts of old-time roads) that you have to climb a set of stairs to reach boarding level. The friendly driver will give you a hand. He'll let you ride shotgun next to him for an up-top view of the park, or you can settle into seats inside as the gentry did in 1890. The stagecoach has been refurbished with 20th-century springs and brakes and is drawn by a team of four spirited horses.

Tips: Those with tired feet will appreciate this gentle ride.

Timber Mountain Log Ride ★★★★★ This is the oldest log flume ride in the United States and one of the most popular attractions in the park. This five-minute float in what appears to be a hollowed-out log begins with an uphill climb, then takes you through the inner workings of a sawmill. While transiting the mountain's misty innards, you pass animated scenes of loggers at a crosscut saw and giant timbers being craned and stacked. It ends with a lickety-split plunge down a 42-foot waterfall, guaranteed to douse everyone in the front seat. Exiting the ride you'll see yourself freeze-framed on a television screen in a photo taken as you nosedived over the falls. The photo, of course, is for sale.

TIPS: Waits can be up to two hours; plan on doing this one early.

Calico Mine Train ★★★★★ You board scaled-down versions of open-ore cars and within seconds are plunged into humid darkness that even smells like you're underground. Blasting noises and the rattle of the train compete with the engineer's running banter as you tour a working coal mine. The beam of the engine light illuminates narrow tunnel walls that widen to reveal animated miners working a glory hole. Dim lights flicker from their hats, casting eerie shadows of swinging ore buckets on the two-story cavern walls. Farther along, stalactites and stalagmites, underground waterfalls and a damp chill (real or imagined?) add to the realism. As you emerge into daylight across a shaky trestle, there's a good view of Ghost Town. Don't look for physical thrills—the fascination here is the feeling of authenticity and the historical sense of the West.

TIPS: Because the entire ride is in darkness, it may be a bit unnerving to the very young and claustrophobic.

GhostRider ★★★★★ Those of us raised on the newfangled looping coasters and inverted feet-free contraptions might tend to be snobbishly nonchalant about riding something as humdrum as an old-fashioned wooden coaster. That is, of course, until you hit the first plunge—the one that makes you feel as if you're falling off the edge of the planet.

Despite its deceptively old-time demeanor, GhostRider stacks right up against its steel and looping counterparts, routinely showing up on coaster fanatic's list of bests. And for good reason. Numerous (sometimes seemingly endless) drops and plummets make the ride an absolute blast—a must for those looking to add something new to their thrill-ride repertoire. The only downside: the inherent bumpiness of the wooden track may leave your bottom end with a few tender spots.

TIPS: My best advice: Tuck the sunglasses, batten down the purses and sit on the hats. This ride is bound to blow that topper right off of your head.

Wild West Stunt Show **** Not as slick and polished as the show at Universal Studios, this presentation provides good entertainment nevertheless. The old-fort setting is suitably realistic. The plot is this: The cowboy stuntman's partner doesn't show up, so he recruits a reluctant "replacement" from the audience, a tourist on his honeymoon. But when the macho stuntman sent from central casting finally makes an appearance, the sparks fly. Fistfights, a high fall and lots of shooting keep the action moving as the hesitant volunteer is picked on from all sides.

TIPS: Arrive at the Wagon Camp early enough and you can garner sheltered seats in the covered wagons that form the 1000-seat theater's periphery. In general, try for seats higher up because those in the front have limited visibility.

Denver & Rio Grande Railroad *** The train is real, and so are the ear-shattering whistle, clanging bell and billows of steam that hiss from its spiffy engine. At trackside, a fatherly conductor ushers you on old Number 40, then yells out the required "All Aboard!" On this narrow-gauge choo-choo, cars are regulation-size with two-and-two seating. About the time you get settled, your journey is interrupted by a pair of marauding outlaws who seem as intent on cracking corny jokes as on holding up the train. (To a youngster with closely cropped hair: "We'll leave you alone, fellah. Looks like you've already been clipped.") The authentic 1880s steam train, complete with cow-catcher and brass trim, does an eight-minute circuit of Ghost Town and The Boardwalk.

TIPS: Here is another chance to get off your feet for a while. Once you board you can make the circuit as many times as you like.

PEEK-IN

Knott's is crammed with nooks, crannies and unexpected surprises like the "peek-ins" in Ghost Town. You can look through windows of rickety buildings for glimpses of an 1800s assay office where gold is being weighed, and a Chinese laundry where hand-washing preceded Maytag by half a century. In the town's telegraph office a dutiful fellow taps out hot bulletins in Morse code.

▼▼▼▼▼▼▼▼▼▼▼▼▼▼▼▼▼▼
Wild Water Wilderness

At just over three acres, this is the smallest of Knott's themed areas, but it does an excellent job of re-creating a California river wilderness park of the early 1900s. The indigenous trees range from California black oak to coast redwood to Torrey pine and are part of a landscape that includes such enchanting wildflowers as California poppy, bluebell, daffodil, larkspur, lily and horsetail. Point Reyes manzanita and star jasmine also grow along the tidy paths. The deciduous trees that change color add a seasonal feeling to the surroundings, and there is an aviary that is home to native dove, quail and ring-neck pheasant. For thrills, check out Bigfoot Rapids. Quieter entertainment can be found at the imaginative Mystery Lodge or at the popular Wilderness Nature Center.

WHAT TO SEE & DO

The **Wilderness Nature Center** is the place to ask the park ranger about Sasquatch, that elusive creature called Bigfoot. He'll show you evidence, in photos and footprints, that such a beast does exist, and you'll hear marvelous tales. The rangers are retired schoolteachers, naturalists and others with a knowledge of the outdoors and an interest in helping kids learn. Hands-on displays of indigenous and exotic insects and native plants plus a glassed-in apiary puts you as close as you'll ever want to get to a working beehive. You can view a honeycomb and watch the industrious insects enter and exit through their own chimney.

Mystery Lodge **★★★★** In this age of stomach-churning roller coasters and thrill rides, Knott's has come up with a winner in this captivating Native North American storytelling presentation. Special effects are employed, not to scare you out of your wits but to suggest the power of imagination, magic and wisdom. The experience begins as guests cross a wooden bridge and pass through a hand-carved ceremonial archway alongside Thunder Falls. Entering a "cave," visitors face a full-size replica of a traditional tribal house front. Sounds of birds and other creatures and water lapping at the lakeshore can be heard; then a flash of lightning and a clap of

LIQUID SKIES

Between Fiesta Village and Ghost Town, the park's Reflection Lake is the site of the **Incredible Waterworks Show**. The sound, light and water extravaganza is similar to the "Dancing Waters" show so popular at state fairs and on the "Ed Sullivan Show" during the 1960s. Hundreds of streams of water, each choreographed to music, soar nearly 100 feet in the air. At night in the same spot, the Peanuts gang hosts **Edison International Electro-Blast**, a lively show featuring music, lasers, special effects and fireworks.

thunder signal an approaching storm. Unfortunately, the mood is broken when the house front opens and you enter the lodge, actually a small modern auditorium, where you'll watch the rest of the presentation. On stage, where the lodge interior has been recreated, a fire glows and the Old Storyteller enters to weave his tale. Images of Raven and other Native totems emerge from the smoke of the fire, dissolving into other forms or dissipating into the air. The effect is gentle and altogether captivating. When it's all over, we are left to believe, as the Old Storyteller has told us, that "if we share the wisdom of elders with the heart of a child, life will be full of wonder and magic."

TIPS: A couple of the effects used to create thunder and lightning may startle small children or infants. Out of respect for the Native traditions, photography and videotaping are not permitted in the Mystery Lodge.

Bigfoot Rapids ***** The sign says, "You WILL get wet, you MAY get drenched." Before this whitewater rafting ride opened, an Olympic kayaker ran the rapids and rated them very challenging. You, of course, do it a bit differently, strapping yourself into a huge, innertube-like craft with as many as five others for a wild, wet jaunt over a series of churning rapids on California's longest manmade whitewater river. A two-story waterfall drops from towering cliffs. If you've ever been whitewater rafting, you'll find the boulders and chutes extremely authentic. Just before returning to civilization, you pass through a misty tunnel that echoes with the roar of the ominous creature for which the ride is named. None of this is really scary, though, unless you have a fear of damp trousers and soggy shoes. Great fun for all ages.

TIPS: To prevent your shoes from getting soaked, brace your feet high up on the center post when a wave hits. Bigfoot Rapids develops long lines during peak periods. Try to do it early or late in the day. There's a 36-inch height restriction.

Wilderness Scrambler ** One of the best things about this ride, which is the same thing as a Scrambler, is the beautiful saltwater aquarium at the entrance. It contains tangs in vivid blue and yellow, a clown fish of brilliant orange, even a small eel hiding in the rocks. The darkness surrounding the aquarium is broken by colored strobe lights that illuminate the whirling cars and create a sense of swirling, churning water.

TIPS: Appeals to teenagers, but adults may find the mashing and slinging more uncomfortable than thrilling. There's a 42-inch height restriction.

The Boardwalk

The area that was known as Roaring 20's was revitalized in 1996 and reborn as The Boardwalk, a colorfully themed area designed to celebrate the vigor and vitality of Southern California's fabled beach culture. Besides the thrill rides HammerHead and Xcelerator, many of the park's old favorites are still here—Boomerang, the Charles M. Schulz Theatre, and Kingdom of the Dinosaurs. Arcade games and other amusements provide familiar diversions throughout the Boardwalk.

WHAT TO SEE & DO

Kingdom of the Dinosaurs ★★★★★ It's the 1920s and Professor Wells is at work in his lab, developing a time machine. His blackboard is scribbled with equations, and bubbling beakers contain his secret formulas. As you glide along a track in a two-person car, the crackle of electrical charges and the sudden shriek of an emergency signal assault your ears. The professor booms frantically, "Something's gone wrong with the time machine!" As he counts off the epochs and eons, you realize you're being drawn further and further into the prehistoric past. On your left the huge jaws of a *Tyrannosaurus rex* seem ready to snap you in two. To the right a prehistoric wolf battles with the ancestor of an elk. Pterodactyls hover overhead, and a long-necked creature eyes you ominously. Ice Age humans huddle in ragged furs. For four minutes a score of gigantic, fully animated robotic figures from 200 million years ago emerge from their twilight world. Just as you think you'll never escape, the professor announces that he has his machine under control and you're on your way home to the 20th century.

TIPS: Even though teenagers find it a bit tame, this is one of the most popular attractions in the park. Long lines move quickly, and the wait is usually not more than ten minutes even at peak periods.

HammerHead ★★★★ If a head-over-heels 360-degree vertical spin that lifts you 82 feet in the air sounds exciting, then get in line. Just to add to the fun, the 42-passenger gondola rotates independently, so you can find yourself hanging upside-down, nearly ten stories above the ground. The ride lasts just over two minutes, but it makes six full 360-degree orbits and gives you a little surprise at the end.

TIPS: The height requirement is 42 inches. Although shoulder-length restraints keep you from falling out, you will definitely lose glasses, hats or anything else not secured in a pocket.

DISCOVERY CENTER

If you saw something in the Kingdom of the Dinosaurs you didn't recognize, this fascinating, laboratory-like center is the place to find out about it. Layered charts explain stages in the earth's development, pointing out when the creatures you've just seen were at their scary best. Displays include petrified wood, touchable fossils and teeth from prehistoric beasts. (Don't miss the mural in front of the Kingdom of the Dinosaurs; it's based on a photo of Los Angeles in 1927.)

Boomerang ★★★★★ This is the ride you've heard about. As you wait in line, its freight-train sound alone can start the adrenaline rushing. When you step into the four-person car and settle under the padded, horseshoe-shaped restraint, you know you're in for a ride to remember (or one you'll never forget). With a lurch, the chain of cars begins to inch to the top of a tower that seems to go nowhere except into space. For a second the car pauses at the top, and then the shrieking begins. You're launched on a terrifying drop from an 11-story height through three loops that not only flip you upside-down but twist at the same time. The cars slow as momentum carries you up a second tower. Is the ride over? Not a chance. Boomerang does it to you again, somersaulting you backwards through the same three loops before jolting to a halt at the exit. This unusual, European-designed roller coaster, which lasts just 33 seconds, gives terror a new twist.

TIPS: There's a 52-inch height restriction. A park favorite of teens and older kids, ride it early on busy days or expect to wait up to an hour during midday.

Xcelerator ★★★★ From the flame-emblazoned fin-tailed cars to the sleek chrome and glass waiting area, this souped-up roller coaster is drenched in '50s nostalgia. Strap yourself into one of the candy-apple red or blazing purple "hot-rods" and blast into the past at 82 m.p.h. In just 2.3 seconds you'll be flung 205 feet into the air and dropped back down again at a stomach-jumping 90 degree angle. No fancy tricks here—just a healthy injection of speedy screamin' fun.

TIPS: At just over a minute long, this thrill-ride will leave die-hard coaster fans panting for more. Teens and other thrill seekers will want run around to the end of the line for a second shot.

Wipeout ★★ This is a fast and furious version of that old carnival classic, the tilt-a-whirl. If zinging around in circles at top speed—while jolting up and down in the air—is your idea of a good time, this one's for you.

TIPS: All that circular motion is dizzying at best; unless your kids have cast-iron stomachs, save this one for *after* lunch.

Sky Cabin ★★ For those who would rather avoid those danger-courting, adrenaline-pumping rides, this is just the ticket. It's simple: an enclosed compartment rises and rotates slowly around the Sky Tower's colorful center pillar. A smashing view awaits you at the top.

TIPS: Take your camera along. There are no sudden jerks or wrenches in the Sky Cabin, and you'll be able to get great shots of the park. There is a 36-inch height restriction.

Supreme Scream ★★★★ The triple threat of this freefall ride is the configuration of three towers—yellow, blue and green—each of which guides you (via open-air lifts) genteelly up the tower before—*foom*—rocketing you back down faster than you can say, "I saw my life flash before my eyes." How high is it exactly that you'll be peaking? Let's say that fans of this contraption have lovingly nicknamed it "L.A.," because, on a clear day, riders—those with their eyes open anyway—can see the entire City of Angels—about 20 miles away. Suffice it to say, daredevils think it's a blast. Those who believe altitude is best viewed from the inside of an airplane window will find it every bit as terrifying as it looks.

TIPS: If you are just the tiniest bit prone to vertigo, this ride is not for you.

Perilous Plunge ★★★ In the annals of theme park attractions, it is the designation of "est"—as in highEST, scariEST, insanEST—that serves as ratings points for a ride. Billed as the world's steepest water ride, Perilous Plunge scores three "ests"—tallest, steepest and wettest—in the world. Though the classifications no doubt are short-term (possibly already passé by the time this makes it to print), thrill junkies will nevertheless relish this 75-degree drop that plummets 24-person boats 115 feet down (just 34 feet shorter than Niagara Falls, for anyone who's interested).

TIPS: Aquaphobes rejoice: the ride is equipped with a switchboard-controlled splash-guard that can tame the dousing on colder Southern California days.

Fiesta Village

Located across the railroad tracks, Fiesta Village has high, tiled arches and wisteria-trellised walkways that create a realistic south-of-the-border atmosphere. In this colorful, exuberant section of the park, strolling mariachis and terra-cotta fountains pay tribute to California's early Spanish heritage. If you time it right, you can order a giant tostada from the Cantina, then settle in to watch a Mexican band or singers, dancers and drummers in traditional American Indian costume perform at Fiesta Plaza. Good Mexican food is available at a number of restaurants. There's a fast-paced feeling here, created by a collection of thrill rides. Fiesta Village is home to one of the park's premier attractions, Montezooma's Revenge.

WHAT TO SEE & DO

Montezooma's Revenge ★★★★★ If you liked Boomerang, you'll love this gut-wrenching experience. Montezooma does it to you with a vengeance. From a standstill in the launching area, a giant flywheel catapults the cars to 55 miles per hour in just over three seconds. The gigantic thriller loops you upside-down, comes to a complete halt, then loops you around again, backwards. At mach speed you race to a second tower, hang at its top at a 90-degree angle, then speed back to the launching area.

TIPS: Do not ride immediately after lunch; in fact, do it early in the day to avoid long lines. There is a 48-inch height restriction.

Jaguar **** "Awesome!" That's the assessment offered by a good many of the riders this attraction was designed for—youngsters and their parents. Rising no more than 60 feet above the ground, this family roller coaster "streaks" out of the Temple of Jaguar Plaza and loops around on 2700 feet of track. The best thing about this ride is that the younger members of your family get to ride on a roller coaster—just like the big kids. Only this one doesn't turn upside-down in gravity-defying feats that leave your stomach in the air. Twenty-four passenger cars leave plenty of room for the entire family to ride together.

The flywheel technology used in Montezooma's Revenge is the same as that used to launch planes from aircraft carriers.

TIPS: Children must be 42 inches high to ride Jaguar. The wait to ride can extend up to an hour or more during peak times.

Merry-Go-Round *** No one's quite sure what it's doing in Fiesta Village, but this beautifully restored 1896 Dentzel seems appropriately sited here on the banks of Reflection Lake. This carousel is one of the few remaining examples of its type in the country, unique because many of the animals aren't horses. Whimsical ostriches, rabbits, zebras, chickens and lions are typical of Dentzel's designs for his grand carousels.

TIPS: One of the few rides that is appreciated by all ages.

Dragon Swing ** This ride is basically a large swing that accelerates sideways to ever-widening arcs until finally you're at right angles to the earth. One adult rider remarked as he disembarked that it made him seasick.

TIPS: Missable, so visit when you run into long lines elsewhere. There's a 42-inch height restriction.

WaveSwinger **** Sling-swings are suspended by a pair of chains from a revolving canopy as centrifugal force flings you out at a 45-degree angle. With your body movement you can control the twists and turns while you dangle tenuously above the watching crowd.

TIPS: Even though you don't reach enormous heights, this is not for those with acrophobia. There's a 42-inch height restriction here.

Hat Dance ** Basically the same ride as Disneyland's Mad Tea Party except that this one involves fiesta-colored bowls topped with sombreros. As the bowls revolve on platforms, they also spin. A center wheel lets you control how fast you whirl.

TIPS: This ride can be as popular with teens as with tots. It seems there's a challenge to seeing just how fast they can get the bowls to spin.

Tampico Tumbler **** The thrill here is feeling like you're on a collision course with the car in front of you. Two-person cars extend from arms that rise from a center stem that revolves as the cars themselves rotate. Halfway through it reverses direction. Fiesta colors of bright red and yellow make the ride interesting to watch. There's a 52-inch height restriction.

Gran Slammer **** From the ground this looks like a simple baby ride, but in fact it simulates a six-story free-fall. You sit in seats at the end of an arm that keeps you parallel to the ground. The arm rotates the seats upwards and out so you go from ground level to a height of 60 feet, then drop back to earth. When your stomach is left at the top and you're at the bottom, you become vividly aware of how deceiving this ride can really be.

TIPS: Another one to avoid immediately after lunch. There's a 42-inch height restriction.

Camp Snoopy

If the kids in your group are six and under, you'll probably have no choice but to make this the first stop on your circuit of the park. As you pass through the main gate, you can go straight ahead into Ghost Town or veer right to Camp Snoopy. If Snoopy or one of his pals is near the entrance, it's a cinch your youngster will drag you in that direction. This is home to the most famous beagle in the world, plus friends Linus, Lucy and Charlie Brown, who regularly stroll the streets to shake hands and pose for photos. Kids might need an explanation that these characters don't talk, but that they have no problem communicating with gestures and hugs on a nonverbal level. Everything is created just for kids. Much of the adult delight comes from watching a child's discoveries here. Themed to the California High Sierra, Camp Snoopy features six scenic acres with rushing waterfalls, a meandering stream, and swaying pontoon and suspension bridges that challenge a child's sure-footedness. Kids can hop on a mini-steamboat for a 15-minute circuit of Reflection Lake, or for a couple of quarters they can pilot their own remote-controlled tugs, dinghies and ocean liners on a quiet bay.

Camp Snoopy is the one area where you must come *under* a maximum rather than *over* a minimum height requirement to go

IT'S SHOWTIME!

The **Charles M. Schulz Theatre** features a variety of entertainment, from big Broadway-style, song-and-dance productions to Snoopy ice shows to special holiday-themed extravaganzas. These shows offer a fun break from the crowds and let little ones, especially, catch their breath before conquering the rest of the park. Check the entertainment schedule or the theater marquee for showtimes.

on many of the rides. Some clearly are labeled "not for parents unless accompanied by a child," and others, like the Huff and Puff, exclude adults altogether. It's a totally happy place, always a family favorite. Senior citizens here for the first time often find some of the rides as exciting as their grandchildren do. Even on crowded days there always seems to be a place to sit to tie a shoe or wipe a face. Many restaurants serve child-sized hamburgers and drinks.

The star rating system here is applied mostly from a small child's point of view and reflects the opinion of a number of two-to-six-year-olds.

WHAT TO SEE & DO

High Sierra Ferris Wheel ★★★ Little ones report that they like being up high so they can see everything. This wheel is an old-fashioned, scaled-down version of those found at state fairs, and sometimes kids can get a bit impatient with the loading and unloading, but once it's off and spinning they're thrilled.

Rocky Road Trucking Company ★★★ For a taste of the trucking life, kids climb aboard shiny, miniature-sized 18-wheelers, honk the blasting air horns and wind through Camp Snoopy. The path even takes you under Montezooma's Revenge in Fiesta Village.

TIPS: There are no restrictions, other than that children must be able to sit properly.

Snoopy's Bounce ★★★ Reaching 38 feet in height, this larger-than-life, inflated Snoopy contains air-filled cushions. The area is constantly in motion as the movement of children shifts air from one chamber to another.

TIPS: To enter, a child must demonstrate basic motor skills.

Log Peeler ★★★ This is a scaled-down and tamer version of the classic ride, the Scrambler. You spin around while moving both forward and backward.

TIPS: Because the ride never leaves the ground, it's a good choice for those afraid of heights.

Woodstock's Airmail ★★★ First, the ratings criteria: this mini-thrill ride, billed as a $1/14$-scale version of Supreme Scream (the two rides actually debuted on the same day), is graded in terms of mini-kid thrills. That said, little ones who will have to wait patiently before passing that all-important height requirement for the grownup version will no doubt have a ball. And hey, to a kid, 19-feet in the air can seem pretty darned supreme.

TIPS: Though it's a kiddie ride, it's still not for everyone. Riders must still pass a height requirement (in this case 36 inches and up). The good news, however, is that with no upper-end requirements, parents may be able to accompany kids for the ride.

Charlie Brown Speedway ★★★ Strap in with Charlie Brown, Lucy and the rest of the gang for this race around a mini track.

The three-minute ride zips you at the speed of Woodstock around a diminutive oval course. Cars are on a track, so you don't really get to steer. But these babies "corner," whipping you around turns fast enough to amuse grownups and kids alike. Tough luck for solo grownups, however: you'll have to be with a kid in order to ride.

TIPS: The wait may look long from the outside, but don't let it scare you away; lines for this ride move pretty quickly.

Beary Tales Playhouse ★★★ A multilevel structure that's home to lovable animated characters whom children can discover while exploring at their own pace. Cave-like corridors, corners and flights of stairs promise a surprise at every turn. At Knott's Berry Farm Canning Company, bears put the famous preserves in jars. Next door, bears in the bakery connive to outwit the wily fox that's after their fresh-baked pies. A favorite area is Weird Woods with its series of distorting mirrors. The Frog and Toddler Path invites tots to crawl into an "animal cage" for a creature's-eye view of spectators outside.

TIPS: A baby center and restrooms are right across from the Beary Tales Playhouse.

Camp Bus ★★★ Resembling a traditional yellow school bus, the Camp Bus offers a thrilling way to get a bird's-eye view of Camp Snoopy. This popular ride, designed with the whole family in mind, soars 20 feet in the air.

TIPS: Because parents may accompany kids, this is a good ride for those too young to ride others, as they can sit on a parent's lap.

Timberline Twister ★★★ Kids who yearn for a ride on Boomerang or Montezooma's Revenge but aren't big enough may find this mini-roller coaster an acceptable substitute. It doesn't have the wild and rowdy curves and speed of the big boys, but there's enough excitement to keep youngsters interested.

TIPS: Teens and adults without kids can skip this one.

Huff and Puff ★ This very basic ride consists of tiny, one-child mine cars that move along a track solely through the efforts of the small fry. Cars meander the brief route through a piney forest as riders push and pull a hand lever. Some children lose interest within the first 30 seconds as they realize they're not seeing any-thing interesting and they're doing all the work. Parents some-times exhort from the sidelines to keep their offspring pumping and prevent them from abandoning the mine cars in mid-track.

Grand Sierra Scenic Railroad ★★★ When it's time for a mid–Camp Snoopy break, hop on this little steam train for a circuit of Reflection Lake. While you catch a rest, the route holds kids' interest as they wind past shrimp-colored flamingos in Fiesta Village and wait for the Walter K Steamboat to pass so the draw-bridge can close. A four-year-old reports he likes the train because "it whistles and makes noise."

TIPS: For shutterbugs, one of the best views of Montezooma's Revenge is from the train as it circles the lake's far shore near the entrance to Fiesta Village.

Edison's Inventor's Workshop ★★ Call this attraction part science museum, part interactive play station. The turn-of-the-20th-century workshop houses nearly a dozen activities, all with gizmos and gadgets on which pint-size tinkerers can experiment with the powers of electricity and magnetism. In the "Light Tower," you use bicycle power to illuminate a tower of light bulbs; the faster you pedal, the more bulbs light up. In "Magnetic Patterns" and "Magnetic Force" you can manipulate magnets to find truth in the phrase "opposites attract." There is also a bunch of authentic Edison artifacts such as an original gramophone, an early experimental light bulb and some of the inventor's handwritten notes, all on loan from Southern California Edison (cosponsor of the attraction) and the Edison Trust. Mr. Edison himself makes periodic appearances, milling about his workshop to answer questions and to tinker alongside visitors.

> When park rides are closed, the explanation posted outside reads: "We're fixing the framus and painting the podar."

TIPS: A rarely crowded attraction. Check with employees at the entrance about Mr. Edison's appearances; the experience is more fun when he's around.

Camp Snoopy Theater ★★★ This little 150-seat outdoor gathering place is home to popular performing-animal shows. "Woodstock's Wildlife Wonders" stars Snoopy's feathered pal, Woodstock. The show features tame forest animals including a timber wolf, raccoons and an owl. The boa constrictor, draped around its trainer's body, is touted as the perfect pet. "You feed him once a month, he doesn't bark or wet and he'll give you a big hug when you need it," winks the trainer.

TIPS: The 20-minute show is so folksy and casual that kids keep leaving their seats to pet the animals.

Petting Zoo ★★ Located next door to the Camp Snoopy Theater, this barnyard-like enclosure houses a variety of docile animals. Even though it's not particularly well-stocked, it can be a source of fascination to small children. There is an Adalbra tortoise, rabbits, goats, sheep and an Asian pot-bellied pig; a boa constrictor under glass and free-running chickens round out the menagerie.

Red Baron ★★★ This ride is very popular with little ones because it's exclusively for them. Kids can choose their own plane and become airborne aces while Snoopy (as the Red Baron) pilots his dog house in the middle of it all. Vintage mini-planes "take off" for a flight filled with gentle dips and swoops.

TIPS: For tykes, this is one of the area's most popular rides, and lines will form on busy days.

Flying Ace Balloon Race ★★★ Another kids-only ride, this is also a favorite because independent-minded youngsters select their own balloon, then hop into the gondola without adult supervision. Huge, colorful pseudo-balloons appear to lift the two-child gondolas six feet in the air, then sink and soar for a three-minute ride.

TIPS: Kids must be at least 3 years old to ride.

Indian Trails

This two-acre attraction, located between Ghost Town and Reflection Lake, is a tribute to American Indians and provides an opportunity for authentic historical and cultural experiences. The hands-on adventure appeals to all ages as kids and adults explore the heritage of American Indians.

Unusual architectural styles have been authentically re-created. They include Salish and Kwakiutl longhouses, Tsimshian totem and potlatch poles as well as the tepees of the Blackfoot, Nez Perce, Cheyenne, Crow and Kiowa tribes. Representing the Southwest Indians are the hogans of the Navajo and adobe buildings of the Pueblo Indians; there also are Chumash dwellings and Gabrieleño wickiups from California.

Artisans at work here include canoe makers, ceremonial-mask carvers, leatherwork artists, face painters, basket makers, potters, weavers, sand painters and silversmiths. Indian Trails is filled with representatives whose ancestry predates Columbus. Food facilities offer Navajo fry bread, buffalo stew and corn roasted in the husk.

WHAT TO SEE & DO

Children's Camp ★★★★ Created especially for youngsters, Children's Camp lets them assist in handcrafting traditional honor bonnets, beadwork and sand paintings. They can listen as storytellers recount living history and have their faces painted in tribal fashion.

Knott's Berry Farm Area Lodging

Within a mile in any direction from Knott's Berry Farm, hotels and motels in all price ranges line Beach Boulevard, Buena Park's Hotel Row and nearby side streets. Because Knott's is just five miles from Disneyland, many visitors headquarter at a single hotel for trips to both parks. Hotels listed here are decidedly closer to Knott's. When booking, ask for special park packages that often include admissions and free gifts.

For convenience it's hard to top the **Radisson Resort Knott's Berry Farm**. The 320-room highrise is literally in Knott's parking lot, a three-minute walk from the main gate, with a complimentary shuttle to Disneyland. Rooms are large and appealing, and, for die-hard "Peanuts" fans, 16 Snoopy-themed rooms are available. The heated pool is a welcome family gathering spot after a day in the park. ~ 7675 Crescent Avenue, Buena Park; 714-995-

Surf's Up at Soak City

If Knott's Berry Farm "wets" your appetite for fun, **Soak City** is sure to drench it. The second park in the Knott's emporium (requiring separate admission unless you buy the Premium Resort Passport), this 13-acre water park has nearly two dozen rides designed to cool you down on those hot Southern California days. Look for tube slides, body slides and other high-speed contraptions. And the monikers leave little to the imagination: Dropoff, Riptide and Banzai Falls, to name a few. Artificial surf can be found in the enormous Tidal Wave Bay, where challenging waves offer the ultimate endless summer experience.

But the place isn't exclusively a daredevil utopia. Some of the most diabolical water hazards are over at the three-level Toyota® Beach House, where just about everything is booby-trapped with sprayers, nozzles and water guns. For less frantic fun, you can loll about on the lazy Sparkletts Sunset River, a one-third-mile long stretch of easy-going rapids. And the Gremmie Lagoon water playground is bound to entertain the littlest ones in your group.

Restaurants like the Salty Dogs and the Edison Electric Grill celebrate Southern California's 1950s surf culture; you'll find souvenirs galore at the Wipeout! Surf Shop.

Soak City is open roughly June through September, but days and times vary. Look for admission discounts after 3 p.m., when the park begins to clear out. Admission. ~ 8039 Beach Boulevard; 714-220-5200; www.soak cityusa.com.

1111, 800-422-4444, fax 714-828-8590; www.radisson.com/buenaparkca. MODERATE.

Embassy Suites Buena Park offers two-room suites with kitchenettes as well as cooked-to-order breakfasts for guests. With a pull-out sofa bed and two double beds, the Spanish-style guest accommodations will comfortably sleep up to six. Well-done natural landscaping surrounds the large pool, which is set in a central courtyard with a barbecue for guests' use. The 201-room hotel is a five-minute walk from the park entrance. ~ 7762 Beach Boulevard, Buena Park; 714-739-5600, 800-362-2779, fax 714-521-9650; www.embassysuites.com. DELUXE.

The 145-room **Courtyard Buena Park** is one of the nicer hotels on Beach Boulevard because it's set back from the street, which helps cut traffic noise. Rooms with private balconies and patios surround a charming inner courtyard landscaped with pine trees and lush plantings. Originally designed to appeal to a business clientele, the hotel now caters to park-goers. The café is open for breakfast, and there is a lounge open in the evenings that serves appetizers and sandwiches. The park is a ten-minute walk away. ~ 7621 Beach Boulevard, Buena Park; 714-670-6600, 800-321-2211, fax 714-670-0360; www.courtyard.com. MODERATE TO DELUXE.

Set back a bit from the busy boulevard, the green-and-white **Innsuites Hotel** has 198 guest rooms and an impressive, two-story lobby with fountain and spiral staircase. The quiet courtyard, with heated pool and spa, is surrounded by multilevel landscaping and palm trees. Opposite the lobby is a video-games arcade. Free breakfast buffet is included. The inn is two blocks from Knott's entrance and will shuttle guests to Disneyland. ~ 7555 Beach Boulevard, Buena Park; 714-522-7360, 800-272-6232, fax 714-523-2883; www.innsuites.com, e-mail buenapark@innsuites.com. MODERATE.

The reliably comfortable **Holiday Inn Buena Park and Conference Center** is always a good, safe family choice. Large rooms

---

CALIFORNIA MARKETPLACE

Knott's California MarketPlace is a separate dining and shopping facility that you pass through before entering the park. This is where Mrs. Knott's Chicken Dinner Restaurant is located, plus two more restaurants. There's a tour de force of Knott's preserves at the Berry Market. Take the time to look twice. Many flavors such as bing cherry, red currant and California plum are available only at the park. Ten intriguing shops make this area an attraction in itself. If you want to explore California MarketPlace and have a bite to eat without entering the park itself, you can park for free for up to three hours.

have an agreeable decor. An extra-large adult pool is set beside a children's wading pool and jacuzzi, both surrounded with a well-kept, palm-studded lawn. There's a complimentary shuttle to Knott's Berry Farm and Disneyland as well as other area attractions. ~ 7000 Beach Boulevard, Buena Park; 714-522-7000, 800-522-7006, fax 714-522-3230. DELUXE.

Red Roof Inn, part of a reliable budget chain, offers no-frills accommodations (children under 18 stay free with adults) plus a free continental breakfast in a plain but friendly atmosphere. The pool and spa are sunny and adequate, and rooms are clean and comfortable. Small pets are allowed in the rooms. ~ 7121 Beach Boulevard, Buena Park; 714-670-9000, 800-633-8300, fax 714-522-7280; www.redroof.com. BUDGET.

Off Beach Boulevard (which means it's quieter), the **Hampton Inn Buena Park** has a young, child-oriented staff that obviously enjoys youngsters. The medium-sized, contemporary-decor rooms and suites have comfortable sitting areas with couches or lounge chairs. Tidily landscaped pool and patio areas are brightened with white umbrella tables. There's no restaurant, but eateries are just next door. ~ 7828 East Orangethorpe Avenue, Buena Park; 714-670-7200, 800-727-7205, fax 714-522-3319. MODERATE.

The **Fairfield Inn Buena Park** is not within walking distance of Knott's, but the 133 medium-sized rooms are comfortably furnished, and the bare-bones pool is adequate. A young, enthusiastic staff takes the time to get involved with kids. ~ 7032 Orangethorpe Avenue, Buena Park; 714-523-1488, 800-228-2800, fax 714-523-8474; www.fairfieldinn.com/lgbbp. BUDGET.

Conveniently located, the **Days Inn Anaheim-Buena Park** is a two-block walk from Knott's. The pool area is a bit sterile, but the 63 rooms are reliably clean. A few family units with two adjoining rooms are available; some are linked by an archway, creating a suite-like arrangement. A continental breakfast is served. ~ 8580 Stanton Avenue, Buena Park; 714-828-5211, 800-646-1629, fax 714-826-3716. BUDGET TO MODERATE.

The **Colony Inn** is a rambling, 100-room, crisp-blue-and-white complex across the street from Knott's. It has a heated pool in addition to efficiency units and suites. ~ 7800 Crescent Avenue, Buena Park; 714-527-2201, 800-982-6566, fax 714-826-3826. BUDGET.

Knott's Berry Farm Area Dining

Inside the park you'll find the usual array of fast-food stands and sit-down restaurants, many with menus a notch above what you'd expect in a theme park. Although lines move quickly, expect a wait during peak lunch and dinner hours.

In Ghost Town, **Auntie Pasta's Pizza Palace** features pasta, salads and sandwiches along with a variety of specialty pizzas.

BUDGET. The **Ghost Town Grill** has a selection of hamburgers, chicken and chili dishes. BUDGET TO MODERATE.

Typically Southern California charbroiled hamburgers, hot dogs and chicken at **Wilderness Broiler** in Wild Water Wilderness satisfy tastes for familiar fare. They'll broil the burgers to order. BUDGET. Among the many restaurants on the Boardwalk, you'll find the '50s-themed **Coaster's Diner**, complete with tabletop jukeboxes and all-American fare such as cheeseburgers, fries and milkshakes. BUDGET.

The giant tostadas at Fiesta Village's **Cantina** have a shell that looks like a sail and are tastily prepared with ground beef and your choice of mild or hot salsa. Enjoy generously sized tacos and burritos while you're serenaded by organ music from the carousel. BUDGET.

In Camp Snoopy at **Lucy's Lunchbox**, you will find child-sized hamburgers and hot dogs. Unfortunately this sit-down restaurant doesn't have mini-prices, but it still falls into the budget category. BUDGET.

Just outside the park main gate in the shopping area called California MarketPlace are some very good sit-down restaurants (714-220-5200 for information on all park restaurants). You can park for free without buying a park ticket. If you're in the park, you can exit and return with a hand stamp. Not to be missed is Cordelia Knott's original **Mrs. Knott's Chicken Dinner Restaurant**. Even on a slow day, lines form to taste the world-famous chicken served here since 1934. Grandmotherly waitresses encourage kids to "eat it all so you have more energy for the park!" Wood booths, "antique" buffets and plate rails with grandma's china create a homey atmosphere. While waiting in line, take a look at the framed menus from those bygone days when an entire dinner was 75 cents. Glassed-in pages from old Knott's guests books bear the signatures and comments of notables including John Wayne and Bob Hope. Lunch begins with baking-powder biscuits

THE SMITHY

At the Blacksmith Shop, a re-creation of a working smithy, the leather-aproned blacksmith will proudly explain how he's hammered out, link by link, the heavy-duty chain across his doorway. He'll explain how the village smithy once was an entire hardware store, the site for forging tools and utensils as well as shoeing horses. He'll show present-day applications of his work, such as iron pothooks and branding irons for steak, and explain that the word "blacksmith," or "blacksmite," has its roots in "hitter, or smiter, of black iron." For a fee he'll even hammer out a horseshoe bearing your name.

and can include a small dish of strawberry/rhubarb sauce (delicious!), two pieces of deep-fried chicken and mashed potatoes and gravy. Try the boysenberry punch for a zippy, refreshing change. The restaurant also serves broiled and roasted chicken as well as chicken salad for those who eschew fried foods. To avoid the lines but sample the chicken, stop by the chicken-to-go window next door. The restaurant also is open early for breakfast (huge, home-style affairs with biscuits and slabs of ham). It puts you within seconds of the park entrance for opening time. BUDGET.

The choice of restaurants within a mile or so of the park runs heavily to budget-priced chains. Several others are priced in the moderate category and have a special fondness for families.

PoFolks epitomizes down-home Southern cookin' and family atmosphere with a hearty, Dixie-style menu. There are turnip greens, black-eyed peas, country-fried steaks, fried chicken and hush puppies. Emphasizing its homespun style are natural-wood booths and tables with blue-and-white-checked tablecloths and a decor that consists of old kitchen paraphernalia. Framed 1920s newspapers decorate the restrooms, and a period model train chugs around the room to the delight of kids. ~ 7701 Beach Boulevard, Buena Park; 714-521-8955. BUDGET.

The wait is worth it at **Claim Jumper**. The Gold Rush theme includes buffalo, moose, elk and deer heads, which peer over your shoulder while you eat. There are mini-burgers with fries and apple garnish, barbecued ribs, grilled cheese, chicken, pasta and chicken fingers. Adults can also dine on baby back pork ribs, meat loaf, rotisserie chicken and great Cobb salads. The baked potatoes weigh over a pound. If you have room, try the Motherlode six-layer chocolate cake. Gigantic portions. ~ 7971 Beach Boulevard, Buena Park; 714-523-3227. MODERATE TO DELUXE.

Located two miles south of Buena Park in Cyprus, **The Olive Garden** is so Italian in ambience that it has gondoliers and white-capped mountains painted on the walls. A profusion of plants and natural-wood tables gives the place an outdoor feel. It can accommodate almost 400 guests but is broken into separate sections, avoiding a barn-like atmosphere. Entrées include ravioli, spaghetti and lasagne. Regular menu offerings come in children's portions, and kids also like the personal-sized pizzas. ~ 6874 Katella Avenue, Cyprus; 714-894-1330. BUDGET TO MODERATE.

Knott's Berry Farm Area Shopping

The expected T-shirts and souvenir mugs with the Knott's logo are available at over 30 shops in the park. Two unusual shopping opportunities stand out. At the **Geode Shop**, bins of "coconuts"—round rocks that may contain an interesting center—are priced according to weight. The lighter, more expensive ones are more likely to contain a hollow quartz and amethyst-filled center. Make your choice and the lapidist will cut it on his diamond-bladed saw, then polish the surface.

The **General Store** in Ghost Town has a great selection of Western wear including classy boots and ten-gallon hats. In Ghost Town's **Magic Shop**, a selection of tricks and gags can turn budding magicians into little Houdinis. If the kids won't leave the park without a Snoopy souvenir, stop at **Snoopy's Campstore** in Camp Snoopy. The famous beagle has his likeness on everything from toys and clothing to illustrated books. Besides plastic totem replicas and other souvenir merchandise, the **Mystery Lodge Store** offers original (and expensive) ceremonial masks, totems and other native crafts.

Immediately outside the park, California MarketPlace is a mecca for shoppers. You'll have to sort through the chachkas and clutter in its 10 shops, but you'll doubtless uncover some wonderful and unusual finds. It's easy to send gifts home from the **Berry Market**. Gift packs of Knott's products are sold in amazing variety. There's no way to miss **Virginia's Gift Shop**, a large, eclectic shop with plenty of souvenir kitsch as well as high-quality crystal, Lladro porcelains and collector baseball cards. The **MarketPlace Emporium** has high-quality Oriental objets d'art in jade and brass. Last thing before you leave, stop by the **Farm Bakery** for a genuine boysenberry pie. It's made with the berry that started it all.

Knott's Berry Farm Area Nightlife

Any after-hours revelry will often include children, and the area outside the park has two guaranteed-to-please options:

It seems hokey at first: dining with your fingers in an imitation 12th-century castle while knights ride into battle. Actually, **Medieval Times** is a brilliant concept, a re-creation of a medieval tournament, complete with games of skill and jousting matches. It can get pretty wild when the knights—highly trained horsemen and stuntmen—perform dangerous jousting and sword-fighting routines. ~ 7662 Beach Boulevard, Buena Park; 714-521-4740; www.medievaltimes.com.

Just up the street at **Wild Bill's Wild West Dinner Extravaganza**, a two-hour musical variety show takes you back to the days of Wild Bill Hickok. While watching the Wild West show, guests get friendly at long, communal tables in Miss Annie's Saloon, chowing down on fried chicken and barbecued ribs from pewter buckets that the guests pass around the table. The show includes Indian dancers, a comical magician and a lasso artist. Audience members get into the act when they become square dancers. ~ 7600 Beach Boulevard, Buena Park; 714-522-6414.

FIVE

Universal Studios Hollywood

If Hollywood is one big fantasy, Universal Studios Hollywood is one big set within the fantasy. Here, movieland unfolds like you won't believe as you see the seaside town of Amity featured in *Jaws*, the damp forests roamed by E.T., Norman Bates's *Psycho* house, Baker Street in London and a Parisian courtyard.

There was little more here than fruit trees and coyotes when Carl Laemmle purchased the barren site in 1915 for a movie studio. The entrepreneur invited visitors to his studio, charging them a quarter for the first Universal tour. For that, guests received a box lunch and sat in bleachers watching early silents being made. In those early days the audience could boo the villain and applaud the heroine, but with the advent of sound, visitors were barred from the set.

In 1964 the tour idea surfaced again, this time allowing a tour company to drive its buses through the lower lot to increase lunchtime business at the studio commissary. That first year, 42,000 guests visited the studio, and top brass realized they were on to something. In 1965 the Upper Lot opened, with a better version of the original stunt show, a live animal show and a "screen test" in which guests became "stars." Today, thousands of visitors a day troop through to get a close-up view of filmland with its sleeves rolled up.

The studio sprawls over a vast lot, flanked by freeways and a small range of hills. The Upper Lot, which also is used for filming, perches atop a hill and down its flanks. From the moment you step out of your car and head for the entrance, you're surrounded with billboards announcing current Universal Studios feature releases.

Technically, the park is split into the Lower Lot and the Upper Lot on the hill. Some areas of the Lower Lot are open to visitors only on the tram tour. The Lower Lot is dominated by the sound stages that house Jurassic Park—The Ride, Backdraft, E.T. Adventure, Lucy: A Tribute and Special Effects Stages.

The much more expansive Upper Lot, where you enter, immediately puts you into a movieland mode as you find yourself strolling the Streets of the World. The weathered, rustic buildings of Western Street, New York's enduring brownstones, Baker Street with its reincarnations of typically London shops, Moulin Rouge and the Parisian courtyard, and '50s America near Mel's Diner are all so amazingly realistic it's hard to fathom that they're just sets. This is, after all, the world's largest movie studio.

Even restaurants continue the fantasy theme; one looks like Bedrock (home of the Flintstones), another is straight out of a Mexican village, and yet another is topped with a revolving windmill. Interspersed with these flights of fantasy are large, comfortable theaters seating as many as 3000 guests. The shows, one of the park's most appealing features, reveal the secrets of movie-making magic.

On the studio's well-known studio tour, you're immersed in silver-screen lore as you drive through streets once haunted by Hollywood greats and catch glimpses of contemporary stars in shows currently in production. Virtually every day (except weekends) it really is possible to witness a motion picture or television show being filmed somewhere on the lot. The authentic-looking sets offer a nostalgic journey from historical films to the screenland homes of the stars of today. Apart from the tour, it's also possible to be an audience guest at the filming or taping of a television show. For most people, though, simply absorbing all the Hollywood imagery and nuances is intoxicating enough. There is a certain excitement and childlike elation in knowing that the line between illusion and reality runs very thin here.

Nuts & Bolts

Universal Studios is located at 100 Universal City Plaza, Universal City (818-622-3801, 800-864-8377; www.universalstudioshollywood.com). If you stay at either the

ARRIVAL Universal Hilton or Universal Sheraton, both of which are on studio property, you simply take a Universal Trolley or walk up the hill to the Studio attraction.

When arriving by car, exit off the Hollywood Freeway (Route 101) at either Universal Studios Boulevard or Lankershim Boulevard. From the freeway, signs direct you about a half-mile to the park entrance.

You'll drive up Universal Hollywood Drive past the Universal Sheraton and the Universal Hilton, pay a parking fee and receive a brochure and parking directions.

TICKETS There are three ticket options here: a one-day pass, a two-week Southern California Value pass (which includes admission to SeaWorld) or an annual pass. Call or check the website for special packages, such as the Director's and VIP tickets.

	Adults	Children 3–11
		(Under 3 years, free)
One-day Pass	$45.00	$35.00
Annual Pass	$54.00	$44.00
Two-week Pass	$79.00	$59.00

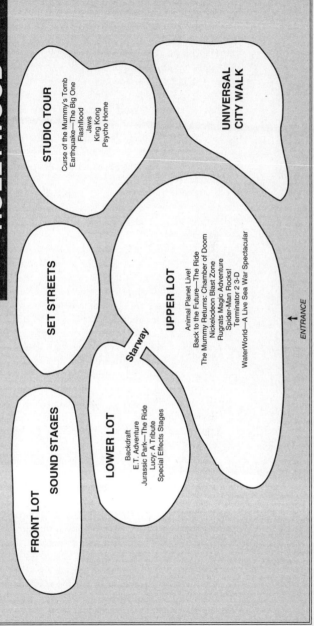

UNIVERSAL STUDIOS HOLLYWOOD

STUDIO TOUR

Curse of the Mummy's Tomb
Earthquake—The Big One
Flashflood
Jaws
King Kong
Psycho Home

UNIVERSAL CITY WALK

SET STREETS

UPPER LOT

Animal Planet Live!
Back to the Future—The Ride
The Mummy Returns: Chamber of Doom
Nickelodeon Blast Zone
Rugrats Magic Adventure
Spider-Man Rocks!
Terminator 2 3-D
WaterWorld—A Live Sea War Spectacular

Starway

FRONT LOT

SOUND STAGES

LOWER LOT

Backdraft
E.T. Adventure
Jurassic Park—The Ride
Lucy: A Tribute
Special Effects Stages

ENTRANCE

GAME PLAN With many major rides and attractions, Universal Studios offers a lot to do in just one day, so make sure you know which rides and attractions are your top priorities and do them first. The following sightseeing strategy is for one day only and hits most of the biggies, but it will make for a full day.

The Universal experience has three distinct parts:

1. The Studio Tour
2. The Lower Lot
3. The Upper Lot

The 45-minute Studio Tour covers the studio, including attractions like King Kong and Earthquake that have been built specifically for the tour. This is where you're most likely to see stars who are working on the lot. Because Universal Studios is a working studio, the route of the tour often changes depending on filming.

The studio back lot occupies a huge, flat acreage with sound stages, offices and equipment-storage buildings. The Lower Lot houses the Jurassic Park ride, the E.T. ride, Lucy: A Tribute and Special Effects Stages.

The Upper Lot houses the Back to the Future ride, Terminator 2:3D, The Mummy Returns, Nickelodeon Blast Zone, WaterWorld and the rest of the attractions.

Weekends and summer months are busiest, and you can expect to move at a snail's pace simply because the park areas are small. But don't be dismayed. Arrive 30 minutes early and get on the first or second tram. This will enable you to get a head start on the lines for the popular rides and attractions.

The Studio Tour departs from the Upper Lot. Once you return you have two options, depending on the show schedules. You can either stay in the Upper Lot and dash to the Back to the Future ride and then attend a WaterWorld show (check the schedule), or head immediately down to the Lower Lot via the Starway and ride Jurassic Park and either E.T. or Backdraft, depending on the lines.

After lunch, check the afternoon show schedule and coordinate afternoon shows with any rides you missed in the morning. Shows are conveniently staggered and repeated several times a day, so if you plan well you should be able to see all of them. It's important to get to a show at least five minutes before it starts (earlier if you want a good seat). Even though the crowds may look horrendous, the theaters are all large and capable of taking hordes of visitors. The gates close as soon as the theater is full and stay closed during the performance, so get there on time.

You can choose from any of the dozen restaurants in the park. Although food is not of table-service restaurant quality, it does rank high in the world of theme-park dining. It's advisable to eat lunch by 11:30 a.m. and dinner at about 4:30 p.m. to avoid the crowds.

General Information   Guest Relations, Universal Studios Hollywood, 100 Universal City Plaza, Universal City, CA 91608; 818-508-9600; www.universalstudioshollywood.com.

Stroller and Wheelchair Rentals   Located at Guest Relations, next to the exit.

Baby Services   Diaper-changing facilities are located in all restrooms throughout the park.

Lockers   Located next to Guest Relations and Jurassic Park—The Ride.

Pets   Bring them to the Information Center and they'll be kenneled for the day at no charge.

Lost Children and Lost & Found   Located at Guest Relations, Security and near the Studio Tour entrance in the Lower Lot.

First Aid   There is a station in the Upper Lot next to Animal Planet Live and near the Studio Tour entrance.

Banking   ATMs are at the main entrance and in the Lower Lot near the Jurassic Cove Café.

GUEST SERVICES

Universal Studios' 415 acres make it the largest film and television studio in the world, but just a small portion is open for on-your-own exploring. You'll see a lot of the grounds on the tram, but when hoofing it you're restricted to the lower and upper lots.

Think of the studio as having an upstairs and a downstairs. You arrive in the Upper Lot, where the tram tour departs. The Starway (a series of four plexi-enclosed escalators a quarter-mile long) connects the Upper and Lower lots.

GETTING AROUND

One of the highlights of any Universal visit is the Studio Tour, which provides a behind-the-scenes glimpse of the cinema world aboard a four-car, open-air vehicle that accommodates 160 guests. Since seating is six across, try to sit on the right side if you want a close-up of King Kong's dental work.

Studio Tour

SEE YOUR TELEVISION HEROES IN THE FLESH

Many television shows and specials are taped before a live audience, and that live audience can easily include you. At any given time (hardly ever on weekends, though) tickets are available for up to 20 current shows including sitcoms, variety shows, talk shows and specials. Tickets are free, and to assure a full house more are distributed than the studios can hold, so once you have your ticket you must show up early to be certain of a seat. Stop by the **TV Audience Ticket Booth** near the Upper Lot exit to see what's available. Tapings are done off the lot, so you should get tickets either for late that same day or for the following day.

As mentioned before, the best strategy is to ride the tram first thing in the morning, before the crowds arrive.

WHAT TO SEE & DO

As you climb aboard the tram, a guide will introduce the studio and let you know what's happening on the lot that day—which stars are around, which films are being shot, which sound stages are "hot" (that is, dressed for filming). As the tram pulls out you'll head to the back lot, which many people find the most fascinating part of the tour. Here you're in another world (or many other worlds) as the tram winds through Jurassic Park, Lake Michigan, Whoville, New York and dozens of other locales familiar to moviegoers. When the tram rounds a corner, each falsefront building is seen for what it is—a mere facade in which bricks are made of foam rubber and chicken wire and many features are simply painted on.

You'll see Brownstone Street where Jerry Seinfeld lived; the clock tower and town square of *Back to the Future* fame; and Spartacus Square, where Kirk Douglas once walked in ancient Rome. The cobblestone streets of Little Europe showed up in *The Deer Hunter*, and Colonial Street was home to such disparate entertainments as *Animal House* and *The Munsters*. Video monitors inside the tram run film clips that vividly illustrate the transformation of each set into famous film locations.

The 30-foot Kong weighs over six tons, has 660 pounds of fur and 10 watts of "growl."

As the tram approaches a large building the guide explains that you're about to enter a sound stage where filming is currently in progress. Once inside this re-creation of a modern subway station, you feel a slight lurch. Then the entire earth shakes as telephone poles topple and power cables emit showers of sparks. The roar becomes deafening when the earth collapses and a truck transporting "highly flammable" material falls through from the street above. Smoke and flames engulf the station. If you're not totally involved by this time, you will be when you see a 15-foot wall of water from a ruptured water main rushing furiously toward you ("use your seat cushions for flotation").

The entire experience graphically simulates an earthquake reaching 8.3 on the Richter scale: 32,000 watts of Sensurround audio power blast you with a thunderous gas explosion and the crackling of a raging fire. Lasting about three minutes, the "quake" is most frightening to those who've actually experienced a trembler because it's so realistic. The entire earthquake stage, which re-sets in 15 seconds, shakes 200 times a day.

Amity, the seafaring village seen in the movie *Jaws*, is another stop on the tour. Just as you get your camera poised for a shot of this tranquil scene, old Jaws himself lunges out of the water within inches of your car. The thrills continue as you travel back in time to the ruins of Hamunaptra—the city of the dead featured in *The Curse of the Mummy's Tomb*. Inside the burial chamber—

a sand-and-stone version of an ancient Egyptian tomb—the tram descends into a spinning tunnel where the evil high priest Imhotep sentences you to spend eternity as one of the living dead. The effect is fun and utterly dizzying, and you'll have to take your tour guide's word for it when he or she explains that it was the tunnel moving, and not your tram.

If that's not enough adventure for one ride, wait until you enter a scaled-down version of New York that has just been devastated by a rampaging King Kong. It's a tense, frightened city where fires burn out of control and a noisy helicopter blares danger warnings over a loudspeaker. Through tenement windows you see television sets broadcasting accounts of the big beast's destruction. Even as you watch, the screen goes blank when the copter crashes into a power line, unleashing a furious shower of electrical sparks and a tunnel of flames.

As the mighty Kong's towering shadow looms along the buildings, you catch your first glimpse of the big ape. Then as the tram inches across the Brooklyn Bridge, you come close enough to the gorilla—three feet from those giant jaws—to smell his banana breath. Hang on tight when he grabs the suspension cables of the bridge.

Assuming you survive this part of the tour, you'll arrive next in a sleepy Mexican village (a setting in the movie *Butch Cassidy and the Sundance Kid*) where you merely have to withstand a flash flood. In true Hollywood style it drains harmlessly away as you continue along to view the house from *Psycho* (complete with Mother Bates rocking in the window), the set from *The Grinch* and many more of Universal's 500 outdoor sets.

Lower Lot

The Lower Lot is the home of several major attractions, including Special Effects Stages, Jurassic Park, Backdraft and E.T. Adventure. It can be seen in under two hours. Unlike the Upper Lot where shows are offered at specific times, attractions in the Lower Lot run continuously. As in the rest of the park, you'll also see some of filmdom's most famous characters—Bride of Frankenstein, Clark Gable, Charlie Chaplin, Woody Woodpecker and others roaming the streets here. They're always willing to pose with you for photos.

WHAT TO SEE & DO

Jurassic Park—The Ride ★★★★★ You know it's only a ride, but the technological sophistication of this $110-million blockbuster attraction will have you believing that the vicious *Tyrannosaurus rex* that was practically breathing down your neck is real enough indeed. The ride begins with a multimedia introduction by host John Hammond, the creator and owner of Jurassic Park (played by Sir Richard Attenborough). Aboard a river raft, your party of explorers navigates through the misty, exotic world inhabited by huge but gentle prehistoric creatures like the 50-foot-high *Ultrasaurus* and playful *Psittacosauruses*. It's all pretty idyllic, with picturesque waterfalls, pools and geysers. Mother and baby *Stegosauruses* seem glad to see you, and small dinosaurs called "compys" shriek their greetings. But then something goes wrong, and the raft spins off-course into Carnivore Canyon, where the ferocious T-rex and vicious *Velociraptors* are supposed to be behind an electrified fence. But they're nowhere to be seen. . . . Well, even if you didn't see the movie, you can guess what's in store. We don't want to give it away, so suffice it to say, the effects are terrifyingly real. But be warned: Somewhere along that five-and-a-half-minute ride, as your raft travels nearly 50 miles an hour, it will plunge down an 84-foot drop in pitch darkness. It took five years and a creative team that included Steven Spielberg, aerospace scientists, paleontologists and robotic engineers to create this ride, which now comprises a six-acre compound. You won't be disappointed.

> Alfred Hitchcock used more than 30 cameras to shoot the famous *Psycho* shower scene.

TIPS: This is the park's centerpiece attraction, so expect big crowds and long waits during peak times. Portions of this ride are not for the faint of heart and may frighten some children (who must be at least 46 inches high to ride).

Backdraft ★★★★ This ride is a stunning special-effects display from the motion picture *Backdraft*. It re-creates the film's climactic warehouse conflagration, putting you literally in the line of fire. Surrounded by ruptured fuel lines, melting metal and scalding heat, guests are "trapped" with flames licking at their heels in a completely controlled situation that can be recycled as many as 15 times per hour. The experience begins with a backdraft flame spinning wildly about the building, triggering massive explosions that cause overhead pipes to burst toward onlookers. Red-hot ashes rain down. Ultimately the firestorm encircles the guests, who are protected by an invisible air curtain.

TIPS: Average wait in line is 15 minutes; visit when other attractions are busy.

E.T. Adventure ★★★★★ Steven Spielberg's celebrated and wildly successful film sets the scene for this airborne bicycle tour to faraway planets. The story line closely follows the movie, with E.T. stranded on earth three million light years from his beloved Green Planet. As you enter the ride, you are asked your first name, then issued a passport that you surrender when you hop onto one of the "bicycles"—cars suspended from above, with handlebars and wheels on the outside. Your first task is to escape government agents and help E.T. save his dying home. As you take flight you feel night winds blow across your face and see the lights of Los Angeles stretch below. You swoop through dizzying star fields en route to E.T.'s eerie home. This spectacular fantasy is created with tens of thousands of fiberoptic stars and 50 cinebotic figures. In what may be the most surprising part of the entire ride, E.T. bids you a fond farewell . . . by your first name.

TIPS: This ride has the best waiting area of any in the universe: a cool, dim forest where the air is scented with evergreen. Considering these surroundings, the typical 30-minute wait isn't so bad after all.

Special Effects Stages ★★★ Most of the Universal experience is about, as the slogan goes, riding the movies. Here's where you get a little info about making them.

In three studios, folks can get the lowdown on the origins of those *Jurassic Park* dinos (alas, it has nothing to do with mosquitos in amber) and the high-tech history of the Mummy. Check out sound tricks (that's "foley" to those in the biz), makeup, miniatures, props and whatever it takes to transform a human (albeit a somewhat surreal, rubber-faced human) into a green, fur-covered Grinch. Audience volunteers get into the act, performing such tasks as creating sound effects for a film clip. Through the magic of a blue screen, one lucky volunteer will get to join Eddie Murphy in the Nutty Professor.

TIPS: The attraction may seem a little high on information for the youngest visitors. At 30 minutes, the length may test their patience. Demonstrations make the events fun, but be prepared to make a getaway if you're toting little ones.

Lucy: A Tribute ★★★ This heart-shaped art deco facility traces the Hollywood career of Lucille Ball from 1933 until her death in 1991. Filled with Lucy memorabilia, the displays portray her years at Columbia Pictures and RKO Studios, with costumes and props from her famous films. There is home video footage of Lucy and her husband Desi Arnaz, plus letters from the comedienne's fans and a collection of her Emmys. True Lucy fans have been known to stand for hours admiring the re-created set from *I Love Lucy* and watching re-runs of the television show. If movie history fascinates you, the interactive "California Here We Come" game lets you test your knowledge of the series while "traveling" with the Ricardos and Mertzes to California.

TIPS: This is a good attraction to visit when waiting for the next tram ride or one of the Lower Lot shows.

This is Universal Studios' major area, where most of the shows and attractions are located, and the place you'll spend the most time. It's a good idea to make a decision about which shows you'd like to see and note the schedule so you can be there on time. Between shows, stroll the **Streets of the World**. There are Baker Street from old London, Western Street,

▼▼▼▼▼▼▼▼▼▼▼▼
Upper Lot

the Moulin Rouge, '50s America where you'll find Mel's Diner and a Parisian courtyard with quiet tables for lunch or a rest.

Among the Upper Lot's numerous attractions you'll encounter is a series of tents housing carnival games. Outside Mel's Diner you can catch the Doo Wop Singers, who croon '50s songs from the seat of a '57 Chevy Bel Air. Clad in hero jackets and sunglasses and sporting outrageous pompadours, they perform "Goodnight Sweetheart," "The Lion Sleeps Tonight" and other familiar favorites from a simpler era. Check the show schedule for performance times.

By comparison, the 15-minute "Blues Brothers Show" simply doesn't measure up. The characters that Dan Ackroyd and John Belushi made famous just never seem to develop the punch of the original. Not even an appearance by Frankenstein, who jives with the black-suited white-soxed duo, can raise this show out of the ordinary.

WHAT TO SEE & DO

The Mummy Returns: Chamber of Doom ★★★★ Universal never likes to do things in a small way. Where Disney's thrill attractions aim to give you a modest jolt, Universal likes to scare the pants off of you. Suffice it to say, this attraction succeeds.

Staged in an old "temple," the walk-through attraction is a haunted house on steroids with movie-style special effects, original movie props, and, yes, lots and lots of Mummies. Live characters literally pop out of the woodwork, scaring some folks right into therapy. The whole thing is reminiscent of the absolutely terrifying Universal Orlando haunted house staged for Halloween in the Bates Motel. Still, you can't help but be enamored of the spooky setup, as if you've walked right into the films. Overall, visitor expressions are a mix of amusement and terror, and not everybody will be so terrorized. Still, you couldn't pay me enough to take my youngest daughter, who is still recovering from a long-age ride through the Mummy section of the backlot tram tour. Bottom line: It's absolutely not for the feint of heart.

TIPS: Movie props are on display just before the queue area, a bonus for the fans of the film who would just as soon skip the maze.

WAITING IN THE WINGS

He's big, he's green and he's coming to Universal Studios. Shrek, the loveable ogre, is the star of his own attraction. Unnamed at press time, the all-new animated show will feature so-called "4D effects"—namely those you see and feel. This one promises to be a hoot. Look for it sometime in mid-2003.

ANOTHER TIP: The truly sadistic can get a few extra laughs towards the end of the maze. Look for a couple of buttons (one to activate a mummy, one to blow a burst of air) allowing you to scare the life out of a couple of unsuspecting visitors elsewhere in the maze. The best part: you get to watch their reactions via the video monitor in front of you.

Terminator 2:3D **** Strap into this larger-than-life theater for the ultimate *Terminator* experience. Based on the two feature films of the same name, the attraction effectively immerses spectators in the action through 3-D film, live action and special effects.

Much of the action explodes from the screen. The 12-minute film, projected onto three 23-by-50-foot movie screens at the front of the theater, was shot just for the attraction. It stars Aahr-nuld (Schwarzenegger) himself and other original cast members. The film literally rocks you in your seat as it ping-pongs the whole audience from present-day Los Angeles to the year 2029, where Arnold and company wage war on Cyberdyne's sinister system.

Although not five-star from start to finish, Terminator 2:3D is a must-see. The finale alone is worth the whole shebang. Not for young kids.

TIPS: Long lines for this attraction can be deceiving as the theater holds hundreds of people at a time. Still, arriving here at park opening and hitting this one first isn't a bad idea.

Animal Planet Live! **** Once upon a time (like back in the days when television was limited to three networks), it would have seemed unlikely that an entire television channel could devote itself to wildlife. Not only has such a thing amply succeeded, but it's made celebrities out of the likes of Steve Irwin (aka The Crocodile Hunter) and Jeff Corwin (my family's personal favorite), who even have fan sites fawning over their naturalist prowess. Alas, neither of the animal experts make appearances here, but this show pays homage to the real stars—the animals themselves. Numerous acts involve various forms of wildlife, many rescued from animal shelters. Lest you forget the program's roots, there are also lots of clips of network favorites such as Emergency Vets, Planet's Funniest Animals and The Jeff Corwin Experience.

TIPS: Kids love this show, and the sit-down nature is a great breather from some of the other attraction's over-stimulating effects.

ANOTHER TIP: The huge amphitheater seats lots of people, but the popular show can fill up. To really appreciate the furry fellows, arrive about 30 minutes early to grab one of the front rows

Back to the Future—The Ride ***** This flight-simulator ride is a super symphony of speed, fantasy, terror and mind-blowing special effects. When it's over, your throat aches because you've unwittingly screamed so long and hard. It's the kind of ride where

12-year-olds do high-fives at the end, then turn to Mom and announce: "We're going again!"

Based on the *Back to the Future* smash-hit trilogy, the five-minute journey hurls you through centuries at supersonic speed. The action begins in a briefing room where the mad scientist Doc Brown tells guests that Biff (the movie's bully) is threatening to end the universe. The pursuit to find him is on. Eight riders climb into a fancy DeLorean Time Machine, which spews liquid-nitrogen fog that looks like ice on fire. Your car eerily floats out of its garage, and suddenly you're enveloped by a room-sized video screen that takes you on a brain-blasting visual trip: you tumble down volcanic tunnels, collide with a glacier and get chomped and spit out by a growling *Tyrannosaurus rex*.

TIPS: This is a *very* rough ride! Children shorter than 40 inches are not allowed to ride. Not recommended for expectant mothers, people prone to nausea or claustrophobia, or those with bad backs. Just about everyone who visits Universal wants to ride *Back to the Future* (even those masochists with queasy stomachs and bad backs). Given this fact, know that unless you ride as soon as the park opens, you'll face up to an hour's wait.

Nickelodeon Blast Zone ★★★★ To fully experience the phenomenon that is Nickelodeon, one has to be doused, dunked, slimed, pelted and subjected to various other substances commonplace on the wildly popular kids' TV network. Thankfully, Universal has dispensed with the green goo. But there's plenty of water and other objects at this new interactive spot to make it way fun even for the biggest kids (aka mom and dad) in your party.

No ho-hum play place, this is the Nick-style, X-treme version. And it's a hoot (if you've been to Curious George Goes to Town in Florida, you've got the idea). Thousands of colorful foam balls are tossed around in the Wild Thornberry's Adventure Temple. Lest you think you'll just be tiptoeing through a ball pit, watch out. If the oversized orangutan doesn't get you (the statue periodically throws things), the other guests taking aim with ball blasters probably will. Fans of SpongeBob SquarePants will be thrilled to find the porous hero milling about Nickelodeon Splash! In Nick speak, the word "Splash" inevitably means "Soak." Water guns apparently weren't enough, so designers diabolically incorporated huge buckets that rain down 12,000 gallons of water per hour. Climb around on multiple levels and find all sorts of faucets, hoses, buckets and anything else that might squirt or spray. The familiar Nickelodeon rocket blasts yet more water.

Younger children not yet ready for the big time can take shelter in the Nick Jr. Backyard play area featuring themes such as Blue's Clues and Dora the Explorer. The gentle spot is a more traditional play place with slides, nets and such (although there's a bit of water play here, too).

The tots that launched it all—Tommy, Angelica, et al. of "Rugrats" fame—perform in the 20-minute "Rugrats Magic Adventure."

Tips: Nickelodeon takes the concept of getting wet very seriously. This isn't a little damping up of the duds—this is a full out dousing! That's what makes it fun. But you'd do well, when dressing in the morning, to think, "quick dry."

Spider-Man Rocks! ★★★ The movie world's newest cash cow comes to life in this rock-and-roll stage show paying homage to the webbed one. All of the hoopla is just an excuse for a revved-up stunt show featuring leaps, flips and special effects. Look for an appearance by Spiderman himself, as well as his arch enemy, the Green Goblin.

Tips: Universal's rock-and-roll shows are notoriously loud. Sitting a few rows back may help a little. If your kids are sensitive to loud noises, skip this one altogether.

WaterWorld ★★★★★ If this live-action extravaganza doesn't impress you, nothing will. It's based on the Kevin Costner movie and has enough action to keep you rapt for the 15 minutes it takes for the show to unfold. All that and a plot, too: The polar ice caps have melted and the survivors live on floating islands— eerie, mist-shrouded structures made of sheet metal, driftwood and debris. Helen, one of the good guys, returns to the floating atoll with the news that she's found dry land. Deacon, leader of the bad guys, attacks, hoping to kidnap her and get to dry land. The battle that ensues involves explosions that send water cascading over the audience, fireballs radiating heat you can feel, a seaplane that practically crashes in spectators' laps, a bullet-spraying gunboat, water cannons and stunts galore. Thundering music and the realistic set add to the excitement.

Tips: This show draws big crowds; some people line up an hour before to get into the 3000-seat outdoor theater. The best seats are in the center section, about halfway up, where you can take in all the action. The first four rows of seats are designated

RUGRATS MAGIC ADVENTURE

After years suspended in animation, Nickelodeon totsters Tommy, Chuckie, Phil, Lil and Angelica have come to life. The fab five star in the fanciful Universal performance, **Rugrats Magic Adventure**. Based on Angelica's wish to become a powerful magician, the 20-minute stage show features some remarkable sleight-of-hand designed by some of the guys responsible for the illusions of David Copperfield and Siegfried and Roy.

as "wet seat" sections. If you sit there, make sure you cover up cameras and video equipment.

Universal Studios Hollywood Lodging

There's no motel row in this area, but two excellent hotels are adjacent to Universal property. Both offer free shuttles to the studio, and their central location puts them within 45 minutes of Six Flags California and ten minutes from Hollywood.

The **Universal Sheraton** rises 21 luxurious stories and overlooks a glistening pool, lush gardens and the San Fernando Valley. It's generally considered the premier place to stay when visiting Universal Studios. The hotel's 438 guest rooms are large and well furnished. Prices at the Sheraton are in the deluxe to ultra-deluxe range, but packages offer a reduced room rate along with tickets to Universal Studios, and weekend rates are available. Children under 17 stay free. ~ 333 Universal Hollywood Drive, Universal City; 818-980-1212, 800-325-3535, fax 818-985-4980. DELUXE TO ULTRA-DELUXE.

A bit taller and farther up the hill, the **Universal Hilton** is a gleaming 24-story tower with guest rooms overlooking Universal Studios, Warner Brothers, Paramount and Disney Studios. Rooms here are spacious and well appointed, and most enjoy spectacular views. Kids love the large pool and jacuzzi. Children under 17 stay free. Although rates are tabbed in the ultra-deluxe range, there are packages available combining Universal Studios tickets with reduced room rates. ~ 555 Universal Hollywood Drive, Universal City; 818-506-2500, 800-444-8667, fax 818-509-2058; www.universalcity.hilton.com. ULTRA-DELUXE.

The **Beverly Garland's Holiday Inn** is a smaller, comfortable place within one and one half miles of Universal Studios that genuinely welcomes families. The seven acres of park-like grounds create a country club–like atmosphere with tennis courts and a pool. Children under 17 stay free and special packages are available. ~ 4222 Vineland Avenue, North Hollywood; 818-980-8000, 800-238-3759, fax 818-766-0112; www.beverlygarland.com. ULTRA-DELUXE.

Universal Studios Hollywood Dining

Universal Studios Hollywood, with some of the best food of any theme park in Southern California, features a full-service restaurant as well as many smaller outlets. They are priced budget to moderate.

In the Upper Lot, restaurants are either cafeteria style or via window service, but there are always eating areas with clean tables and chairs nearby. Family meals that serve four people, with fried chicken, mashed potatoes, gravy and biscuits, are available at **Doc Brown's Fancy Fried Chicken**. BUDGET TO MODERATE. Right next door, the **Hollywood Cantina** has traditional Mexican tor-

Universal CityWalk

As if there wasn't already enough to do at Universal, along comes **Universal CityWalk**, a complex with blocks of places to shop, dine and play. Stroll down the middle of this "city street" and behold a collection of vintage neon signs and wacky, eclectic architecture. In the central court, located by Tony Roma's, kids enjoy darting in and out of jets of water shooting up from the sidewalk fountain. Occasionally, street performers entertain here, too. ~ 1000 Universal Studios Boulevard, Universal City; 818-622-4455; www.citywalkhollywood.com.

Retail outlets purvey goods ranging from surfing duds to knickknacks and just about everything in-between. **Wound & Wound Toy Co.** (818-509-8129) features thousands of whirring wind-up toys. At **Glow** (818-761-3270) you'll find an inventive assortment of things that—what else?—glow in the dark, including jewelry, paint, stickers and stones. Skaters in the family will gravitate to the **Atomic Garage** (818-505-9961), which is full of the latest, hippest skate- and snowboard gear.

Restaurants include the Wolfgang Puck Café, Buca di Beppo, Tony Roma's and more. You'll also find numerous quick-service eateries, such as **Jody Maroni's Sausage Kingdom** (818-622-5639), a gourmet hot-dog stand serving exotic concoctions like Bombay curried lamb and Portuguese fig and pine-nut versions. Traditionalists (your five-year-old included) will appreciate the hearty beef and turkey dogs. BUDGET.

Hard Rock Cafe Hollywood (818-622-7625) forms another link in the famous restaurant chain devoted to music memorabilia. One of the prized possessions here is Bill Clinton's autographed gold saxophone. As far as the eats go, choose between a variety of salads, sandwiches, burgers and entrées, which include barbecue chicken, ribs and fresh fish of the day. MODERATE.

Every Sunday at noon, folks flock to **B. B. King's Blues Club** (818-622-5464) for an unusual (and uplifting) dining experience: the gospel brunch. In the evenings people choose from an eclectic menu of soul food with a twist and hear top-notch blues musicians spilling their hearts out. MODERATE.

Among the entertainment options: a six-story **IMAX** theater, **Jillian's Hi-Life Bowling** (818-985-8234), what Universal dubs "multimedia rock-and-roll bowling," and **NASCAR Silicon Motor Speedway** (818-766-2323), a revved-up virtual race track.

tillas, tacos and burritos. You can eat in Bedrock-style surroundings at the **Flintstone's Drive-In**, where giant turkey legs are a "stone age" specialty. BUDGET. On the Lower Lot, the **Jurassic Cove Café** features teriyaki dishes as well as the more traditional burgers and fries. BUDGET TO MODERATE.

The most entertaining park restaurant is **Mel's Diner**, an extravaganza complete with neon and chrome trim, quilted metal walls and a black-and-white-checkered floor. There's no curbside service, but helpers in roller skates bus trays and wipe tables. Hot dogs and hamburgers (with a tiny American flag on top) are served in red plastic baskets with a side of fries. BUDGET TO MODERATE.

Dining Outside Universal Studios Hollywood

Places outside the park tend to cluster on Cahuenga and Ventura boulevards in Universal City/Studio City within a mile of the studio. The neighborhood is filled with both starving actors and wealthy hill-dwellers, and restaurants reflect their mixed tastes.

For a glimpse of a rising star or celebrity, the funky **Good Neighbor Restaurant** is as likely a place as any. This low-key, no-frills coffee shop has standard American fare. Breakfast and lunch only. ~ 3701 Cahuenga Boulevard West, Studio City; 818-761-4627, fax 818-761-0619. BUDGET.

The decor at **Teru Sushi** is as inviting as the cuisine. Hand-painted walls and carved figures combine with slat booths and a long dark wood sushi bar. The sushi menu includes several dozen varieties; they also serve a selection of traditional dishes. There is a beautiful garden dining area with a koi pond. No lunch on Saturday and Sunday. ~ 11940 Ventura Boulevard, Studio City; 818-763-6201, fax 818-763-5016. DELUXE TO ULTRA-DELUXE.

Miceli's Restaurant is noisy and a bit Italian-kitschy with its stained-glass windows and opera-singing waiters, but the food is excellent. Try the pizza and spaghetti and don't miss the hot dinner rolls. ~ 3655 Cahuenga Boulevard West, Universal City; 818-508-1221. MODERATE.

Thai BBQ Restaurant prepares broccoli chicken, chicken satay, beef dishes and a host of other Southeast Asian entrées.

ALL QUIET ON THE SET!

Because Universal is a working studio, the tram route may change from day to day to avoid areas where shooting is in progress. Some directors love an audience and encourage visitors on their set; you could be lucky and get a close-up look at a popular show.

While some meals are very spicy, many are mild enough for children. ~ 3737 Cahuenga Boulevard West, Universal City; 818-760-9691. BUDGET TO MODERATE.

▼▼▼▼▼▼▼▼▼▼▼▼▼▼▼▼

Universal Studios Hollywood Shopping

Inside the park, shops have more Universal Studios Hollywood T-shirts, mugs and other logo-emblazoned merchandise than you ever imagined. A few stores, however, are noteworthy. Information about all the stores may be obtained by calling 818-622-3716. If you get home and wish you'd bought something, don't despair. Just call the studio mail-order department at 800-447-0373.

In the Lower Lot, the **Backlot** is a multimedia shopping experience. You can watch clips from your all-time favorite television shows while browsing through the shop. At the **E.T. Toy Closet** there are giant tinker toys that hold such intriguing items as articulated robot hands. **Jurassic Outfitters** features the widest array of dinosaur merchandise imaginable.

The largest store in the park, **Universal Studios Store** offers souvenirs from every attraction in the park. **Silver Screen Collectibles**, also located in the Upper Lot, features a "Wardrobe Dept." where little girls can buy "dress-up" clothes (glittery, chiffony fairy princess–like dresses, sequined tiaras, gold and silver slippers, hats with feathers and fancy hair clips). There's also movie memorabilia; collectors can pick up framed, signed photos of stars (Brando, Hepburn, Crawford), plus lobby cards, publicity stills and limited-edition animation cels. There's a Wizard of Oz scarf depicting all the movie's characters, which was a promotional item when the film opened in 1939. It's framed, and the asking price is $5000. **Animal Stars**, a menagerie of stuffed creatures, has mounted lion and tiger "trophy" heads for children's rooms, plus leopard, lion and zebra print T-shirts.

Kids of all ages should head over to **Cartooniversal** for clothing and souvenirs sporting their favorite cartoon characters.

SIX

SeaWorld

San Diego attracts thousands upon thousands of tourists with its winning combination of surf, sand and sea. For many of these visitors, SeaWorld, a manmade aquatic wonderland, is number one on the itinerary. The 189-acre adventure park, chock full of shows and attractions that probe the puzzles of the deep, is the jewel of San Diego's Mission Bay.

The 20,000-plus marine residents of SeaWorld hail from as close as San Diego Bay and as far as Antarctica. Here at the best-known oceanarium on earth are whales the size of your house and clown fish the size of your toe. Add to them slick black seals and pink-fringed invertebrate, clever dolphins and endearing penguins, whiskered sea lions and mischievous otters. There are not-so-familiar characters, too, such as puffins and aracaris, unicorn fish and blue sea stars.

Many of the critters hang out in big, blue pools that dot SeaWorld's lush landscape. Every day thousands of people file into the park's stadiums to watch the fascinating animals play while they work: whales that whistle and do somersaults, sea lions that smile and dolphins that swim the backstroke.

Amphibious actors (plus a few human performers) steal the shows that have made SeaWorld world-famous. But this place is much more than shows. The multimillion-dollar aquatic park and research center boasts over 25 attractions that delve into underwater mysteries. From the mammoth World of the Sea aquarium and chilly Penguin Encounter to the den of scary sharks, they paint a poignant portrait of the sea.

Outside the attractions, the park looks like a seaside painting in motion. Seagulls shriek overhead, and salty breezes shift across lawns of soft grass. Rock ponds weave through palmy gardens, and pink flamingos make clawprints on patches of sand. SeaWorld's definitive landmark, the 320-foot Skytower, affords visitors a panoramic view of the city's skyline, foothills, bays and beaches.

Within this briny setting you can stroke a slippery, slimy bat ray. You can handfeed a hungry dolphin or get wet on a river rapids ride. Or you can lunch on the shady patio of the Shipwreck Reef Café.

If this sounds like quintessential Southern California tourist-ing, it is. Since SeaWorld opened in 1964, it has offered marine-life education with a kick-back-and-take-your-shoes-off attitude. Today, SeaWorld endures as an old-style California theme park. Unlike Disneyland, that big mouse house nearby, SeaWorld offers less in the way of high-tech attractions and more in the way of low-key, old-fashioned fun.

> SeaWorld's penguin population gobbles about 8000 pounds of fish every day.

But those are really the best things about SeaWorld. Life here is more relaxed, more tuned to the out-of-doors. This is a place where you can downshift into slow gear and think about what happens below sea level. A place that, for many people, is the only real thread to that strange, liquid cosmos.

Nuts & Bolts

ARRIVAL

Hurray! SeaWorld is easy to find: It's right off SeaWorld Drive on Mission Bay, about five miles north of down-town San Diego. From Route 5, exit west onto SeaWorld Drive. From Route 8 heading west, exit onto West Mission Bay Drive and then go east on SeaWorld Drive. Remember to *make a note of where you park* (rows are numbered) so you'll be able to find your car at the end of the day. There is a fee for parking.

TICKETS

You can buy a one-day ticket, two-day ticket or one of several annual "passports" with various benefits attached.

	Adults	Children 3–9
		(Under 3 years, free)
One-day Ticket	$42.95	$32.95
Two-day Ticket	$46.95	$36.95
One-year Silver Passport	$74.95	$59.95
One-year Platinum Passport	$109.95	$89.95
Two-year Gold Passport	$124.95	$99.95

GAME PLAN

As a first-time visitor, you may expect the same crowd craze faced at Disneyland and Universal Studios. Don't. Laidback SeaWorld rarely has gridlock and is so well-planned it hardly ever has lines. The main thing to know is that the big attractions are shows, so you should plan your day around their starting times. Allow at least 45 minutes between shows. This gives ample time for rest-room stops and enjoying the "walk-through" exhibits such as the Forbidden Reef and Penguin Encounter. It also lets you arrive 20 minutes early for each show so you get a seat. Some shows fill up fast, particularly during midday. If you have small children, take a seat near an aisle so you can easily make restroom or other emergency trips during the shows. SeaWorld helps you decide what to see and when to see it with a computer-generated Map and Show Schedule, which are passed out as you enter the park.

Parents also will want to schedule a midday stop at Shamu's Happy Harbor playground. Children love all the nifty activities, and you'll be happy to take a break in the shade. Above all, don't rush from show to show. Half the fun of SeaWorld is taking the leisurely way around and enjoying the "walk-through" exhibits.

GUEST SERVICES

General Information   Ticket Information, SeaWorld, 500 SeaWorld Drive, San Diego, CA 92109; 619-226-3901; www.seaworld.com.

Stroller and Wheelchair Rentals   Both are available in the entrance plaza just inside the main entrance.

Baby Services   There are changing tables next to or in most restrooms.

Cameras   Forgot your camera? Disposable cameras can be purchased inside the park.

Lockers   Located near the Information Center. Lockers cost 75 cents each time you open them.

Lost Children   Report lost children to the Information Center inside the main entrance.

Lost & Found   Contact the Information Center

First Aid   The First Aid Center is located in the exit plaza near Dolly Dolphin Emporium and behind Shipwreck Rapids.

Banking   ATMs are located at the main entrance and in between the Rocky Point Preserve and the Skytower.

Package Pickup   This free service lets you shop without having to tote the bags around all day. Just inform any SeaWorld store clerk you want package pickup, and they will send your purchases to the Dolly Dolphin Emporium where you can pick them up on your way out of the park.

GETTING AROUND

SeaWorld is a breeze. Just think of it as a lopsided doughnut. The doughnut's center is marked by the Skytower; the hole is made up of a circle of eateries, marine-life pools, Rocky Point Preserve, Forbidden Reef and the Sea Lion and Otter Stadium. Along the doughnut's outer edge are 12 other major attractions and shows. Traveling clockwise they are Shamu Closeup, Shamu Stadium, Shipwreck Rapids, Cirque de la Mer, Pirates 4-D, Shark Encounter, Manatee Rescue, Dolphin Stadium, Dolphin Interaction Program, Penguin Encounter, Wild Arctic, Pets Rule and Shamu's Happy Harbor.

If you're in a wheelchair, SeaWorld is easy to navigate. Paths are broad, and ramps are abundant and gently sloped. Stadiums and attractions offer plenty of wheelchair seating (often front-row).

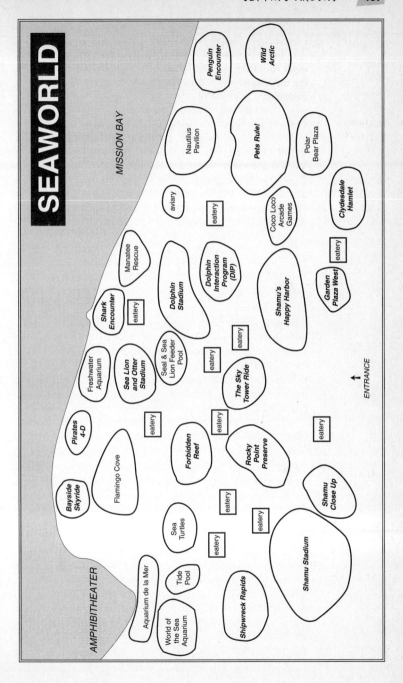

The Shows

**WHAT TO
SEE & DO**

Shamu Stadium ★★★★★ Outside the Disney domain, no theme-park character has gotten more hype than Shamu the killer whale. Not to worry: Everything you've heard is true. SeaWorld's best-loved mammal—all 8000 pounds of him—lives up to his reputation in this splendid attraction called, "The Shamu Adventure." Black and white and glossy all over, the big guy does a graceful underwater ballet and waves to the crowd with his tail, then sends a mini-tidal wave over the first few rows. He also parks himself on the platform so audience members can see. During the show, Shamu is often joined by Baby Shamu (born September 1, 2001, the 15th killer whale to be born at the SeaWorld family of adventure parks) and their friends. The action is captured on state-of-the-art cameras that broadcast Shamu's feats (and the crowd's reactions) on a 300-square-foot video screen above his pool.

TIPS: This is the only attraction that regularly fills up well before show time. Consider arriving at the stadium 20 or even 30 minutes ahead of time. The folks at SeaWorld tell us that the afternoon shows are the least crowded. Be advised that spectators sitting in the first 15 rows will undoubtedly be drenched. Not to be missed.

Cirque de la Mer ★★★★ Nothing about this show in the Amphibitheater is what you'd expect—particularly since it's performed entirely by humans. Nevertheless, it is entertaining, a mix of the exotic—dramatic fire twirlers, a breathtaking hand-to-hand act—with more traditional circus antics. Good views can be had from virtually anywhere you sit, but if you choose the front row, you may be hauled on stage as part of a wildly funny "boxing" routine.

TIPS: The show is fun, but the preshow is even better. Plan to arrive at least 15 minutes early to fully appreciate the hysterical "Sea Sprites" who become part of the main act later on. But beware: those not on their guard may be mercilessly toyed with.

Dolphin Stadium ★★★★★ Remember that SeaWorld television commercial where the dolphin rockets into the air and does a really great triple flip? It was a teaser for this "Dolphin Discovery" show that reveals just how clever dolphins can be. For 20 minutes the jovial creatures perform gracefully on command, doing backstrokes, acrobatics and even the hula. The crowd oohs and aahs at just the right times, like when a child from the audience does a flipper shake with a dolphin. Pilot whales do some pretty neat things, too, such as taking their trainer on a high-speed spin around the pool. The show climaxes with a multispecies finale. If you've ever doubted the intelligence of whales or dolphins, this show will change your mind.

Pirates 4-D ★★★★ Three-dimensional whales aren't the only vivid experience at SeaWorld—now you've got four-dimensional pirates, too. Pirates 4-D follows a group of hapless scalawags as they search for treasure in the Caribbean. The totally immersing film (shown on enormous screens) was written by Monty Python alum Eric Idle, who also stars. That means you can count on a dose of silliness—not to mention a swarm of hornets, some sprays of water and a barrage of surprising special effects.

TIPS: With a theater for about 700, long lines move faster than you might think. Regardless, the show is worth the wait.

Dolphin Interaction Program ★★★ Dolphin lovers have been lining up in droves since SeaWorld inaugurated its Dolphin Interaction Program (DIP), the event that invites guests 6 and older to stand nose to bottlenose with these popular aquarian mammals.

The two-hour program begins with an hour-long class on dolphin anatomy, husbandry and training techniques, followed by a wetsuit fitting and a few minutes of calisthenics. Then it's everybody into the pool. After everyone has acclimated to the 55° salt water (even with a wetsuit, it's c-c-cold!), trainers take you through a series of training signals where dolphins respond with such behaviors as shaking flippers, doing flips, jumping and stopping on a dime.

Program creators are careful to refer to DIP as an "interaction" rather than a "swim" with the dolphins (the rule here is "two feet on the floor at all times"), which is an important distinction for those who have visions of frolicking around with Flipper. Though the whole program lasts two hours, only 20 to 25 minutes are actually spent in the water, wading at that. Still, such encounters with dolphins are rare and many visitors are genuinely enamored of the whole experience. For my money, the $135 per person price tag is a little steep for the reward.

TIPS: SeaWorld's DIP has been a popular sell since it first opened in 1995. The program is limited to 12 people so if you are interested, two months ahead is not too early to make your reservation.

◆◆◆

IT'S CHOW TIME

Want to get close to SeaWorld's animals? Just feed them. Buy a tray of herring, squid or smelt and head over to the Forbidden Reef, Rocky Point Preserve or the Seal and Sea Lion feeding pool attractions. The California bat rays and dolphins will eat right out of your hand, and you can even pet them. The sea lions and seals put on a real show, barking for food and rolling on their backs. Get there late in the day and you'll see the whiskered fellows all fat and happy and snoozing in a big heap.

Sea Lion and Otter Stadium ★★★ A mischievous sea lion, an oversized walrus, and an otter in a toilet—what's not to love about "Fools with Tools"? Kids particularly get a big kick out of the animal high jinks as the hapless host (ostensibly the star of a home-improvement type show) tries to keep her assistants in check. As with all SeaWorld shows: audience volunteers, beware of getting doused.

TIPS: Large theater though it is, the stadium has a tendency to fill up. And this is a show you don't want to miss. The moral: come early!

ANOTHER TIP: Watch out for the "soak" seats: they mean it!

Pets Rule! ★★★ You can't help smiling through this old-time show that showcases some of SeaWorld's non-aquatic animals. Cats, dogs, birds and even a pig wreak havoc on bewildered humans, who don't understand the rules of animal behavior. For example, rule number eight, Cats Are In Control At All Times, produces a precarious highwire act. Sometimes it can be predictable. But kids won't be able to resist the furry critters and parents won't want to miss their reactions. The fact that these talented kitties and pups were all adopted from local animal shelters sends a nice side message. In short: Vaudeville never looked so cute.

TIPS: Be sure to stick around after the show when kids can get up close and fur-sonal with some of the show's star performers.

The Exhibits

WHAT TO SEE & DO

Forbidden Reef ★★★★★ This fascinating exhibit affords a safe, wonderful way to experience some creatures you would probably not want to encounter in the wild. Outside the entrance, slippery bat rays glide through a shallow pool; their stingers have been surgically removed so they're safe to touch. The slimy creatures even seem to enjoy being stroked as they swim around the pool's perimeter. Inside, the mood is darker and eerier as giant aquariums hold enormous, dark-rock formations. A closer look reveals hundreds of snake-like figures emerging from holes in the rock. These moray eels stay almost motionless, suspended in the water, half-emerged from their hiding places. Their beady eyes and needle-like teeth are frightening but mesmerizing. It's difficult to drag the kids—and sometimes even the adults—out of this one.

TIPS: The bat rays can take a while to swim over to the edge of the pool. Be patient and they'll come around. Don't miss out on touching one of these intriguing creatures; they feel like slimy velvet.

Rocky Point Preserve ★★★★★ Resembling the rocky California coastline, this 700,000-gallon pool houses the world's largest display of Atlantic and Pacific bottlenose dolphins. Visitors are invited to participate in their feedings and observe them surfing waves created by a machine. Residing in an adjacent pool are Californian sea otters

The Penguin Encounter **** SeaWorld's most charming creatures live here in an icy den of snow-capped rocks, freezing waters and blustery breezes. As visitors drift by on a moving walkway, the little guys waddle across the floor, dive into their seapool and zoom around underwater. Occasionally they cock their heads at you through the viewing window as if to say, "What's the big deal?" To many people, the Penguin Encounter is a big deal. The simulated polar world is the largest penguin home away from home. Hundreds of the flightless birds live where the light is Antarctic-dim and the air is a penguin-comfy 25°F. Next door in a similar room are dozens of alcids, Arctic birds that look like a cross between a parrot and a duck. Actually a relative of penguins, alcids have wonderfully bizarre names like puffins, smews and murres. If you have small kids, take them to the alcids: They'll love seeing the strange creatures and learning to pronounce their names.

TIPS: After stepping off the beltway, guests can take longer looks at the birds from a separate viewing area.

Shamu's Happy Harbor **** "I wish you hadn't shown them this. I'll never get them out," lamented one mom after dad brought the kids here. Getting small fry to leave is a common problem, and little wonder: It's filled with stuff kids love best. There are tunnels to roam and water muskets to fire, bells to clang and wheels to turn. There are shallow pools and rigging-net ladders, and rooms where children can wade thigh-high in plastic balls. All day, jubilant kids pour across the two-and-a-half-acre playground, testing one gadget after another. The crowd favorite is a 55-foot pirate galleon with zillions of places to run, climb and hide. For parents, there's a sheltered area with good views of the kids and (yes!) plenty of seats for resting those aching feet.

TIPS: To play, kids must be between 37 and 61 inches tall.

A SEA LION OR A SEAL?

How can you tell a sea lion from a seal? If you don't know, sign up for SeaWorld's **Behind-the-Scenes** tour. The 90-minute, guided excursion features oodles of sea life trivia and a backstage look at SeaWorld attractions. You'll see animals that were injured and rescued by the park, and the place where penguins incubate. The tour costs $10 for adults, $8 for seniors and children ages 3–9 (plus park admission) and is offered several times a day. To sign up, visit the Reservations Center near the main entrance. (P.S. A sea lion is a seal with earflaps.)

Clydesdale Hamlet ★★ What has four legs, is six feet tall and weighs more than a ton? Answer: A Clydesdale, and SeaWorld is home for ten of these huge animals. Horses at a marine park? Go figure. The world-famous animals are owned by SeaWorld's parent company, Anheuser-Busch, which is how they ended up sharing their turf with Shamu.

TIPS: Small children delight in these creatures as their sheer size and bulk are really something to see.

Shark Encounter ★★★★ This spectacular attraction allows visitors to view sharks from above, below and within their environment. No, you're not expected to dive in, but you'll actually walk along an acrylic tunnel through the center of the shark tank. There's nothing like being face to face with nine-foot sandtiger sharks and hundreds of tropical fish. You enter the exhibit along a sandy path surrounded by palms. In the distance you'll see ominous-looking shark fins circling about a lagoon. The path takes you down into a 280,000-gallon tank filled with lemon, nurse, pacific black-tip and white-tip reef sharks. Don't miss the chance to see these sea scaries up close.

TIPS: Kids of all ages give this attraction high marks because, as one eight-year-old said, "It's like being inside a big aquarium." They also like being able to walk through again—and again—and again.

Manatee Rescue ★★★★ It's hard not to be affected by the teddy-bear looks of a manatee. Bulbous and benevolent, these denizens of warm shallow waters are facing extinction at the hands of developers and unwary boaters. This three-and-a-half acre attrac-

SEAWORLD'S WORLD OF THE SEA

In addition to all the shows and exhibits, SeaWorld's landscape is dotted with smaller ponds, pools and aquariums filled with thousands of intriguing sea critters. Turn a corner and you may encounter a thriving colony of flamingos, a frisky bunch of otters or ancient sea turtles basking in the sun. SeaWorld is also home to four aquariums that simulate the natural habitats of aquatic creatures from all over the globe. The **Aquarium de la Mer** features hundreds of ocean fish, a chambered nautilus and a giant Pacific octopus. The **Freshwater Aquarium** houses creatures from Africa, Asia and the Amazon River basin, including a large tank of archerfish, capable of shooting airborne prey with liquid "arrows." At the **World of the Sea Aquarium**, four 55,000-gallon tanks feature kelp-bed fish, a coral reef and numerous species of sportfish. At **Manatee Rescue**, a freshwater tank is home to several of these gentle mammals.

tion features a 300,000-gallon naturalistic habitat and a circular theater where visitors are treated to an engrossing manatee's eye view of the world projected on the walls and ceiling. The exhibit is both heart-warming and heartwrenching as you learn about these mysterious and imperiled creatures.

TIPS: Allow yourself at least a half-hour to see and appreciate these wonderful mammals. Also, don't miss the 126-foot underwater viewing window.

Wild Arctic **** SeaWorld has creatively packaged this exhibit of Arctic animals into a theme attraction featuring an interactive ride. Visitors first board the jet helicopter (à la flight simulator) for a flight over the frozen north, soaring over rocky glaciers and tumbling through an avalanche. The helicopter lands, and guests exit into Base Station Wild Arctic, where resident scientists are ostensibly there to explore two capsized sailing ships from a century-old wreck. The base station has lots of neat areas to explore, as well as windows and decks for above- and below-water viewing of native Arctic mammals such as polar bears, walruses, beluga whales and foxes.

Creators have taken great pains to carry out the research station theme here, from the long johns hanging on the clothesline to the snowshoes and jackets piled hastily in a corner. The vast pools of chilled (and chilly!) salt water are nattily disguised, with plenty of "ice" and "glaciers" to simulate the Arctic. If you're lucky, you may catch a glimpse of "researchers" venturing out into the terrain via kayak, and there are plenty of "resident scientists" on hand to answer questions. There are also interactive touch screens and cameras for getting a closer look. Interestingly, the attraction is based on a real event; the disappearance of the sailing ships *Erebus* and *Terror* in the Arctic in 1845. One little extra: Being that it's in the Arctic, this is one of the coolest places in the park.

TIPS: The attraction has two theaters for the helicopter portion: one with motion and one without (ask which line is for which). If you'd like to skip the helicopter ride entirely, you can ask to be let into the Base Station through the gift shop.

Shipwreck Rapids **** Shamu may be big, but apparently not big enough to carry the park by himself. Today's theme-park visitors seem to want a little thrill ride with their animal entertainment. With ShipWreck Rapids, SeaWorld obliges. Oversized inner tubes give classic spins down the rapids, drenching riders via waterfalls and a hefty dose of splashing. Nine-person rafts leave virtually no rider unscathed—but then, that's the fun. Though the rapids aren't quite as cold as Shamu's tank,

The Rides

WHAT TO SEE & DO

you'll either want to bring a raincoat, or save this adventure for a warm day.

TIPS: Given that this is the park's first (and, to date, only) thrill ride, lines are inevitable. Go early and you can minimize the lines —but you may spend the day in squishy sneaks.

The Skytower ★★★ Often called "the needle in the sky," this ink-blue tower rises a skinny 320 feet from the center of the park. A round, windowed elevator ferries people back and forth to the summit and looks like a top in slow motion spiraling up and down a string. A ride on the Skytower will cost you $2.75 extra. The five-minute vertical voyage is quiet, leisurely and scenic, and the view from the top is enough to make your day. Whether it's worth the extra bucks is, of course, a matter of opinion.

TIPS: Some preschoolers are frightened when they see the ground start to shrink below. Older kids, however, love it.

Bayside Skyride ★★★ Almost every theme park in America has one of these skyrides where you board a hanging gondola for a bird's-eye view of the activity below. SeaWorld's gondola ride reaches a height of 100 feet for a half-mile roundtrip journey over the park and Mission Bay. Like the Skytower, this attraction costs an extra $2.75.

TIPS: Small children and even adults who are afraid of heights may find this ride a bit unnerving.

SeaWorld Dining

For a quick low-cost meal, SeaWorld visitors have the choice of several casual cafeteria and takeout eateries. **The Ranch House Grill** serves up decent salads and smoked, mesquite-grilled chicken and ribs. BUDGET. **Mama Stella's Italian Kitchen** is a large, efficient cafeteria serving pizza, pasta and other Italian specialties. BUDGET. Freshly carved turkey and roast beef sandwiches are featured at the **Hospitality Center Deli.** BUDGET. **Shipwreck Reef Cafe** serves up a little entertainment with your lunch and dinner. Tropically themed dining areas look out among some of the park's wildlife including ibises, sea turtles and flamingos. The food? A tasty selection of

GLASS WITH CLASS

Tucked away in a small shop between the Skytower and the Forbidden Reef, a true artisan practices her craft. Sandra Duchery-O'Neil fashions delicate whales, dolphins, seals and other marine creatures out of shimmering handblown glass. A third-generation glassblower, she has been creating these works of art at SeaWorld since 1969. Stop by and see this very talented woman do her thing.

freshly grilled seafood, veggies and meats, as well as sandwiches and salads. MODERATE.

SeaWorld Shopping

SeaWorld's few shops are of the souvenir variety and offer little in the way of interesting browsing. For those who insist on a campy memento, there are stuffed Shamus, dolphins and sea lions, shark hand puppets and an assortment of ocean-themed T-shirts.

SeaWorld Nightlife

San Diegans usually wait until the summer season to visit SeaWorld, when the park comes alive after dark with Mystique de la Mer, a park-wide extravaganza. Special night shows are offered at both Shamu Stadium and Sea Lion and Otter Stadium. Acrobats, jugglers and live bands perform throughout the park, and every evening concludes with a fireworks spectacular that reflects in the pools, ponds and adjacent bay. Mystique de la Mer takes place Memorial Day through Labor Day; the park is open until 10 p.m. weeknights and 11 p.m. on weekends; the show is included with regular admission.

SEVEN

Orange County Day Trips

If you need an escape—or just a breather—from the ultimate escape itself, you don't have to travel far to find it. Active cities, picturesque towns, beaches, parks, the ocean, museums, theater—you name it, they're all practically on your doorstep. Disneyland and Knott's Berry Farm are by no means the only things going in Orange County.

Within only a few miles of the theme parks, Anaheim and Buena Park offer numerous attractions. Away from the urban crush, Orange County has soft beaches galore, curving hills, ocean bluffs and towns along its fabled "Gold Coast" that are separate and unique. Do not fail to take a leisurely drive along Route 1, the coast road that parallels the ocean through most of the state and is lovingly known as the Pacific Coast Highway. It may just lead you to the perfect California beach town.

Seal Beach, Orange County's answer to small-town America, is a pretty community with a sense of serenity. To the south lies Huntington Beach, a place that claims the nickname "Surfing Capital of the World." The social capital of this beachside society is Newport Beach.

There's more. Corona del Mar is a model community with quiet streets and a placid waterfront. Laguna Beach shelters an artist colony, along with spectacular beach coves. Dana Point represents an ultramodern marina development. San Juan Capistrano, a small town surrounding an old mission, is closer to its roots than any place in this futuristic area.

Among them these coastal towns offer an amusement park, marine preserves, fishing piers, shopping malls, historic sights and miles of white-sand beach. All are splendid diversions when you tire of the hot, crowded theme-park scene. Since Newport Beach and Laguna Beach are located so conveniently close to the Disneyland area, you might even consider alternating days at the theme park with days at the beach. Or spend some time touring Orange County's inland realms, where you'll discover parks, children's museums and roads that lead east into the distant mountains.

Far from being the only visitor attractions in the inland reaches of Orange
County, the theme parks themselves
have spawned the growth of other travel destinations.

▼▼▼▼▼▼▼▼▼▼▼▼▼▼▼▼▼▼▼
Anaheim–Buena Park Area

SIGHTS

Hobby City looks like a miniature Knott's Berry Farm, anchored
by a "perfect half-scale replica" of the White House and featuring
a doll and toy museum. There are thousands of dolls from around
the world including special exhibits dating back to the time of the
Egyptian pharaohs. Arranged in chronological order, the doll exhibits sweep through the Middle Ages all the way up to the height
of the Cabbage Patch dynasty and the late Barbie period. A special display features dolls of the first ladies from Martha Washington through Jackie Kennedy. The entire complex is encircled
by the wee tracks of the "Adventure City Train," a mini-train for
kids. Also featured is an intriguing array of about 20 specialized
shops, each devoted entirely to the hobbyist and collector, and
housed in specially constructed theme buildings. Among them are
baseball card, stamp, coin, gem, antique, reptile and doll stores.
Perhaps the most unique is a shop devoted to miniatures all built
on the scale of one inch to the foot. Admission. ~ 1238 South
Beach Boulevard, Anaheim; 714-527-2323.

Fans of celluloid should pay a visit to **Movieland Wax Museum**.
There are more than 300 wax celebrities here ranging from Charlie
Chaplin to Michael Jackson to Arnold Schwarzenegger. Hokey?
Sure. But it's also pretty entertaining, especially those figures set
up in scenes from the "Beverly Hillbillies" and "Star Trek." Most,
but not all, of the figures are realistic (though some are a little
on the laughable side); you're bound to have a ball anyway. Parents,
take note: the Chamber of Horrors section is truly frightening. A
complete tour takes about two hours. Admission. ~ 7711 Beach
Boulevard, Buena Park; 714-522-1155, fax 714-739-9668; www.
movielandwaxmuseum.com.

If Movieland is a tribute to film, **Ripley's Believe It or Not!** is a
tribute to weird. Eight-legged pigs and maggot-infested jewelry are
among the entrées at this bizarre and wonderful museum. Some of
the exhibits are educational (you'll learn a bit about entomological
anatomy), some just plain gross (such as the aforementioned insect-
covered ornamentation) but none of it is dull. Its distastefulness, as
a matter of fact, might be the very thing that enamors young kids
("Mommy, it's disgusting . . . I love it" is a direct quote from a child
I know). Ask about discounted joint passes to the two museums.
Admission. ~ 7850 Beach Boulevard, Buena Park; 714-522-7045;
www.ripleys.com/buenapark2.htm, e-mail pnhut@aol.com.

Located on a prehistoric fossil field that may be as extensive as
the famed La Brea Tar Pits, **Ralph B. Clark Regional Park** offers

tours of centuries-old fossil beds. Admission charge for tours (by reservation). This unique facility also features an interpretive center with fossil displays and a working paleontology lab. Providing marvelous educational opportunities, the digs and lab activities are structured as part of an organized tour program. Parking fee. ~ 8800 Rosecrans Avenue, Buena Park; 714-670-8045.

Who says kids go to the mall just to shop? At **The Block at Orange** they go to skate, too. Amid all the retail and eateries of this vast retail complex is Vans Skate Park (714-769-3800), a 46,000-square-foot indoor/outdoor palace for skateboards and inline skates. Bystanders can enjoy the show from the upper-level mezzanine. ~ 20 City Boulevard, Orange.

Huntington Beach

There are many ways to enjoy the beautiful coastline here: you can pedal the bike paths, dig for Pismo clams, hike in a wetlands preserve and warm up at beach bonfires in the evening. But no matter what you do, you'll encounter surfing in some shape or form.

SIGHTS   It's hard to beat a stretch of coastline that's up there in the mythology of surfing with Hawaii's Waimea Bay and the great breaks of Australia. Since the 1920s, surfers with boards have been as much a part of the seascape as blue skies and billowing clouds. They paddle around **Huntington Pier**, poised to catch the next wave that pounds the pilings. First built in 1904 for oil drilling, the pier has been damaged by storms and extensively repaired four times. The pier's newest incarnation, which opened in July 1992, is 1856 feet long and 38 feet above the water. ~ End of Main Street.

Stop in at the **International Surfing Museum** for a historic perspective on Southern California's favorite pastime. The showplace sits two blocks away from the beach and features boards, boards and more boards as well as an array of surfing paraphernalia. Closed Tuesday and Wednesday in winter. Admission. ~ 411 Olive Street; 714-960-3483; www.surfingmuseum.org, e-mail intsurfing@earthlink.net.

At the **Newland House Museum** visitors can see what life in 19th-century Huntington Beach was all about. Listed on the National Register of Historic Places and built in 1898, the house is filled with antiques from the town's early days. Closed Monday, Tuesday and Friday, as well as on rainy days. ~ 19820 Beach Boulevard; 714-962-5777.

In addition to its many beaches, Huntington Beach features **Bolsa Chica Ecological Reserve**. An important wetlands area dotted with islands and overgrown in cord grass and pickleweed, this 300-acre preserve features a mile-and-a-half long loop trail. Among the hundreds of animals inhabiting or visiting the marsh are egrets, herons and five endangered species. There is an interpretive center with scientific displays, educational materials and trail guides. Reserve is always open; interpretive center is closed Monday. ~ Accessways across from the entrance to Bolsa Chica State Beach and at 3842 Warner Avenue; 714-846-1114; www. bolsachica.org, e-mail adrienne@bolsachica.org.

At **Spark Woodfire Cooking**, you can dine on fine Italian cuisine for reasonable prices. Try one of their fresh pasta dishes, such as rigatoni with grilled vegetables tossed in olive oil, or a California-

DINING

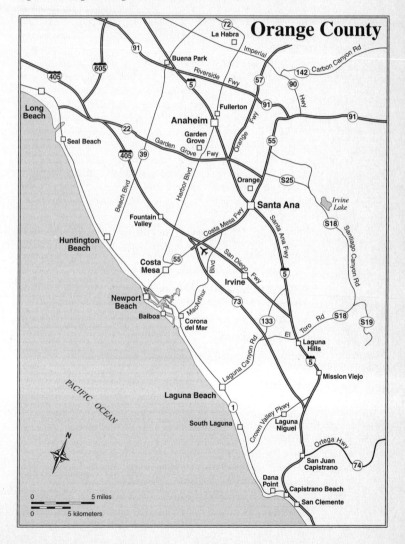

style pizza with one of their inventive salads. The restaurant is open and airy with modern decor, plenty of windows and a patio overlooking the ocean for open-air dining. A Sicilian family-style menu is available for parties of four or more—a fun way to try a variety of dishes. ~ 300 Pacific Coast Highway, Huntington Beach; 714-960-0996; www.sparkwoodfirecooking.com. MODERATE.

HIDDEN ►

The **Harbor House Café** is one of those hole-in-the-wall places packed with local folks. In this case it's "open 24 hours, 365 days a year" and has been around since 1939. Add knotty-pine walls covered with black-and-whites of your favorite movies stars and you've got a coastal classic. The menu, as you may have surmised, includes hamburgers and sandwiches. Actually, it's pretty varied— in addition to croissant and pita-bread sandwiches there are Mexican dishes, seafood platters, chicken entrées and omelettes, with the option of kid-sized portions. ~ 16341 Pacific Coast Highway, Sunset Beach; 562-592-5404. BUDGET TO MODERATE.

For something different in a Mexican restaurant, try the **Yucatan Grill**, specializing in dishes from the Mexican Caribbean such as *cochinita pibil* (pork barbecued in banana leaves with a tangy sauce) and Mayan *dorado* (mahimahi with a pungent orange sauce). There are also offerings from other parts of the Caribbean, such as Jamaican jerk chicken and steak *cubano*. With seating both indoors and out, the atmosphere is supercasual. ~ 12147 Seal Beach Boulevard, Seal Beach; 562-430-4422. BUDGET TO MODERATE.

BEACHES & PARKS

SEAL BEACH A local favorite tucked in between Huntington Beach and Long Beach, Seal Beach has a swath of fine-grain sand and a fishing pier. The swimming is good, and surfers can be seen riding the good breaks at the pier around 13th Street.

BOLSA CHICA STATE BEACH With three miles of fluffy sand, this is another in a series of broad, beau-

AUTHOR FAVORITE

Serpentine descents, tube rides, swimming pools and jacuzzis make **Wild Rivers** Orange County's ultimate waterfront attraction. Flume rides, swirling rapids, waterslides, wading pools, river safaris and bodysurfing are all part of the fun. One ride, The Abyss, plunges ten stories through a pitch-black tunnel. Some popular rides, like the whitewater trip down Wild Rivers Mountain, are off-limits for small children. But miniature versions of the most popular thrill rides do give the little ones a taste of big-time fun. The major pools all have lifeguards, and a wave pool creates an ideal boogie-boarding environment. Open daily from June through August; weekends and holidays only in May and September. Admission. ~ 8770 Irvine Center Drive, Irvine; 949-768-9453; www.wildrivers.com.

tiful beaches. There are seasonal grunion runs and rich clam beds here; the beach is backdropped by the **Bolsa Chica Ecological Reserve**, an important wetlands area. Since the summer surf is gentler here than at Huntington Beach, Bolsa Chica is ideal for swimmers and families. You'll find picnic areas, restrooms, lifeguards, outdoor showers, snack bars and beach rentals—and all these facilities do come with a cost. The fishing is good year-round at Bolsa Chica; swimming is better in the summer. For surfing, there are small summer waves and big winter breaks. Parking fee, $6. ~ Located along Pacific Coast Highway between Warner Avenue and Huntington Pier in Huntington Beach; 714-846-3460.

▲ There are 57 sites with water and electric hookups; $18 per night. Reservations required, call 800-444-7275.

HUNTINGTON CITY BEACH 🚴 🏊 🏄 🎣 An urban continuation of the state beach to the south, this strand runs for several miles. This is one of the most famous surfing spots in the world. The Huntington Pier is the pride of the city. The surrounding waters are crowded with surfers in wet suits. A great place for water sports and people-watching. This surfer heaven gives way to an industrial inferno north of the pier where the oil derricks that plague offshore waters climb right up onto the beach, making it look more like the Texas coast than the blue Pacific.

So stay south of the pier and make use of the fire pits, lifeguards, restrooms and outdoor showers, volleyball courts and beach rentals. Swimming is good if you can find a time when the swells aren't too big, but the surf pumps year-round here, and international surfing competitions are held throughout the summer months and in September. Fishing tackle shops are nearby in Huntington Beach; if you're aiming to angle, try the pier. Day-use fee, $7 to $9. ~ Located along Pacific Coast Highway in Huntington Beach with numerous accesses; 714-536-5281, fax 714-374-1500.

HUNTINGTON STATE BEACH 🚶 🚴 🏊 🏄 🎣 One of Southern California's broadest beaches, this strand extends for three miles. In addition to a desert of soft sand, it has those curling waves that surfer dreams (and movies) are made of. Pismo clams lie buried in the sand, a bike path parallels the water, and there is a five-acre preserve for endangered least terns. Before you decide to move here permanently, take heed: these natural wonders are sandwiched between industrial plants and offshore oil derricks. Nonetheless, your visit will be made more comfortable by the restrooms, fire rings, lifeguards, outdoor showers, dressing rooms, snack bars, volleyball and beach rentals. The fishing is good here, and the surfing is excellent. Swimming is prime when the surf is low. Day-use fee, $3. ~ Located along Pacific Coast Highway in Huntington Beach; entrances are at Beach Boulevard, Newland Street, Brookhurst Street and Magnolia Street; 714-536-1454, fax 714-536-0074.

▼▼▼▼▼▼▼▼▼▼▼▼
Newport Beach

The main resort town on the Orange County coast, Newport Beach is a mélange of manmade islands and peninsulas surrounding a small bay. Although virtually the entire shoreline of the lower bay is developed, the upper bay is a protected wetlands, and it offers perhaps the only escape from the constant flow of boat traffic of the lower bay.

SIGHTS

For help finding your bearings, contact the **Newport Harbor Area Chamber of Commerce**. Closed Saturday and Sunday. ~ 1470 Jamboree Road; 949-729-4400; www.newportbeach.com, e-mail info@newportbeach.com. The **Newport Beach Conference & Visitors Bureau** is closed Saturday and Sunday, except in summer. ~ 3300 West Coast Highway; 949-722-1611, 800-942-6278; www. newportbeach-cvb.com, e-mail info@newportbeach-cvb.com.

Although it cannot compete with Laguna Beach as an art center, the town does offer the **Orange County Museum of Art**. Specializing in contemporary art, this facility possesses perhaps the finest collection of post–World War II California art in existence. Closed Monday. Admission. ~ 850 San Clemente Drive; 949-759-4848; www.ocma.net, e-mail ocma@pacbell.net.

HIDDEN ►

The richness of the natural environment is evident as well when you venture through **Upper Newport Bay Ecological Reserve**. The road passes limestone bluffs and sandstone hills. Reeds and cattails line the shore. Southern California's largest estuary, the bay is a vital stopping place for migrating birds on the Pacific Flyway. Over 200 species can be seen here, and six endangered species, including Belding's savannah sparrow and the light-footed clapper rail, live along the bay. Guided walking, canoeing and kayaking tours are available year-round. Closed Monday. ~ 2301 University Drive; 714-973-6820; www.newportbay.org, e-mail info@newportbay.org.

One of Newport Beach's prettiest neighborhoods is **Balboa Island**, comprising two manmade islets in the middle of Newport Bay. It can be reached by bridge along Marine Avenue or via a short ferry ride from Balboa Peninsula. Walk the pathways that circumnavigate both islands and you will pass clapboard cottages, Cape Cod homes and modern block-design houses that seem made entirely of glass. While sailboats sit moored along the waterfront, streets that are little more than alleys lead into the center of the island.

The central piece in this jigsaw puzzle of manmade plots is **Balboa Peninsula**, a long, narrow finger of land bounded by Newport Bay and the open ocean. High point of the peninsula is **Balboa**

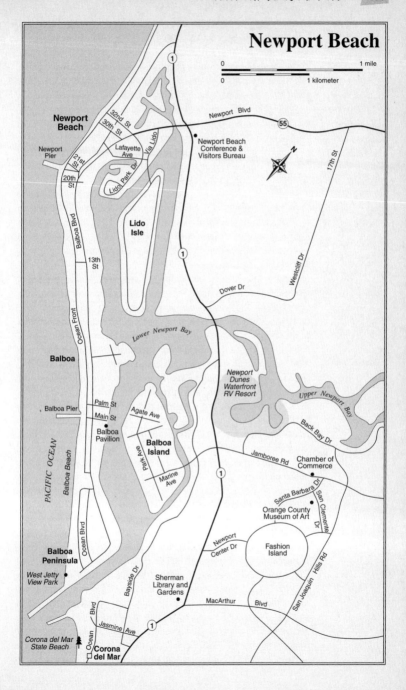

Newport Beach

0   1 mile

0   1 kilometer

Newport Beach

Newport Blvd

55

Newport Pier

32nd St
30th St

21st St

20th St

Lafayette Ave

Via Lido

Lido Park Dr

17th St

Newport Beach Conference & Visitors Bureau

N

Lido Isle

Balboa Blvd

13th St

Westcliff Dr

Dover Dr

Ocean Front

Lower Newport Bay

Balboa

Newport Dunes Waterfront RV Resort

Upper Newport Bay

Balboa Pier

Palm St

Main St

Agate Ave

Balboa Pavilion

Balboa Beach

PACIFIC OCEAN

Park Ave

Balboa Island

Marine Ave

Back Bay Dr

Jamboree Rd

Chamber of Commerce

Santa Barbara Dr

San Clemente Dr

Orange County Museum of Art

Ocean Blvd

Balboa Peninsula

West Jetty View Park

Bayside Dr

Newport Center Dr

Fashion Island

San Joaquin Hills Rd

Sherman Library and Gardens

MacArthur Blvd

Blvd

Ocean Blvd

Jasmine Ave

Ocean

1

Corona del Mar State Beach

Corona del Mar

Pavilion (end of Main Street), a Victorian landmark that dates back to 1905 when it was a bathhouse for swimmers in ankle-length outfits. Marked by its well-known cupola, the bayfront building once created its own dance sensation, the "Balboa."

Today Balboa Pavilion is the home of a waterfront amusement park, the **Fun Zone**, where kids can practice defensive driving in a bumper car, ride the Ferris wheel and merry-go-round or take a dark ride through the funhouse. In addition, they can try their hand at skee ball, video games and pinball machines. To see more of the harbor area, rent a pedal or pontoon boat. ~ 600 East Bay Avenue, Balboa; 949-673-0408.

Balboa Pavilion hosted the nation's first surfing tournament in 1932.

Cruise ships to Catalina Island debark from the dock here, and there are harbor cruises offered by **Catalina Passenger Service** aboard the *Pavilion Queen*, a mock riverboat that motors around Newport Bay. Admission. ~ 400 Main Street, Balboa; 949-673-5245; www.catalinainfo.com, e-mail betsy@catalinainfo.com.

This is also home to the **Balboa Island Ferry**, a kind of floating landmark that has shuttled between Balboa Peninsula and Balboa Island since 1919. A simple, single-deck ferry that carries three cars (for about $1.25 each) and sports a pilot house the size of a phone booth, it crosses the narrow waterway every few minutes.

The beach scene in this seaside city extends for over five miles along the Pacific side of Balboa Peninsula. A broad, white-sand beach lined with lifeguard stands and houses reaches along the entire length. The centers of attention and amenities are **Newport Pier** (Balboa Boulevard and McFadden Place) and **Balboa Pier** (Balboa Boulevard and Main Street). At Newport Pier, also known as McFadden's Pier, the skiffs of the **Newport Dory Fishing Fleet** are beached every day while local fishermen sell their catches. This flotilla of small, wooden boats has been here so long it has achieved historic landmark status. At dawn the fishermen sail ten miles offshore, set trawl lines and haul in the mackerel, flounder, rock fish and halibut sold at the afternoon market.

To capture a sense of the true beauty around you, take a walk out to **West Jetty View Park** at the tip of Balboa Peninsula. Here civilization meets the sea. To the left extend the rock jetties forming the mouth of Newport Harbor. Behind you are the plate-glass houses of the city. A wide beach, tufted with ice plants and occasional palm trees, forms another border. This is also the place where the truly courageous (or the truly crazy) challenge the waves at "The Wedge." Known to bodysurfers around the world, the area between the jetty and beach is one of the finest and most dangerous shore breaks anywhere, the "Mount Everest of bodysurfing." ~ Ocean Boulevard at Channel Road, Balboa.

Orange County Kids' Museums

Sure, Southern California has theme parks, water parks and moviedom. But when your kids look like they need something a little less over the top (you'll know it's time by the bug-eyed, overstimulated expressions on their little faces), you're in luck: Orange County has that, too.

No less than four kid-friendly museums dot the landscape. **The Bowers Kidseum** gives a new twist to the children's museum genre, adding a dash of multicultural flair through activities, play things and performances. Despite its diminutive size, the place ignites the imagination with dress-up, puppets and scads of crafts and activities. Visit on a Saturday and you might just happen upon one of the family festivals (one Saturday each month). And there's always the interesting (albeit decidedly more grown-up) Bowers Museum next door with art and artifacts from around the world. Admission. ~ 2002 North Main Street, Santa Ana; 714-567-3600, fax, 714-567-3603; www.kidseum.org, e-mail info@bowers.org.

Budding scientists can experiment with the physical world at the **Discovery Science Center** in Santa Ana. This science playground is gizmo and gadget heaven: 59,000 square feet of space with activities from a bed of nails (illustrating the principles of weight dispersion) to electronic finger painting. Admission. ~ 2500 North Main Street, Santa Ana; 714-542-2823.

If newfangled science isn't your thing, go back in time at the **Discovery Museum of Orange County**. The century-old abode has household items and knickknacks from a bygone era: old-fashioned games, a Victrola and even a washboard you can try. Outside the main structure, a 12-acre spread has a nature center and blacksmith shop. Closed Monday, Tuesday and some Saturdays. Admission. ~ 3101 West Harvard Street, Santa Ana; 714-540-0404.

For plain-old modern thrills, you can't beat the **Children's Museum** in La Habra. In a renovated train depot, this cozy spot is kid heaven, where little ones can get in the driver's seat of an actual city bus (don't worry, it doesn't go anywhere!) or play operator on an old-time switchboard. There's lots (and lots and lots!) more. The highlight: a well-stocked stage (complete with lighting, props and microphone) where pint-sized thespians can get ready for their closeups. An extra perk for moms and dads: such imagination-fueled activities let beleaguered parents sit back and watch for a while. Admission. ~ 301 South Euclid Street, La Habra; 562-905-9693; www.lhcm.org.

And hey: it doesn't hurt that all of these places are a mite (okay, a lot!) cheaper than the theme parks.

LODGING   You'd have a heckuva time docking your boat at the **Little Inn by the Bay**. Actually it's on an island, but the "island" is a median strip dividing the two busiest streets on the Balboa Peninsula. Offering 17 standard motel rooms, the inn is a block from the beach and walking distance from many restaurants. It's also just one mile from the rides and arcade games of the Fun Zone at Balboa Pavilion. ~ 2627 Newport Boulevard; 949-673-8800, 800-438-4466, fax 949-673-4943. MODERATE.

By way of full-facility destinations, Southern California–style, few places match the **Hyatt Newporter Resort**. Situated on a hillside above Upper Newport Bay, it sprawls across 26 acres and sports three swimming pools, three jacuzzis, a nine-hole pitch-and-putt course, a tennis club and ping-pong. Within walking distance is the Back Bay area featuring playgrounds, excellent beaches and swimming. Beautifully landscaped with a series of terraced patios, the resort features a lavishly decorated lobby. Guest rooms are modern in design, comfortably furnished and tastefully appointed. An inviting combination of elegance and amenities. ~ 1107 Jamboree Road; 949-729-1234, 800-233-1234, fax 949-644-1552; www.hyattnewporter.com, e-mail info@hyattnewporter.com. ULTRA-DELUXE.

The **Balboa Inn,** next to the beach at Balboa Pier, is a Spanish-style hotel built in 1929. With its cream-colored walls and tile-roofed tower, this 34-room hostelry is vintage Southern California. Adding to the ambience is a swimming pool that looks out on the water. Kids will have a ball building sandcastles and paddling around in the Pacific. At night they can head over to join the crowd at the Fun Zone. The rooms, some of which have ocean views, are furnished in knotty pine, decorated with colorful prints and supplied with jacuzzis, brass fixtures and fireplaces. Suites are ideal for families. ~ 105 Main Street, Balboa; 949-675-3412, 877-225-2629, fax 949-673-4587; www.balboainn.com, e-mail rod@balboainn.com. DELUXE TO ULTRA-DELUXE.

DINING   With a bakery on the premises, you know that the pastries at **Haute Cakes** must be fresh. Enjoy the daily waffle special in a cozy, simple setting, or have a hot scrambler out in the courtyard. If you're in the mood for lunch, the grilled-eggplant-and-vegetable salad with a sandwich hits the spot. No dinner. ~ 1807 Westcliff Drive; 949-642-4114. BUDGET TO MODERATE.

Ironically enough, one of Newport Beach's top dining bargains lies at the heart of the region's priciest shopping malls. Encircling the lower level of **Fashion Island** is a collection of stands dispensing sushi, soup and sandwiches, Mexican food, pasta salads, burgers and other light fare. ~ Newport Center, 401 Newport Center Drive; 714-721-2000; www.fashionisland-nb.com, e-mail brigitte@irvine.com. BUDGET TO MODERATE.

Around **Balboa Pavilion** you'll find snack bars and amusement-park food stands that are particularly convenient for families.

A place nearby that's worth recommending is **Newport Landing**, a double-decker affair where you can lounge downstairs in a wood-paneled dining room or upstairs on a deck overlooking the harbor. The upper deck features live music. Serving lunch, dinner and weekend brunch, Newport Landing specializes in fresh fish and also features hickory-smoked prime rib and chicken with artichokes. Special kids' choices include hamburgers and grilled-cheese sandwiches. ~ 503 East Edgewater Avenue; 949-675-2373, fax 949-675-0682; www.newport-landing.com. MODERATE TO DELUXE.

Who could imagine that at the end of Balboa Pier there would be a vintage 1940s-era diner complete with art-deco curves and red plastic booths? **Ruby's Diner** is a classic. Besides that it provides 270 views of the ocean. Of course, the menu, whether breakfast, lunch or dinner, contains little more than omelettes, hamburgers, sandwiches, chili and salads. Kids' meals include chicken fingers and grilled cheese sandwiches with fries. ~ 1 Balboa Pier, Balboa; 949-675-7829, fax 949-673-3237; www.rubys.com. BUDGET.

Because there are very few restaurants on Balboa Island, one place stands out: **Amelia's**, a family-run restaurant serving Italian dishes and seafood, is a local institution. At lunch you'll find them serving a handful of pasta dishes, fresh fish, sandwiches and salads. Then in the evening the chef prepares calamari stuffed with crab, scallops, Icelandic cod, bouillabaisse, veal piccata and another round of pasta platters. Dinner is served daily; lunch on Friday and Saturday. Sunday brunch. Child-sized portions are available. ~ 311 Marine Avenue, Balboa Island; 949-673-6580, fax 949-673-5395; www.calenderlive.com/amelia. MODERATE TO DELUXE.

◄ *HIDDEN*

AUTHOR FAVORITE

You won't miss **The Crab Cooker**. First, it's painted bright red; second, it's located at a busy intersection near Newport Pier; last, the place has been a local institution since the 1950s. Actually, you don't *want* to miss this crabby place. The informal eatery, where lunch and dinner are served on paper plates, has crab (surprise!) as well as fish, scallops, shrimp and oysters. A skewer of cod comes on the children's plate. A fish market is attached to the restaurant, so freshness and quality are assured. ~ 2200 Newport Boulevard; 949-673-0100, fax 949-675-8445. MODERATE TO DELUXE.

If you were hoping to spend a little less money, **Wilma's Patio** is just down the street. It's a family-style restaurant—open morning, noon and night—that serves multicourse American and Mexican meals. Kids can order from a special menu that has space on the back for crayon artwork. Smaller portions of many items, ranging from dollar pancakes to hot dogs, are available year-round. ~ 203 Marine Avenue, Balboa Island; 949-675-5542, fax 949-675-7243. BUDGET TO MODERATE.

BEACHES & PARKS

In addition to the beach that extends the entire length of Balboa Peninsula, you'll want to consider several other spots.

NEWPORT DUNES WATERFRONT RV RESORT This resort has a broad, horseshoe-shaped beach about a half-mile in length. It curves around the lake-like waters of Upper Newport Bay, one mile inland from the ocean. Very popular with families and campers, it offers a wide range of possibilities, including playground activities, volleyball, a swimming pool, jacuzzi, and boat and watersport rentals. Lifeguards are on duty in the summer. Other facilities include restrooms, a café, groceries, picnic areas and laundry. The park is very popular, so plan to come for the attractions, not peace and quiet. Parking fee, $7. ~ 1131 Back Bay Drive, Newport Beach; 949-729-3863, 800-765-7661, fax 949-729-1133; www.newportdunes.com, e-mail kdobbs@catamaranresort.com.

▲ There are 405 sites for freestanding tents and RVs (all with hookups, some with cable TV and phone access); $23 to $95 per night.

CORONA DEL MAR STATE BEACH Located at the mouth of Newport Harbor, this park offers an opportunity to watch sailboats tacking in and out from the bay. Bounded on one side by a jetty, on the other by homes, with a huge parking lot behind, it is less than idyllic, yet it is also inevitably crowded. Throngs congregate because of its easy access, landscaped lawn and ex-

SURF'S UP

In the 1960s, brassy sounds of Newport Beach's Big Bands surrendered to the twanging strains of electric guitars as the Orange Coast earned the nickname "Surfer Heaven." Dick Dale, the "King of the Surf Guitar," hit the top of the charts with "Pipeline," setting off a wave that the Beach Boys and Jan and Dean rode to the crest. Down in Dana Point, local boy Bruce Brown contributed to the coast culture in 1966 with a surf flick called *The Endless Summer*, which achieved cult status and earned for its director a reputation as "the Fellini of foam."

cellent facilities, which include restrooms, picnic areas, lifeguards, showers, concession stands, beach rentals and volleyball courts. It's well protected for swimming and also popular for surfing and fishing—cast from the jetty bordering Newport Harbor. Skin-diving is also good around the jetty. If the crowds are driving you crazy, you will find one possible escape valve: there are a pair of pocket beaches on the other side of the rocks next to the jetty. Parking fee, $6. ~ Located at Jasmine Avenue and Ocean Boulevard in Corona del Mar; 949-722-1611.

LITTLE CORONA DEL MAR STATE BEACH

Another in the proud line of pocket beaches along the Orange Coast, this preserve features the **Corona del Mar Tidepool Reserve,** where sea stars, urchins, crabs and octopuses serve as the entertainment. The bluff to the north consists of sandstone that has been contorted into a myriad of magnificent lines. There's a marsh behind the beach thick with reeds and cattails. Unfortunately you won't be the first explorer to hit the sand; Little Corona is known to a big group of locals. The beach is also popular with swimmers, surfers, snorkelers and skindivers; for anglers, try casting from the rocks. ~ There is an entrance to the beach at Poppy Avenue and Ocean Boulevard in Corona del Mar; 949-722-1611.

Laguna Beach Area

Another stop on Orange County's cavalcade of coastal cities is Laguna Beach. Framed by the San Joaquin hills, the place is an intaglio of coves and bluffs, sand beaches and rock outcroppings. It conjures images of the Mediterranean with deep bays and greenery running to the sea's edge. Little wonder that Laguna, with its wealthy residents and leisurely beachfront, has become synonymous with the chic but informal style of Southern California. Its long tradition as an artist colony adds to this sense of beauty and bounty.

SIGHTS

Part of Laguna's artistic tradition is the **Festival of the Arts and Pageant of the Masters,** staged every year during July and August. While the festival displays the work of 160 local artists and crafts-people, the Pageant of the Masters is the high point, an event you *absolutely must not miss*. It presents a series of *tableaux vivants* in which local residents, dressed to resemble figures from famous paintings, remain motionless against a frieze that re-creates the painting. Elaborate make-up and lighting techniques flatten the figures and create a sense of two-dimensionality. Admission. ~ Irvine Bowl, 650 Laguna Canyon Road; 714-494-1145, 800-487-3378, fax 949-494-9387; www.foapom.org.

During the 1960s, freelance artists, excluded from the more formal Festival of the Arts, founded the **Sawdust Festival** across the street. Over the years this fair, too, has pretty much joined the establishment, but it still provides an opportunity to wander along sawdust-covered paths past hundreds of arts-and-crafts displays accompanied by musicians and jugglers. It also runs from July to late August and has hands-on craftsmaking booths for children. Admission. ~ 935 Laguna Canyon Road; 714-494-3030; www. sawdustfestival.org, e-mail sawdust@deltanet.com.

Laguna Beach's artistic heritage is evident in the many galleries and studios around town. The **Laguna Beach Visitors Bureau and Chamber of Commerce**, with its maps and brochures, can help direct you. They can also assist with hotel and restaurant reservations. Closed Sunday, except in July and August. ~ 252 Broadway; 800-877-1115, fax 949-376-0558; www.laguna beachinfo.org.

Beauty in Laguna is not only found on canvases. The coastline is particularly pretty and well worth exploring. One of the most enchanting areas is along **Heisler Park**, a winding promenade set on the cliffs above the ocean. Here you can relax on the lawn, sit beneath a palm tree and gaze out on the horizon. There are broad vistas out along the coast and down to the wave-whitened shoreline. Paths from the park descend to a series of coves with tidepools and sandy beaches. The surrounding rocks, twisted by geologic pressure into curving designs, rise in a series of protective bluffs. ~ Located on Cliff Drive.

DANA POINT   South on Route 1, you will pass through Dana Point. This ultramodern enclave, with its manmade port and 2500-boat marina, has a history dating back to the 1830s when Richard Henry Dana immortalized the place. Writing in *Two Years Before the Mast*, the Boston gentleman-turned-sailor described the surrounding countryside: "There was a grandeur in everything around."

Today much of the grandeur has been replaced with condominiums, leaving little for the sightseer. There is the **Ocean Institute** with a small sea-life aquarium, a modern research vessel and a 130-foot replica of Dana's brig, *The Pilgrim*. They also lead evening cruises (admission) on weekends and selected weekdays. The aquarium and ships are open weekends only. ~ 24200 Dana Point Harbor Drive; 949-496-2274, fax 949-496-4296; www. ocean-institute.org.

SAN JUAN CAPISTRANO   Seventh in the state's chain of 21 missions, **Mission San Juan Capistrano** was founded in 1776 by Father Junípero Serra. Considered "the jewel of the missions" it is a hauntingly beautiful site, placid and magical.

There are ponds and gardens here, ten acres of standing adobe buildings and the ruins of the original 1797 stone church, destroyed by an earthquake in 1812. The museum displays American Indian crafts, early ecclesiastical artifacts and Spanish weaponry, while an Indian cemetery memorializes the enslaved people who built this magnificent structure.

The highlight of the mission is not the swallows, which are vastly outnumbered by pigeons, but the chapel, a 1777 structure decorated with Indian designs and a baroque altar. The oldest continually used building in California, it is the only remaining church previously used by Father Serra.

Of course the mission's claim to fame is the 1939 ditty, "When the Swallows Return to Capistrano." The tune, like many schmaltzy songs about California, seems to remain eternally lodged in the memory whether you want it there or not. The melody describes the return of flocks of swallows every March 19. And return they do, though in ever-decreasing numbers and not always on March 19. There is also a living-history program (admission) on the last Saturday of every month, with costumed "characters" playing the role of Father Serra and others, and craftspeople showing how old-time crafts were made. On select Saturday nights during the summer, you can hear live music under the stars. Admission. ~ Camino Capistrano and Ortega Highway; 949-248-2048; www.missionsjc.com, e-mail mission@fea.net

> For a lighthouse keeper's view of the harbor and coast, take in the lookout points at the end of Old Golden Lantern or Blue Lantern streets.

At the **O'Neill Museum**, housed in a tiny, 1870s Victorian, there are walking-tour maps of the town's old adobes. Within a few blocks you'll discover about a dozen 19th-century structures. The museum is furnished with Victorian decor. Closed Monday and Saturday. Admission. ~ 31831 Los Rios Street; 949-493-8444, fax 949-240-8091.

The **Capistrano Depot** appeared a little later in the century but is an equally vital part of the town's history. Still operating as a train station, the 1895 depot has been beautifully preserved. Built of brick in a series of Spanish-style arches, the old structure houses a variety of railroad memorabilia, as well as a restaurant and a saloon. An antique pullman, a brightly colored freight car and other vintage cars line the tracks. ~ 26701 Verdugo Street; 949-487-2322, fax 949-493-4243.

LODGING

Boasting 70 rooms, a pool, a spa and a sundeck overlooking the sea, the **Inn at Laguna Beach** offers great ocean views from its blufftop perch. Rooms are small, the construction uneven and the furnishings modern at this coastside property. But continental breakfast and a local paper are brought to your room gratis. ~ 211 North Coast Highway; 949-497-9722, 800-544-4479, fax 949-497-9972; www.innatlagunabeach, e-mail info@innatlaguna beach.com. MODERATE TO ULTRA-DELUXE.

Even if you never stay there, you won't miss the **Hotel Laguna**. With its octagonal tower and Spanish motif, this huge, white-

Orange County's Outback

To explore the last vestiges of Orange County's open country, plan to spend a day wandering the ridges and valleys of the Santa Ana Mountains along the county's southeastern fringes. It's your final chance to catch a glimpse of Orange County as it looked back in 1769 when the Spanish first probed the region's rugged, chaparral-covered mountains. But at the rate new housing tracts are pushing into the region, you'd better hurry!

LIVE OAK CANYON   Heading south on Route 5, exit onto El Toro Road (Route S18) and head northeast toward those lovely mountains. Continue for about seven miles to Live Oak Canyon Road, turn right, and you'll slip beneath a canopy of live oaks. This leafy tunnel into Orange County's distant past is also the way to **O'Neill Regional Park**, a 3100-acre preserve that makes a perfect spot for a picnic lunch. This county park straddles Trabuco and Live Oak canyons in a delightfully undeveloped region of the Santa Ana Mountains. Topography varies from oak-lined canyon bottomlands and grassy meadows to chaparral-covered hillsides. Opossum, raccoon, rabbit and coyote are frequently seen from the hiking trails, as are hawk, quail, dove and roadrunner. Returning to El Toro Road, which becomes Santiago Canyon Road, the route curves up what locals call Modjeska Grade, leaving in its wake a spate of subdivision projects that spoil the view for solace seekers.

washed building dominates downtown Laguna Beach. The oldest hotel in Laguna, it sits in the center of town, adjacent to Main Beach. In addition to 65 guest rooms there are a restaurant, lounge and a casual lobby terrace. For a place on the water *and* at the center of the action, it cannot be matched. Kids will enjoy the playground on the beach in front of the hotel. ~ 425 South Coast Highway; 949-494-1151, 800-524-2927, fax 949-497-2163; www.hotellaguna.com. MODERATE TO ULTRA-DELUXE.

The premier resting place in Laguna Beach is a sprawling, 164-room establishment overhanging the sand. The **Surf & Sand Hotel** is a blocky, 1950s-era complex, an architectural mélange of five buildings and a shopping mall. The accent here is on the ocean: nearly every room has a sea view and private balcony, the pool sits just above the sand, and the beach, perfect for the kids, is a short step away. A full-service hotel, the Surf & Sand has an oceanfront restaurant and a lounge; baby-sitting services are also available. Guest rooms are understated but attractive with raw-silk furnishings, unfinished woods and sand-hued walls. ~ 1555

TUCKER WILDLIFE SANCTUARY   Turn right on Modjeska Valley Road, another winding lane, then left at the junction of Modjeska Canyon and Foothill roads (there's a large tree forming between the two streets). Proceed through the rustic town of Modjeska; a mile farther along Modjeska Canyon Road lies Tucker Wildlife Sanctuary, a 12-acre refuge that's home to more than 170 species of birds and animals, which can be viewed along a series of short loop trails. Tucker is best known for its hummingbirds; all seven varieties known to exist in California can be seen here. An island of conservation in a sea of development, the preserve is also home to hawks and woodpeckers. Guided tours (fee) are available during the week only. ~ 714-649-2760.

IRVINE LAKE   Back on Santiago Canyon Road, continue northwest to Irvine Lake, a 731-acre private lake. Stocked and maintained with the serious angler in mind, these waters have produced a state record 59-pound catfish as well as trophy-sized triploid rainbow "super trout" in the 20-pound range. Bass up to nearly 15 pounds have been caught, and there are bluegill and white sturgeon as well. Admission. ~ 714-649-9111. To wrap up this backcountry adventure, continue for four miles on Santiago Canyon Road to Chapman Avenue, turn left and go three miles to the Newport Freeway (Route 55), then proceed south to Route 5 or 405. Either will carry you back to the civilization from which you temporarily escaped.

South Coast Highway; 949-497-4477, 800-524-8621, fax 949-494-2897; www.jcresorts.com. ULTRA-DELUXE.

Accommodations with kitchen facilities are hard to come by in Laguna Beach. You'll find them in most of the units at **Capri Laguna**, a multilevel, 46-unit motel on the beach. It provides contemporary, motel-style furnishings, plus a pool, a sauna, a workout room and a sundeck with barbecue facilities ideal for families. Continental breakfast is included. ~ 1441 South Laguna Coast Highway; 949-494-6533, 800-225-4551, fax 949-497-6962; www.caprilaguna.com. ULTRA-DELUXE.

The **Ritz-Carlton Laguna Niguel**, set on a cliff above the Pacific, is simply the finest resort hotel along the California coast. Built in the fashion of a Mediterranean villa, it dominates a broad sweep of coastline, a 393-room mansion replete with gourmet restaurants and dark-wood lounges. An Old World interior of arched windows and Italian marble is decorated with one of the finest hotel collections of 19th-century American and English art anywhere. The grounds are landscaped with willows, sycamores and a spectrum of flowering plants. Tile courtyards lead to two swimming pools, a pair of jacuzzis, four tennis courts and a fitness and massage center. There are special supervised kids' programs as well as private baby-sitting services. The guest rooms are equal in luxury to the rest of the resort. ~ 1 Ritz-Carlton Drive, Dana Point; 949-240-2000, 800-241-3333, fax 949-240-1061. ULTRA-DELUXE.

Most motels have a stream of traffic whizzing past outside, but the **Dana Marina Inn Motel**, situated on an island where the highway divides, manages to have traffic on both sides! The reason we're mentioning it is not because we're mean but because rooms in this 29-unit facility are inexpensive. The accommodations are roadside-motel style. ~ 34111 Coast Highway, Dana Point; 949-496-1300. BUDGET.

While San Juan Capistrano is lacking in accommodations, you'll find several places in neighboring San Clemente. **Algodon Motel** is a standard-type, 18-unit facility several blocks from the beach. Some units have kitchens. Not much to write home about, but it is clean and affordable. ~ 135 Avenida Algodon; 949-492-3382. BUDGET.

DINING   Laguna Beach is never at a loss for oceanfront restaurants. But somehow the sea seems closer and more intimate at **Laguna Village Cafe**, probably because this informal eatery is partially outdoors, with about half of the tables placed at the very edge of the coastal bluff. The menu is simple: egg dishes in the morning, and a single menu with salads, sandwiches and smoothies during the rest of the day. There are also house specialties like calamari, abalone, scallops amandine, teriyaki chicken, Chinese-style chicken and skewered shrimp dumplings. Closed at dusk. ~ 577 South Coast Highway, Laguna Beach; 949-494-6344. BUDGET TO MODERATE.

AUTHOR FAVORITE

A secluded canyon is the home of **Aliso Creek Inn and Golf Resort**, an appealing, 83-acre resort complete with swimming pools, jacuzzi, restaurant, lounge and nine-hole golf course. Particularly attractive for families, every unit includes a sitting area, patio and kitchen. Removed from the highway but within 400 yards of a beach, the resort is surrounded by steep hillsides populated by deer and raccoon. Tying this easy rusticity together is a small creek that tumbles through the resort. ~ 31106 South Coast Highway, Laguna Beach; 949-499-2271, 800-223-3309, fax 949-499-4601; www.alisocreekinn.com, e-mail hotel@alisocreekinn.com. DELUXE TO ULTRA-DELUXE.

The **Penguin Malt Shop** is from another era entirely—the 1930s, to be exact. A tiny café featuring counter jukeboxes and swivel stools, it's a time capsule with a kitchen. Breakfast and lunch are all-American affairs from ham and eggs to hamburgers and milkshakes. It's affordable, so what have you got to lose? Step on it and order a chocolate malt with a side of fries. No dinner. ~ 981 South Coast Highway, Laguna Beach; 949-494-1353. BUDGET.

The White Tavern and House seems nearly as permanent a Laguna Beach fixture as the ocean. Dating to early in the 20th century, this simple, wooden structure serves as bar (with live music seven nights a week), restaurant and local landmark. Paneled in dark wood and trimmed with wallpaper, the White House is lined with historic photos of Laguna Beach and works by local artists. You can drop by from early morning until late evening to partake of a menu that includes pasta, steak, chicken and seafood dishes. ~ 340 South Coast Highway, Laguna Beach; 949-494-8088, fax 949-494-0986. MODERATE.

Choose one place to symbolize the easy elegance of Laguna and it inevitably will be **Las Brisas**. Something about this whitewashed Spanish building with arched windows perfectly captures the natural-living-but-class-conscious style of the Southland. Its cliffside locale on the water is part of this ambience. Then there is the dual kitchen arrangement that permits formal dining in a white-tablecloth room or bistro dining on an outdoor patio. The menu consists of Continental-Mexican seafood dishes and other specialties from south of the border, as well as chicken, steak and pasta. Out on the patio you can choose from sandwiches, salads and appetizers. ~ 361 Cliff Drive, Laguna Beach; 949-497-5434, fax 949-497-9210. MODERATE TO DELUXE.

The most remarkable aspect of the **Cottage Restaurant** is the cottage itself, an early-20th-century California bungalow. The place has been neatly decorated with turn-of-the-20th-century antiques, oil paintings and stained glass. Meal time in this historic house is a traditional American affair. They serve traditional breakfasts, while lunch consists of salads and sandwiches plus specials like top sirloin, fresh fish and steamed vegetables. For dinner there are chicken fettuccine, top sirloin, broiled lamb, fresh shrimp and swordfish as well as daily fish specials. Special entrées for the small fry include a junior breakfast featuring dollar-sized pancakes as well as dinner specialties like linguine and hamburgers. ~ 308 North Coast Highway, Laguna Beach; 949-494-3023, fax 949-497-5183. MODERATE.

The **Harbor Grill**, located in spiffy Dana Point Harbor, lacks the view and polish of its splashy neighbors. But this understated restaurant serves excellent seafood dishes. The menu includes fresh swordfish and salmon with pesto sauce, but the real attraction is the list of daily specials. These might include sea bass with black-bean sauce, gumbo and other fishy delights. Lunch, dinner and Sunday brunch are served in a light, bright dining room with contemporary artwork. Patio dining and a full bar are also options here. For the kids, they serve grilled cheese sandwiches, burgers, fish and chips, or a half order of anything on the menu. ~ 34499 Golden Lantern Street, Dana Point; 949-240-1416; www.harbor grill.com, e-mail grillman@home.com. MODERATE TO DELUXE.

If you'd prefer to dine alfresco overlooking the harbor, there's **Proud Mary's**, a hole-in-the-wall where you can order sandwiches, salads, hamburgers and a few chicken and steak platters, then dine on picnic tables outside. Breakfast is served all day and there is a separate kids' menu. No dinner. ~ 34689 Golden Lantern Street, Dana Point; 949-493-5853, fax 949-493-3911. BUDGET.

One of San Juan Capistrano's many historic points, the 19th-century building **El Adobe de Capistrano** has been converted into a restaurant. The interior is a warren of whitewashed rooms, supported by *vigas* and displaying the flourishes of Spanish California. The menu includes lunch, dinner and Sunday brunch. The cuisine is primarily Mexican, but it also includes a number of American steak and seafood dishes. There's a special children's dinner. ~ 31891 Camino Capistrano, San Juan Capistrano; 949-493-1163, fax 949-493-4565. BUDGET TO MODERATE.

BEACHES & PARKS

CRYSTAL COVE STATE PARK 🧍 🚲 ⛵ 🎣 ⚓ 🛶 This outstanding facility has a long, winding sand beach which is sometimes sectioned into a series of coves by high tides. The park stretches for over three miles along the coast and extends up into the hills. Grassy terraces grace the sea cliffs and the offshore area is designated an underwater preserve. Providing long walks along an undeveloped coastline and on upland trails in El Moro Canyon, it's the perfect park when you're seeking solitude. Facilities are limited to lifeguards and restrooms. Onshore fishing is permitted

MAIN BEACH

You'll have to venture north to Muscle Beach in Venice to find a scene equal to this one. It's near the very center of Laguna Beach, at Coast Highway and Broadway, with shopping streets radiating in several directions. A sinuous boardwalk winds along the waterfront, past basketball players, sunbathers, volleyball aficionados, little kids on swings and aging kids on rollerblades. Here and there an adventuresome soul has even dipped a toe in the wa-wa-water. In the midst of this humanity on holiday stands the lifeguard tower, an imposing, glass-encased structure that looks more like a conning tower and has become a Laguna Beach icon.

(with a valid California driver's license), and swimming is good. For surfing, try the breaks north of Reef Point in Scotchman's Cove. Day-use fee, $6. ~ Located along the Coast Highway between Corona del Mar and Laguna Beach. There are entrances at Pelican Point, Los Trancos, Reef Point and El Moro Canyon; 949-494-3539, fax 949-494-6911; www.crystalcovestatepark.com.

▲ Environmental camping is permitted at three campgrounds, a two- to four-mile hike inland from the parking lot; $11 per night. No open campfires allowed.

DOHENY STATE BEACH 🚲 ⛵ 🏊 ⛵ This park wrote the book on oceanside facilities. In addition to a broad swath of sandy beach there is a five-acre lawn complete with private picnic areas, beach rentals, restrooms with changing areas, lifeguards, horseshoe pits, volleyball courts and food concessions. The grassy area offers plenty of shade trees. Surfers work the north end of the beach, leaving plenty of room for swimmers to the south. Dana Point Harbor, with complete marina facilities, borders the beach. For fishing, try the jetty in Dana Point Harbor. Swimming is good here, and surfing is comfortable for beginners, particularly on a south swell. Day-use fee, $3. ~ Located off Dana Point Harbor Drive in Dana Point; 949-496-6171, fax 949-496-9469; www.dohenystatebeach.org.

▲ There are 121 tent/RV sites (no hookups), including 32 beach sites. All sites cost $12. Call 800-444-7275 for reservations.

SAN CLEMENTE STATE BEACH 🏊 ⛵ 🏊 ⛵ Walk down the deeply eroded cliffs guarding this coastline, and you'll discover a long narrow strip of sand that curves north from San Diego County up to San Clemente City Beach. There are camping areas and picnic plots on top of the bluff. Down below a railroad track parallels the beach and surfers paddle offshore. You can stroll north toward downtown San Clemente or south to the late President Nixon's old home. Beach facilities include lifeguards, picnic areas and restrooms. Surf fishing is best in spring, and surfers will find year-round breaks at the south end of the beach. Swimmers should beware of rip currents. Day-use fee, $6. ~ Located off Avenida Calafia in San Clemente; 949-492-3156.

▲ There are 160 tent/RV sites (71 with hookups); $18 for tents, $24 for hookups.

Whether you want to snatch a tuna or watch a spouting whale, the Orange County coast offers plenty of possibilities.

Outdoor Adventures

SPORTFISHING & WHALE WATCHING

Davey's Locker offers half- and full-day sportfishing charters for yellowtail, bass and barracuda. ~ 400 Main Street, Balboa; 949-673-1434; www.daveyslocker.com. For trips to Catalina and Clemente islands for bass, dorado and tuna, contact **Dana Wharf**

Sportfishing. ~ 34675 Golden Lantern Street, Dana Point; 949-496-5794; www.danawharfsportfishing.com. Dana Wharf Sportfishing and Davey's Locker also sponsor two-hour whale-watching cruises during migratory season (December to late March).

DIVING

The coastal waters abound in interesting kelp beds rich with sea life; several companies are available to help you through the kelp.

For diving lessons and rentals on Catalina contact **Aquatic Center.** ~ 4537 West Coast Highway, Newport Beach; 949-650-5440. This full-service scuba center also operates a 24-hour surf and water condition line. ~ 949-650-5783; www.aquaticcenter.net. **Laguna Sea Sports** rents equipment and provides lessons. ~ 925 North Coast Highway, Laguna Beach; 949-494-6965; www.scuba-superstore.com.

SURFING & WIND-SURFING

Orange County is surfer heaven, so when you're in the area, don't miss out on its wild waves.

For surfboards, boogieboards, wetsuit rentals, sales and repairs, contact **Huntington Surf and Sport.** ~ 300 Pacific Coast Highway, Huntington Beach; 714-841-4000; www.huntingtonsurfandsport.com. **Hobie Sports** also rents boards and wetsuits. ~ 24825 Del Prado, Dana Point; 949-496-2366. **Stewart's Surf Boards** sells and rents surfboards, boogieboards and wetsuits. Inquire about lessons—many of the employees offer private instruction. ~ 2102 South El Camino Real, San Clemente; 949-492-1085.

KAYAKING & BOATING

With elaborate marina complexes at Huntington Beach, Newport Beach and Dana Point, this is a spectacular area for boating. If you yearn to make some waves, call one of the outfits listed below.

Sailboats and powerboats (including fishing skiffs) are available for rent at **Davey's Locker.** ~ 400 Main Street, Balboa; 949-673-1434; www.daveyslocker.com. In Newport Beach, try **Marina**

SURFER'S PARADISE

Practically all the beaches in Orange County are surfable; these are just a few spots to get you started. Early risers head to Newport Pier at Newport Beach. World-renowned Huntington City Beach hosts international surfing competitions in the summer. The south end of San Clemente State Beach offers great breaks any time of the year. Beginners choose to learn at Doheny State Beach. If bodysurfing is your thing, the Wedge at West Jetty View Park is the place to do it. For surf reports call 949-673-3371. See "Surfing & Windsurfing" for equipment rental information.

Sailing for lessons or six-passenger charters. ~ 300 Pacific Coast Highway, Suite F, Newport Beach; 949-548-8900. Electric boats, motorboats, sailboats, kayaks and offshore runabouts can be rented at **Balboa Boat Rentals**. ~ 510 Edgewater Avenue, Balboa; 949-673-7200; www.boats4rent.com. **Embarcadero Marina**, located at the public launch ramp, rents sailboats, fishing skiffs and an electric boat. ~ 34512 Embarcadero Place, Dana Point; 949-496-6177.

If you'd rather shake up the cellulite than the water, you can do it on Orange County's miles of beaches and running trails.

JOGGING

Mecca for Orange County runners is the **Santa Ana Riverbed Trail**, a smooth asphalt ribbon stretching 20.6 miles from Anaheim to Huntington Beach State Park. There are par courses and excellent running trails at both **Laguna Niguel Regional Park** (La Paz and Aliso Creek Road) and **Mile Square Regional Park** (16801 Euclid Avenue in Fountain Valley). In Mission Viejo there's a beautiful two-and-a-half-mile trail around **Lake Mission Viejo**. And then there are the miles and miles of beaches for which Orange County is renowned.

The inland sections of Orange County feature numerous golf links. Among them is **Dad Miller Golf Course**. ~ 430 North Gilbert Street, Anaheim; 714-765-3481. Visit the **Anaheim Hills Golf Course**, which features a double-decker driving range. ~ 6501 East Nohl Ranch Road, Anaheim; 714-998-3041. A natural creek running along 14 of the 18 holes at **Fullerton Golf Course** ensures lots of water hazards. ~ 2700 North Harbor Boulevard, Fullerton; 714-871-7411. For a flat, wide-open, 18-hole walking course, visit **Mile Square Golf Course**. ~ 10401 Warner Avenue, Fountain Valley; 714-968-4556.

GOLF

On the coast you can tee up in Newport at the 18-hole executive **Newport Beach Golf Course**, but expect to carry your own clubs: this course has no electric carts. ~ 3100 Irvine Avenue, Newport Beach; 949-852-8681. The enchanting nine-hole **Aliso Creek Golf Course** is set in the middle of a steep canyon with a creek winding through it. ~ 31106 Coast Highway, Laguna Beach; 949-499-1919; www.alisocreek.com. The coastal course at **The Golf Links at Monarch Beach** is designed by Robert Trent Jones, Jr., and has a beautiful view of the water. ~ 33033 Niguel Road, Dana Point; 949-240-8247. If you're looking for a dry course with ocean views, visit the **San Clemente Municipal Golf Course**. ~ 150 East Avenida Magdalena, San Clemente; 949-361-8384. Situated in a narrow canyon, the public, par-72 **Shorecliffs Golf Course** has a driving range and putting green. The greens are small and the course is fast and in good condition. Carts are mandatory. ~ 501 Avenida Vaquero, San Clemente; 949-492-1177.

TENNIS

Even though public courts are hard to find in this area, who says Orange County is elitist? There are still many private clubs, and given the wonderful climate and the way you'll fit in wearing those white shorts and tennis sweaters, it's probably worth the club fee after all.

The **Anaheim Tennis Center** offers 12 lighted courts. Fee. ~ 975 South State College Boulevard, Anaheim; 714-991-9090. In Buena Park, **Ralph B. Clark Regional Park** has four lighted courts. ~ 8800 Rosecrans Avenue, Buena Park; 714-670-8045.

The swallows returning to Capistrano come all the way from Argentina!

In Newport Beach, you can try one of the eight lighted, plexi-paved courts at **Hotel Tennis Club**. A pro is available for lessons. Fee. ~ Marriott Hotel, 900 Newport Center Drive, Newport Beach; 949-729-3566. Laguna Beach's **Moulton Meadows Park** has two courts. ~ Del Mar and Balboa avenues, Laguna Beach; 949-497-0716. **Laguna Niguel Regional Park** features four lighted tennis courts. ~ 28241 La Paz Road, Laguna Niguel; 949-831-2791. There are eight lighted courts at **Dana Hills Tennis Center**. ~ 24911 Calle de Tenis, Dana Point; 949-240-2104.

Strangely enough, San Clemente is the one Orange County town that does seem to have an abundance of public courts. **Bonito Canyon Park** offers two lighted courts. ~ 1304 Calle Valle at El Camino Real, San Clemente; 949-361-8264. There are four lighted courts at **San Luis Rey Park**. ~ 109 Avenida San Luis Rey, San Clemente; 949-361-8264. **San Gorgonio Park** has two unlit courts. ~ 2916 Via San Gorgonio, San Clemente; 949-361-8264. **Verde Park** also has two courts for day use only. ~ 301 Calle Escuela.

BIKING

Wind and wheels are a perfect blend with Southern California's weather, and you can avoid adding to the smog and sitting in traffic by tooling around on a bike rather than in a car. Whether you like road riding or mountain biking, you'll find a suitable place to cycle in Orange County. **Route 1**, the Pacific Coast Highway, offers cyclists an opportunity to explore the Orange County coastline. The problem, of course, is the traffic. Along **Bolsa Chica State Beach**, however, a special pathway runs the length of the beach. Another way to avoid traffic is to mountain-bike; **Moro Canyon** in Crystal Cove State Park is a favorite off-road riding area.

Skirting the **Upper Newport Bay Ecological Reserve** are about ten miles of bikeway, with some hills, but nothing too strenuous. You can park for about $7 at Newport Dunes (an RV resort) or try for one of the spots in the small Big Canyon lot in the reserve. Back Bay Drive, a multi-use paved roadway, has a double-wide bike route; it links up with a dedicated bike route around the northern perimeter of the reserve. Eventually, along the western flank, the bike route gives way to a bike lane on city streets to complete the loop around the reserve. ~ Back Bay Drive at Jamboree Road.

Call the **Newport Beach Department of Public Works** and ask for a copy of the "Bikeways" map; it shows all the trails in Newport Beach. ~ City Hall, 3300 Newport Boulevard; 949-644-3311.

Other interesting areas to explore are **Balboa Island** and the **Balboa Peninsula** in Newport Beach. Both offer quiet residential streets and are connected by a ferry which permits bicycles. A popular inland ride is along **Santiago Canyon Road**; leaving from Orange the route skirts Irvine Lake and Cleveland National Forest.

Bike Rentals   **Sandpiper Bicycle Repair** is a full-service shop renting hybrids, tandems and inline skates. ~ 231 Seal Beach Boulevard, Seal Beach; 562-594-6130. **Rainbow Bicycle Company** rents, repairs and sells mountain bikes. ~ 485 North Coast Highway, Laguna Beach; 949-494-5806.

EIGHT

San Diego Day Trips

The experts agree that San Diego is one of the best family vacation cities in the United States. Who are we to argue? Famous for its zoo and wild animal park, beaches and missions, San Diego is one of California's most entertaining and relaxing destinations. You could spend a week exploring the museums of Balboa Park and still not see all that this cultural hub has to offer. And when it comes to family attractions you'll have a hard time beating delights like SeaWorld, Scripps Museum, Horton Plaza and Coronado.

The San Diego County Coast, with 76 sparkling miles stretching from the San Clemente area to the Mexican border, is the place to see the rare Torrey pines, ride one of the West Coast's two remaining classic roller coasters and visit California's first mission. With bays and beaches bathed in sunshine 75 percent of the time, less than ten inches of rainfall per year and average temperatures that mirror a proverbial day in June, San Diego offers the casual outdoor lifestyle that fulfills vacation dreams. There's a beach for every taste ranging from broad sweeps of white sand to slender scimitars beneath eroded sandstone bluffs.

Although waterfront resorts are a prime attraction, the San Diego region also offers many inland attractions. Old Town San Diego State Historic Park, Heritage Park, the Children's Museum of San Diego and the Aerospace Museum and Hall of Fame are just a few of the unique features of this alluring destination.

San Diego is also famous for its zoo, considered the world's best. It takes at least a day to get an overview of the lush habitat that is home to 800 species. Like the 2100-acre Wild Animal Park in northern San Diego County, the zoo is a center of wildlife conservation and offers a close look at the quiet war being waged to save the world's endangered species.

The city's downtown is a delight as well, thanks to attractions like Horton Plaza, an offbeat urban mall that doubles as a living museum showcasing more than a dozen architectural styles from the Renaissance to the postmodern. The nearby Gaslamp Quarter historic district and the shops of Seaport Village also invite leisurely exploration.

Although they are within the boundaries of the city of San Diego, the seaside communities of Ocean Beach, Mission Beach and Pacific Beach have developed their own identities, moods and styles. "OB," as the first is fondly known, exults along with its two sister beach communities in the sunny, sporty, Southern California lifestyle fostered by nearby Mission Bay Park—home of SeaWorld. These neighboring communities are fronted by broad beaches and an almost continuous boardwalk that is jammed with joggers, skaters and cyclists.

The region's most upscale beach town, La Jolla, is scented with jasmine and hibiscus and looks like it was imported from Italy's Amalfi Coast. This university town makes an excellent base for exploring the best of San Diego's beaches, galleries, restaurants and family attractions.

Coronado, nestled on a peninsula jutting into San Diego Bay and connected to the mainland by a narrow sandbar known as the Silver Strand, is another community ideal for the sporting life.

All of these choices might make San Diego sound daunting. But in many ways this big city is like a small town, easy to navigate and surprisingly affordable. No matter where you go in this family-oriented region you'll likely only be minutes away from another great waterfront restaurant, a promising bike path or a marina that can rent you a ski or sailboat. Now, if you're ready, let's get started on the day trips that could easily turn into overnights.

The San Diego Zoo

The San Diego Zoo has long been heralded as the best zoo in the world. But this glorious, 100-acre zoological park is not resting on its laurels. Having celebrated its 85th anniversary in 2001, it is in the midst of a multimillion-dollar rebuilding and reorganization into several bioclimactic zones. Many of these climate zones are already in place and have met with resounding success.

In addition to the lions, tigers and bears so common in zoos around the world, the animal population here includes many rare and endangered species that you'll be hard-pressed to find elsewhere; you'll see giant pandas, Australian koalas, New Zealand kiwis and Fiji Island iguanas. You'll also witness the curious habits of feisty sun bears, acrobatic siamangs and playful meerkats.

The best thing about the zoo is that the animals seem relatively content to be here. You won't see any species cooped up in barred cages. Instead, the residents live in spacious, barless, moated enclosures carefully landscaped with plants from their native habitats.

NUTS & BOLTS

Arrival   The zoo is just north of downtown San Diego on the east end of Balboa Park. Take the Park Boulevard exit off Route 163 and go north, following the signs to the zoo. The parking lot is located right off Park Boulevard. Parking is free and plentiful but be sure to make a note of where you left your car; each row is marked by a different animal. There is also a bus stop right in front of the zoo. Call San Diego Transit Information (619-233-3004) for route information.

Tickets Visitors can choose between a one-day pass ($19.50 for adults, $11.75 for children ages 3–11) or an annual membership ($66 for single adults or $84 for two adults in the same household, $21 for children ages 3–15), which allows unlimited visits to both the San Diego Zoo and the San Diego Wild Animal Park; children under 2 are free. Also available is a deluxe ticket package ($32 for adults, $19.75 for children ages 3-11), which includes admission, a guided bus tour, express bus service and a roundtrip ride on the Skyfari Aerial Tram.

Elephants have 40,000 muscles in their trunks alone.

Game Plan Covering a whopping 100 acres, the zoo seldom seems overcrowded. The most you have to worry about is having to crane your neck a little to see over the crowds that gather around the most popular enclosures. People don't linger in one spot for more than a few minutes, so you should always be able to work your way to the front for a good view.

Everyone is handed a map upon entering the zoo. You'll find it detailed and easy to follow. Signage within the zoo is so good that you might not even have to look at the map very often.

Some visitors find navigating zoo terrain to be a challenging physical exercise. This zoo is no exception, spread out over several hills and canyons, which means stairs, inclines and lots of walking. Several moving sidewalks carry visitors up the steepest inclines, but if you have a small child or an elderly relative, you may want to consider taking the 40-minute bus tour, which is described in greater detail below.

Guest Services For recorded zoo information, call 619-234-3153; to reach a switchboard operator (in other words, to speak to a real person), call 619-231-1515; or write San Diego Zoo Guest Relations, P.O. Box 1220551, San Diego, CA 92112. Wheelchair and stroller rentals are located just inside the main gate to the left. Here you'll also find an Information Center, Security, Lost & Found and a Camera and Film Shop. Lockers and First Aid are located by the Reptile House. Telephones, drinking fountains and restrooms with handicapped access are scattered throughout the zoo and clearly marked on the map. No animals are allowed.

Getting Around This zoo is an enormous place, and it's possible that you may not get to see all the animals in one day. So it's a good idea to first consult the map and go directly to the animals and shows that you most want to see.

For a great bird's-eye view of the entire facility, climb aboard the **Skyfari Aerial Tram** ($2 each way). A station is located to the left of the main entrance. From your aerial cabin you'll see lush rainforests on one side, dry savanna on the other. Children love

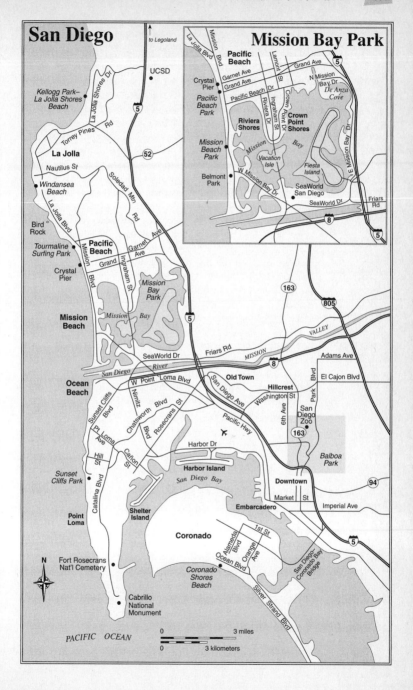

San Diego

to Legoland

UCSD

Kellogg Park–
La Jolla Shores
Beach

La Jolla Shores Dr

Torrey Pines Rd

La Jolla

Nautilus St

Windansea
Beach

Bird
Rock

La Jolla Blvd

Soledad Mtn Rd

Tourmaline
Surfing Park

Pacific
Beach

Crystal
Pier

Mission Blvd

Garnet Ave

Grand

Ingraham St

Mission
Beach

Mission Bay

Mission
Bay
Park

Ingraham Ave

Mission Bay Park

Pacific
Beach

Crystal
Pier

Grand Ave

Lamont St

Grand Ave

N Mission
Bay Dr

De Anza
Cove

Pacific Beach Dr

Garnet Ave

Ingraham St

Crown Point Dr

Riviera Dr

Riviera
Shores

Crown
Point
Shores

Mission
Beach
Park

Mission

Bay

Belmont
Park

W Mission Bay Dr

Vacation
Isle

Fiesta
Island

SeaWorld
San Diego

E Mission Bay Dr

Friars
Rd

SeaWorld Dr

163

805

VALLEY

SeaWorld Dr   Friars Rd   MISSION

8

Adams Ave

El Cajon Blvd

San Diego   River

Ocean
Beach

W Point   Loma Blvd

Nimitz   Blvd

Sunset Cliffs Blvd

Chatsworth Blvd

Rosecrans St

Old Town

San Diego Ave

Pacific Hwy

Hillcrest

Washington St

6th Ave

Park Blvd

San Diego
Zoo

163

Balboa
Park

94

Pt Loma
Ave

Hill
St

Cañon
St

Harbor Dr

Harbor Island

San Diego Bay

Downtown

Market   St

Imperial Ave

Sunset
Cliffs Park

Catalina Blvd

Shelter
Island

Coronado

Embarcadero

1st St

Alameda
Blvd

Orange
Ave

5

Point
Loma

N

Fort Rosecrans
Nat'l Cemetery

Ocean Blvd

Coronado
Shores
Beach

Silver Strand Blvd

San Diego–
Coronado Bay
Bridge

Cabrillo
National
Monument

PACIFIC   OCEAN

0   3 miles

0   3 kilometers

to look down over the enclosures and identify all the animals scurrying about below.

The 40-minute **Guided Bus Tour** is another alternative to seeing the entire zoo on foot, although it will cost you $8.50 for adults, $4 for children ages 3-11. Double-decker buses cruise slowly through the canyons, giving passengers a chance to spot many animals. An extremely knowledgeable guide narrates the tour, giving the names and birthdays of celebrity animals, species anecdotes, conservation information and other interesting and often amusing bits of trivia. The information alone is worth the price of the tour. The seats on the top deck offer the best views, though you'll have to wait longer for them.

The **Express Bus** follows the same route as the Guided Bus route, but it has stops at eight locations throughout the zoo. Included in the price of a Guided Bus tour ticket, this service allows you to hop on and off the bus all day. This is ideal for families with small children because they can walk for a while and then get back on the bus to rest their feet and enjoy the commentary on the animals. Express Bus passes are limited and can sometimes sell out during peak season. In summer, when the zoo is open late, you might want to check back in after 4 p.m., when space on the buses sometimes frees up.

WHAT TO SEE & DO

Just inside the entrance to the left is **Tiger River**. A winding, downhill path takes you through a simulated Southeast Asian rainforest with lush, live foliage. Hidden sprinklers provide cool, ambient mist along the way. Reaching the bottom of the path, you'll be treated to glimpses of such rainforest natives as Malaysian tapirs and a 100-pound python. You will also see the playful "fishing cats," one of the only feline species that enjoys the water. But the stars of Tiger River are, of course, the magnificent Indochinese tigers, housed in a lush, green environment that slopes up the side of a hill. Visitors view these striped beasts from behind plexiglass at the

ALL THE ZOO'S A STAGE

The zoo has two different shows to choose from, each taking place several times daily. Thankfully, you won't see costumed animals starring in silly, contrived skits. These shows aim to educate as well as entertain. At Hunte Amphitheater in Cat Canyon, the **Wild Ones** focuses on a variety of critically endangered species, such as the cheetah and the cloud leopard. Wildlife native to California's offshore islands take to the Wegeforth Bowl pool for a splashy, informative **Wegeforth National Park Sea Lion Show** that focuses on the natural abilities of these animals to adapt to their environment and to one another.

bottom of the slope or from across an open moated area. You should be willing to linger here awhile, as these animals spend much of the day napping in the upper confines of their enclosure and are sometimes difficult to spot. But patience pays off when one of them suddenly rises to stretch its legs or get a drink of water.

Because hippopotamuses spend the majority of their day submerged, when you stop by **Ituri Forest** that's likely how you'll find them: underwater and doing their infamous hippo ballet. As you watch the memorable moves of Funani and Jabba through the 105-foot-long observation window, you'll likely discover that they're just as curious about you as you are about them. The river hippos share this African marsh–like habitat with many fish and several species of birds including sacred ibis, African spoonbills and white-breasted cormorants. Adjacent to the hippos are the rare forest-dwelling okapi from central Africa (they are the closest living relative of the giraffe).

Around the corner from the Ituri Forest is the **Pacific Bell Giant Panda Research Station** (you'll know it by the long line to get in), home to temporary residents Bai Yun and Shi Shi (both on loan from the People's Republic of China). In August 1999, the two pandas became the happy parents of Hua Mei, the first surviving panda baby in the U.S. (a fact about which the San Diego Zoo is understandably proud). The little girl has been a focal point of zoo activity. Sadly, she is scheduled to move to China in August 2002.

But the parents are out every day, with varying viewing times throughout the year. If you don't catch them up close, you may be able to see them in their exercise yards via "Panda Cam," and there's always some sort of video playing if the bears aren't available at all. Summer, when the bears are out for many hours at a time, is a particularly good season to see them. On busy days, you can count on long lines. You'll have the best luck (and the shortest wait) if you arrive at the beginning of the scheduled viewing times or wait until later in the day. Those who fall in love with these furry cherubs can check on their progress by viewing the Panda Cam on the Zoo's website (www.sandiegozoo.org).

Overlooking the Giant Panda Research Station and Ituri Forest is **Gorilla Tropics**, a two-and-a-half acre simulated African rainforest that houses gorillas and thousands of African plants. Superstar primates Memba and Alvila and family are truly a privileged bunch; behind the scenes, their state-of-the-art home includes skylights, heated floors, custom-designed sleeping platforms and a 96-speaker compact disc stereo system that plays sounds recorded in actual African rainforests. The animals spend most of their time in the outdoor habitat—a hillside clearing surrounded by bamboo, fig and banana trees, where frequent feedings afford visitors up-close views of the apes.

The **Owens Rainforest Aviary** features flying denizens of the tropics. A particularly tranquil area, the 65-foot-high enclosure gives you a treetop-level look at colorful fliers such as black-and-crimson orioles and blue-backed fairy bluebirds.

A popular addition to Gorilla Tropics, **Pygmy Chimps at Bonobo Road**, is a replica of an African rainforest. Exhibits include the African crowned eagle and a variety of other birds. The stars are bonobos (also called pygmy chimpanzees) who entertain visitors with their antics.

Sun Bear Forest, judging from the crowds, is one of the most popular and entertaining zones within the zoo. Rambunctious lion-tailed macaques (rhymes with "attacks") swing from intertwined ropes and branches to the delight of crowds pressed up against the plexiglass wall of their enclosure. A sign informs visitors of these creatures' lofty heritage—some are descendants of a colony of macaques once owned by Prince Rainier of Monaco.

But the real celebrities are their neighbors, the sun bears. The world's smallest bear, this creature gets its name from the cream-colored starburst on its chest. Their long claws look threatening, but these clumsy, roly-poly bears seem anything but menacing. They appear to be the happiest creatures alive as they play in the waterfall and pools, and lumber about their spacious home, pestering their slumbering mates.

While you'll seldom see koalas doing much more than munching eucalyptus leaves, these creatures have always been among the most lovable residents of the zoo. Most of the time they stay curled up in a ball, doing what they do best—snoozing. This enclosure is also home to other intriguing creatures from Down Under, including several adorable wallabies and tree kangaroos.

The western end of the zoo, also known as **Horn and Hoof Mesa**, is reserved for giraffes, gazelles, buffalo and antelope. Continue south and you'll find more hoofstock such as deer, impala and rare takin from China.

EARLY BIRDS AND NIGHT OWLS

From the end of June through August, the San Diego Zoo features expanded hours that allow a peek into the lives of animals who might otherwise be getting shuteye. Early morning hours include close encounters with koalas, giraffes and camels. Indochinese tigers, snow leopards and lorises are just a few of the "night owls" you might want to see; evenings also feature a variety of entertaining shows, from musical events to magic and storytelling acts. Expanded hours are roughly 9 a.m. until 9 p.m., but check before you go.

To visit **Polar Bear Plunge** is to be transported to the northern coast of Alaska in the summertime. At the center of this simulated Arctic tundra are the polar bears. As you watch them swimming gracefully underwater in their deep saltwater bay, you would never guess that they are fierce and persistent predators. Look closely at their fur. It's not the white or cream color that it appears; it's actually translucent and hollow, allowing sunlight to penetrate it. Other Arctic species that inhabit this wondrous exhibit are reindeer, Arctic foxes, yellow-throated martens and a variety of waterfowl.

In addition to these not-to-be-missed attractions, the zoo has hundreds of other intriguing animals to see should time permit. Up the hill from Sun Bear Forest you'll find **Elephant Mesa**, home to several rhinos and, of course, a herd of African and Asian elephants. Continue north and you'll pass bats, camels and tree kangaroos. The nearby **African Kopje Exhibit**, another of the zoo's bioclimatic zones, contains miniature antelope called klipspringers, dwarf mongooses, rock hyrax and a pair of majestic Verreaux's eagles. And don't miss the amusing meerkats just around the corner from the Kopje. These frisky critters are real crowd-pleasers, wrestling around in the dirt, standing on their hind legs and playing leapfrog.

Down the hill is **Dog and Cat Canyon** where you'll find several species of felines including the snow and Persian leopards, and a pair of stunning jaguars.

Crocodilians, tortoises and various rare frogs make their homes on **Reptile Mesa**. And don't forget to visit the slithering inhabitants of the **Reptile House** where dozens of varieties of snakes and lizards live in glass enclosures. Be sure to check out the rare Fiji island iguana.

Wind down your day with a visit to the **Children's Zoo**. As in most zoos, this enclosure has the familiar petting paddock, filled with docile goats, sheep, deer and even pot-bellied pigs. But there's much more, like dozens of downy newborn chicks for touching; rabbits, guinea pigs and a miniature horse; and a nursery where newborn animals sometimes spend their first few months. Don't miss the pygmy marmosets housed in a glass enclosure at the entrance to Children's Zoo. The world's smallest monkeys, these tiny creatures weigh in at only four ounces when full grown.

DINING

The food at the zoo has improved greatly over the years. You'll find many favorite gourmet snacks such as frozen yogurt, Häagen-Dazs ice cream and Michelangelo calzones. The newest alternatives to the standard hot dogs, hamburgers and limp chicken sandwiches are found in the Treehouse, designed to recall a turn-of-the-20th-century African manor house. On the upper level is the **Treehouse Café**, a buffet-style restaurant serving salads, sandwiches and hot dishes. BUDGET. All the seating is on open-air decks. On the lower level is **Albert's Restaurant**, named for the gorilla who once occupied the area where the Treehouse now stands. This sit-down eatery offers a variety of salads, sandwiches, pizzas, fresh pastas and fish and meat entrées. There is a children's menu. MODERATE. For cuisine and ambience, the **Canyon Café**, at the bottom of Bear Canyon, tops our culinary list. This outdoor eatery is right next door to the Giant Panda Research Station. And in addition to the hamburgers, the menu includes some pretty decent fish tacos—a favorite dish of San Diegans. BUDGET. **Sydney's Grill**, near the koalas, has Italian food. MODERATE.

You can also grab a budget-priced bite at the handful of snack bars. **Safari Kitchen** near the Flamingo lagoon serves up burgers and chicken sandwiches. BUDGET. Just inside the main entrance, the **Lagoon Terrace** serves specialty hot dogs. BUDGET. The **Flamingo Cafe** offers sandwiches and vegetarian fare served up cafeteria-style. BUDGET.

San Diego Wild Animal Park

If you've always fantasized about going on an African safari, the San Diego Wild Animal Park—an 1800-acre sanctuary 30 miles north of San Diego—is the place for you. As your shaded monorail snakes slowly through the foothills, herds of antelope, rhinoceros, giraffes and zebras roam the vast plains below. Unlike most conventional zoos, the park's 3600-plus animals live together, creating one of the most realistic recreations of the wild you could think of anywhere.

Imagine a herd of giraffes, wildebeest or antelope charging pell-mell across the plains; a pair of young male gazelles locking horns, playfully sparring for territorial rights; mountain goats springing straight up a 100-foot rocky incline in mere seconds. These are just some of the things you can hope to see at this wonderful park.

NUTS & BOLTS

Arrival The park is at 15500 San Pasqual Valley Road in San Diego, near Escondido. From San Diego, take Route 15 to Via Rancho Parkway. From Los Angeles take Route 5 south to Route 78, then follow it east and pick up Route 15 south to Via Rancho Parkway. From Via Rancho Parkway a series of carefully placed signs leads you six more miles to the park. There is a fee for parking. (For information call 760-747-8702.)

Tickets Choose between a one-day pass ($26.50 for adults, $19.50 for children ages 3–11) or an annual membership ($66 for single adults, $84 for adult couples, $21 for children ages 3–11, $25 for children 12-17), which allows unlimited visits to both the San Diego Wild Animal Park and the San Diego Zoo.

Game Plan Both humans and animals have plenty of space to roam, so the Wild Animal Park seldom seems congested. However, the 50-minute Wgasa Bush Line Railway, the highlight of the park, is what everyone heads for first. On slow days the wait usually runs about 20 minutes; when it's crowded you could be waiting twice as long. So it's best to take the train ride first. This will also give you an overview of the entire park and help you decide which animals you wish to return to later. The best strategy is to arrive at the park just as it opens and head immediately for the station. When the ride is over, you can spend the rest of the day leisurely strolling through the park's many gardens, discovering pockets of wildlife around every corner.

One important thing to take into consideration: The San Diego Wild Animal Park is so far inland that temperatures reach the scorching point during late summer and early fall. Generally, the hotter the weather, the less active the animals. If possible, visit anytime from November through May, when the weather is cooler. Or go during the extended nighttime hours from June through August, when the park is open until 10 p.m.

Yuck!!! Giraffes clean their ears and eyeballs with their long, black tongues.

Guest Services   For general park information call 619-234-6541 or 760-747-8702, or write San Diego Wild Animal Park Guest Relations, 15500 San Pasqual Valley Road, Escondido, CA 92027. Lockers, strollers and wheelchair rentals are located just inside the main entrance. The Information Center (619-234-6541), situated north of the Wgasa Bush Line Railway in the administration building, houses Lost & Found and a First Aid station. Major credit cards are accepted at the admission gate, in the gift shops and in some of the eateries. There are ATMs in Mombasa Market, Heart of Africa and in the administration building. An information packet for visitors with disabilities is available at all ticket windows. Animals are not allowed, except for qualified service dogs. Kennels are available for pets.

Getting Around   After entering the park, you'll find yourself in Nairobi Village. This is the main pedestrian area of the park and where you'll find all the shops, restaurants, restrooms and the homes of some of the park's smaller animals. The village, together with the railway, the Heart of Africa experience, the Kilimanjaro Safari Walk and the Animal Shows, are the Wild Animal Park's central attractions.

RAILWAY RIDE   The 50-minute, five-mile Wgasa Bush Line Railway Ride is the core of the Wild Animal Park experience. The tour is a relaxing journey narrated by a knowledgeable guide who successfully mixes factual information with interesting anecdotes.

WHAT TO SEE & DO

The shaded monorail travels through several sections of the park, each designed to simulate a different habitat. First you'll pass through the **Eastern Africa** and **Asian Plains** sections, home to elephants, giraffes, Sumatran tigers and zebras. Watch carefully for Indian rhinos; you may mistake them for large boulders.

Next you'll see the **Asian Waterhole** where European bison and fallow deer live together. Look closely on the other side of the train or you might miss the many goats and sheep living in the **Mountain Habitat**. Camouflage is their best weapon against predators. That and speed: According to the guide they can scale this rocky mountain in under 20 seconds.

In **Southern Africa,** crowned cranes, rhinos, zebras and wildebeests peacefully coexist. To the other side of the train is a smaller habitat called the **Mongolian Steppe**. This area is reserved for a large herd of rare Przewalski's horses. The progenitor of domestic horses, there are only about 500 of these animals left in the world.

Shortly before the conclusion of the rail journey, you'll pass a colony of **Western Lowland Gorillas**. Because the view from the train is largely obscured, you'll want to make sure you visit this enclosure later on foot. These somber beasts are undoubtedly the most popular residents of the park. About a dozen of the creatures loll about on a grassy hillside stretching, rolling on their backs and yawning, giving visitors a frightening display of teeth.

NAIROBI VILLAGE After the rail tour, you'll want to explore the park on foot. Walking trails wind all over the facility, through various habitats and nearly a dozen botanical gardens. After a visit to the gorillas, make your way along the **Bridge of Birds**, a wooden walkway that passes around an aviary.

Continuing through Nairobi Village, walk the path along **Mombasa Lagoon** and the **Congo Fishing Village** for a view of Chilean flamingos, Dalmatian pelicans and shoebill storks. A colony of adorable lemurs is right at home on **Lemur Isle**, in the center of the lagoon.

UP CLOSE AND PERSONAL

How'd you like to get nose to nose with a rhino or eye to eye with an oryx? On a **Wild Animal Park Photo Caravan** anything is possible. Designed for photography buffs, these special tours take visitors into the animal habitats on a flatbed truck for close encounters with gazelles, giraffes, rhinos and more. Visitors have their choice of three tours, ranging from one-and-three-quarters to three-and-a-half hours. The journeys are $98.95 to $145 per person (park members receive a 15 percent discount), but true nature buffs will tell you they're well worth it. The price includes park admission and a species-identification guide. Children must be at least 8 years old (ages 8 through 17 must be accompanied by an adult). Reservations required. ~ 619-718-3050.

Children in particular enjoy the **Petting Kraal**, where they can stroke and feed deer, antelope and gazelle. Next door, the **Animal Care Center** houses newborns that can be seen through large glass windows. Try to be on hand for the 11 a.m. or 4 p.m. feedings. Hundreds of insects, birds, amphibians, plants and reptiles inhabit the indoor rainforest of the **Hidden Jungle**. Visitors can observe these creatures in their natural environment, each performing a vital role in maintaining this 8800-square-foot ecosystem. A springtime favorite among the visitors is the collection of butterflies from rainforests all over the world.

At **Lorikeet Landing** visitors can experience hand-feeding rainbow lorikeets. Lorikeet food is available for purchase. Nairobi Village is also dotted with enclosures containing gibbons, spider monkeys, meerkats and red river hogs. Don't miss the chance to see any of these playful mammals.

HEART OF AFRICA With this attraction, the folks at the San Diego Wild Animal Park have taken their safari concept one giant step closer to the real thing. With lazy pathways winding through 32 acres of animal habitats, Heart of Africa is about the closest thing you'll get to the Serengeti without actually being there; exotic African wildlife seemingly roam as freely as the people. There are more than 200 animals here—cheetahs, rhinos, giraffes and gazelles, to name a few—all ambling together (as they would in the wild) in authentically re-created homes flourishing with exotic African plants. The whole walk takes about an hour, and park staff are on hand at the area's research station, where you'll have your best chance of actually interacting with some animals.

Designers of Heart of Africa have taken great pains to create the feeling of openness, installing camouflaged animal barriers that are largely imperceptible. Though the animals feel within reach, their accessibility is an illusion. Those cheetahs can't exactly come up and eat from your hand (although giraffes do occasionally make their way over to guests to be fed). But with invisible, low-lying boundaries such as trenches and brush-covered fences, it feels as if they can, and the effect is both real and startling.

KILIMANJARO SAFARI WALK This mile-and-three-quarter trek through the eastern portion of the park passes lookout points that offer spectacular views of elephants, giraffes, lions, tigers and zebras. It also meanders through the park's many gardens, including a bed of herbs fragrant with culinary aromas. You can venture into **Tropical Asia**, where hundreds of exotic birds live in the canopy overhead.

The Kilimanjaro Safari Walk ends at the park's far northeast corner. There you'll find a **Fuchsia Garden** as well as a **Bonsai Pavilion** and **Conifer Garden**. Right next door is **Condor Ridge**, one of the few places in the world where it's possible to view these majestic birds. Its elaborately landscaped trails are where you'll find the enormous California birds (their ten-foot wingspans make them the largest birds in North America) for which the area is named, as well as parrots, owls and a bunch of non-airborn critters. The area also features an observation deck with telescopes for a closer look. After this last stop, double back and Nairobi Village is just a short hike away.

ANIMAL SHOWS   The **Bird Show** at Benbough Amphitheater is truly entertaining, with celebrity Amazon parrots that have appeared on the "David Letterman" show. These feathered creatures ham it up onstage, singing "I Left My Heart in San Francisco" and mimicking the sounds of sirens and human laughter. If you have small children along, be sure to catch this show; the tots delight in these crazy bird stunts.

> The Wild Animal Park dispenses six tons of animal food daily at a cost of over $60,000 a month.

The **Elephant Show** takes place on the outskirts of Nairobi Village along the Kilimanjaro Safari Walk. The Asian elephants are the stars of the show, which aims to educate the audience about the natural behavior of these behemoths.

Wild Discoveries is an informal, gather-round question-and-answer session. A trainer brings out a variety of animals, such as foxes, reindeer and parrots, and fields questions about the creatures from onlookers. Wild Discoveries can be heard several times daily at various locations throughout the park.

DINING

Wild Animal Park fare is surprisingly good, a cut above the food served at most other theme parks. It's also apparent that a lot of thought went into creating a scenic atmosphere for each restaurant.

Our hands-down favorite lunch spot is the **Thorn Tree Terrace**. The one-third-pound gourmet hamburgers with onion rings are tasty, and the setting is sublime. Just across a moat from the shady patio tables, a group of playful spider monkeys puts on a lively floor show, swinging from their tails and pouncing on one another. MODERATE.

The **Mombasa Cooker** is another scenic dining spot with a spacious patio overlooking the park's central lagoon. Best meals include the chicken sandwiches and pizza, pasta and stir-fry. MODERATE.

There are half a dozen other snack bars and food stands throughout Nairobi Village. If you're in the mood for a hot dog, head for the **Congo Kitchen**, just north of the lagoon.

San Diego

The San Diego area is not as eccentric and sophisticated as San Francisco, nor as glamorous and fast-paced as Los Angeles. But those who still perceive it as a laidback mecca for beach bums—or as a lunch stop en route to Mexico— are in for a huge surprise.

SEAWORLD AREA One of the nation's largest and most diverse city-owned aquatic recreational areas, and home to SeaWorld, **Mission Bay Park** has something to suit just about everyone's interest. Here, visitors join with residents to enjoy swimming, sailing, windsurfing, waterskiing, fishing, jogging, cycling, golf and tennis. Or perhaps a relaxing day of kite flying and sunbathing. It is a mecca for San Diego's athletic set, a recreational paradise dotted with islands and lagoons and ringed by 27 miles of sandy beaches.

Key locations in this 4600-acre wonderland are as follows: **Dana Landing** and **Quivira Basin** make up the southwest portion of the park. Most boating activities begin here, home to port headquarters and a large marina. Adjacent is **Bonita Cove**, used for swimming, picnicking, softball and volleyball. Mission Boulevard shops, restaurants and recreational equipment rentals are within easy walking distance. **Ventura Cove** houses a large hotel complex, but its sandy beach is open to the public. Calm waters make it a popular swimming spot for small children.

Vacation Isle and **Ski Beach** are easily reached via the bridge on Ingraham Street, which bisects the island. The west side contains public swimming areas, boat rentals and a model-yacht basin. Ski Beach is on the east side and is the favorite spot in the bay for waterskiing. **Fiesta Island** is on the southwest side of the

SIGHTS

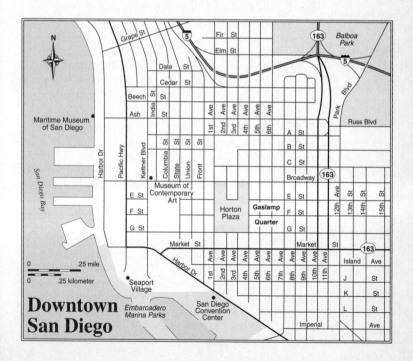

Downtown San Diego

park. It's ringed with soft-sand swimming beaches and laced with jogging, cycling and skating path—a favorite spot for fishing from the quieter coves and for kite flying.

Over on the **East Shore** you'll find landscaped picnic areas, playgrounds, a physical-fitness course, a sandy beach for swimming and the park information center. **De Anza Cove**, at the extreme northeast corner of the park, has a sandy beach for swimming plus a large private campground. **Crown Point Shores** provides a sandy beach, picnic area, nature-study area, physical-fitness course and waterski landing.

Sail Bay and **Riviera Shores** make up the northwest portion of Mission Bay and back up against the apartments and condominiums of Pacific Beach. Sail Bay's beaches aren't the best in the park and are usually submerged during high tides. Riviera Shores has a better beach with waterski areas.

Santa Clara and **El Carmel points** jut out into the western-most side of the bay. Santa Clara Point is of interest to the visitor with its recreation center, tennis courts and softball field. A sandy beach fronts San Juan Cove between the two points.

Just about every facility imaginable can be found somewhere in the park: catamaran and windsurfer rentals, playgrounds and parks, frisbee and golf. For further information contact the **Mission Bay Aquatic Center**. ~ 619-221-8900, fax 619-581-9984.

Not far from Mission Bay Park, the historic, 1925 "Giant Dipper" has come back to life after years of neglect at **Belmont Park**. One of only two West Coast seaside coasters, this beauty is not all the park has to offer. You'll also find a carousel, a video arcade, an enormous indoor swimming pool and a host of shops and eateries along the beach and boardwalk. ~ 3146 Mission Boulevard and West Mission Bay Drive; 619-491-2988; www.bel montpark.com, e-mail info@belmontpark.com.

SAN DIEGO HARBOR   San Diego's beautiful harbor is a notable exception to the rule that big-city waterfronts lack appeal. Here, the city embraces its bay and presents its finest profile along the water.

The best way to see it all is on a harbor tour. Many vessels can be found near Harbor Drive at the foot of Broadway. **San Diego Harbor Excursion** provides leisurely trips around the 22-square-mile harbor, which is colorfully backdropped by commercial and naval vessels as well as the dramatic cityscape. A ferry to Coronado Island from downtown is also operated by Harbor Excursion. Fee. ~ 1050 North Harbor Drive; 619-234-4111, 800-442-7847, fax 619-522-6150; www.sdhe.com. A sunset cruise is offered aboard the 151-foot yacht *Lord Hornblower*. Fee. ~ 1066 North Harbor Drive; 619-234-8687.

All along the cityside of the harbor from the Coast Guard Station to Seaport Village is a lovely landscaped boardwalk called the **Embarcadero**. It offers parks where you can stroll and play, a floating maritime museum and a number of waterfront diversions.

Near the south end of the Embarcadero sits the popular shopping and entertainment complex known as **Seaport Village**. Designed to replicate an early California seaport, it comprises 14 acres of bayfront parks and promenades, shops and galleries. On the south side, overlooking the water, is the 45-foot-high Mukilteo Lighthouse, official symbol of the village, a re-creation of a famous lighthouse in Washington state. Nearby is the Broadway Flying Horses Carousel, a hand-carved, turn-of-the-20th-century model that originally whirled around Coney Island. ~ Kettner Boulevard and West Harbor Drive; 619-235-4013; www.seaportvillage.com.

The **Maritime Museum of San Diego** is composed of three vintage ships. The most familiar is the 1863 *Star of India*, the nation's oldest iron-hulled merchant ship still afloat. Visitors go aboard for a hint of what life was like on the high seas more than a century ago. You can also visit the 1898 ferry *Berkeley*, which helped in the evacuation of San Francisco during the 1906 earthquake, and the 1904 steam yacht *Medea*. Admission. ~ 1306 North Harbor Drive; 619-234-9153, fax 619-234-8345; www.sdmaritime.com.

The Marine Center presents colorful **military reviews** most Fridays. Marching ceremonies begin at exactly 10 a.m. at the Marine Corps Recruiting Depot (619-524-1772). The center may be reached from downtown by going north on Pacific Highway to Barnett Avenue, then left to Gate 1.

The **San Diego Convention Center** looks like an erector set gone mad. An uncontained congeries of flying buttresses, giant tents and curved glass, it is fashioned in the form of a ship, seemingly poised to set sail across San Diego Harbor. This architec-

FLORAL FROLIC

An explosion of color takes place every spring at **The Flower Fields**, just down the road from Legoland. Coordinated displays of Giant Tecolote Ranunculus flowers burst into bloom for approximately six to eight weeks each year, from early March to early May. Rolling hills, covering nearly 50 acres, show off imaginative floral designs and provide plenty of room for kids to run around. After they've tired themselves out, jump on the antique tractor for an old-fashioned spin around the grounds. A morning coffee cart keeps the grownups wide awake, while the weekend snackbar offers lots of goodies (sandwiches, salads, hamburgers and ice cream) for the whole family. Admission. ~ 5704 Paseo Del Norte, Carlsbad; 760-431-0352; www.theflowerfields.com, e-mail info@theflowerfields.com.

tural exclamation mark is certainly worth a drive by or a quick tour. ~ 111 West Harbor Drive; 619-525-5000, fax 619-525-5005; www.soccc.org.

The **Children's Museum of San Diego** offers hands- and mind-on activities for the whole family. At Cora's Rainhouse, kids can work with clay, watch videos or listen to storytellers. The art studio featuring recycled materials is a good place for young people to try their hand at finger painting, mask making and quilting. In the Improv Theater your child will be a star. Every month there are new exhibits and programs. In addition, a gift shop offers toys, games and books the kids will enjoy during their travels. Closed Sunday and Monday. Admission. ~ 200 West Island Avenue; 619-233-5437; www.sdchildrensmuseum.org.

DOWNTOWN SAN DIEGO Within the compact city center there's Horton Plaza, an exciting example of avant-garde urban architecture, and the adjacent Gaslamp Quarter, which reveals how San Diego looked at the peak of its Victorian-era boom in the 1880s.

Horton Plaza is totally unlike any other shopping center. It has transcended its genre in a whimsical, multilevel, open-air, pastel-hued concoction of ramps, escalators, rambling paths, bridges, towers, piazzas, sculptures, fountains and live greenery. Mimes, minstrels and fortunetellers meander about the six-block complex performing for patrons.

Horton Plaza was inspired by European shopping streets and districts such as the Plaka of Athens, the Ramblas of Barcelona and Portobello Road in London. In all, 14 different styles, ranging from Renaissance to postmodern, are employed in the design. ~ Bounded by Broadway and G Street and 1st and 4th avenues.

The **Gaslamp Quarter** is one of America's largest national historic districts, covering a 16-block strip along 4th, 5th and 6th avenues from Broadway to the waterfront. Architecturally, the Quarter reveals some of the finest Victorian-style commercial buildings constructed in San Diego during the 50 years between the Civil War and World War I. It was this area, along 5th Avenue, that became San Diego's first main street. The city's core began on the bay where Alonzo Horton first built a wharf in 1869.

During its redevelopment, the city added wide, brick sidewalks, period streetlamps, trees and benches. In all, more than 100 grand Victorian buildings have been restored to their original splendor.

BALBOA PARK Home of the renowned San Diego Zoo, Balboa Park came about in 1868 when city fathers with a view to the future set aside 1400 acres for the public. The park's eventual development, and most of its lovely Spanish Baroque buildings, came as the result of two world's fairs—the Panama–California

Exposition of 1915–16 and the California–Pacific International
Exposition of 1935–36.

Today, Balboa Park ranks among the largest and finest of
America's city parks. Wide avenues and walkways curve through
luxurious subtropical foliage leading to nine major
museums, three art galleries, four theaters, picnic
groves, the zoo, a golf course and countless other
recreation facilities. Its verdant grounds teem with
cyclists, joggers, skaters, picnickers, weekend artists
and museum mavens.

> The Spreckels Organ in
> Balboa Park has 4416
> pipes, making it one of
> the world's largest
> outdoor instru-
> ments.

The main entrance is from 6th Avenue onto Laurel
Street, which becomes El Prado as you cross Cabrillo
Bridge. Begin your visit at the **Balboa Park Visitors Center**,
on the northeast corner of Plaza de Panama. They provide free
pamphlets and maps on the park. ~ 619-239-0512; www.balboa
park.org.

From here you can stroll about, taking in Balboa Park's main
attractions. To the right, as you head east on the pedestrian-only
section of El Prado, is the **Casa de Balboa**. It houses the **San Diego
Model Railroad Museum**, which features the largest collection of
small-gauge trains in the world. Closed Monday. Admission. ~
619-696-0199, fax 619-696-0239; www.sdmodelrailroadm.com.

Continuing east to the fountain, you'll see the **Reuben H. Fleet
Science Center** on your right. Among the park's finest attractions,
it features one of the largest planetariums and most impressive
multimedia theaters in the country. The hands-on galleries contain various exhibits and displays dealing with modern phenom-
ena. Admission. ~ 619-238-1233, fax 619-658-5771; www.
rhfleet.org.

Located just across the courtyard is the **San Diego Natural
History Museum** with displays devoted mostly to the Southern
California environment. There are also fossils (whales, dinosaurs,
land mammals) galore. Admission. ~ 619-232-3821, fax 619-232-
0248; www.sdnhm.org.

Going back along El Prado, take a moment to admire your
reflection in the Lily Pond. With the old, latticed **Botanical Building** in the background, the scene is a favorite among photographers.
The fern collection inside is equally striking. Admission.

The grandest of all Balboa Park structures, built as the centerpiece for the 1915 Panama–California Exposition, is the 200-foot
Spanish Renaissance **California Tower**. The **Museum of Man**, at
the base of the tower, is a must for anthropology buffs and those
interested in American Indian cultures. Admission. ~ 619-239-
2001, fax 619-239-2749; www.museumofman.org.

Another museum not to be missed is the **San Diego Aerospace Museum** several blocks south of the plaza. It contains over
65 aircraft including a replica of Charles Lindbergh's famous *Spirit*

of St. Louis, the original of which was built in San Diego. Admission. ~ 619-234-8291, fax 619-233-4526; www.aerospacemu seum.org, e-mail sdam.admin@usa.net.

Sports fans will want to take in the **Hall of Champions Sports Museum** in the historic Federal Building. It houses the Breitbard Hall of Fame and exhibits that feature world-class San Diego athletes from more that 40 sports. The museum also has an interactive sports center. Admission. ~ 2131 Pan-American Plaza; 619-234-2544, fax 619-234-4543; www.sandiegosports.com.

Balboa Park's museums charge an admission fee, but every Tuesday select museums can be visited free.

CORONADO   An isolated and exclusive community in San Diego Bay, Coronado is almost an island, connected to the mainland only by the graceful San Diego–Coronado Bay Bridge and by a long, narrow sandspit called the Silver Strand.

Once known as the "Nickel Snatcher," the Coronado Ferry for years crossed the waters of San Diego Harbor between the Embarcadero and Coronado. All for five cents each way. That fare is history, of course, but the 1940-vintage, double-deck *Silvergate* still plies the waters. The **San Diego Bay Ferry** leaves from the Bay Café on North Harbor Drive at the foot of Broadway and docks 15 minutes later at the Ferry Landing Marketplace on the Coronado side. Fee. ~ 619-234-4111, fax 619-522-6150; www.sdhe.com.

The town's main attraction is the **Hotel del Coronado**, a red-roofed, Victorian-style, wooden wonder, a century-old National Historic Landmark. Explore the old palace and its manicured grounds, discovering the intricate corridors and cavernous public rooms. It was Elisha Babcock's dream when he purchased 4100 acres of barren, wind-blown peninsula in 1888 to build a hotel that would be the "talk of the Western world." Realizing Babcock's dream from the beginning, it attracted such famous guests as Thomas Edison, Robert Todd Lincoln, Henry Ford and a dozen U.S. presidents. ~ 1500 Orange Avenue; 619-435-6611, fax 619-522-8262; www.hoteldel.com.

POINT LOMA   The Point Loma peninsula forms a high promontory that shelters San Diego Bay from the Pacific Ocean. It also

HERITAGE PARK

On the outskirts of Old Town lies **Heritage Park**, an area dedicated to the preservation of the city's Victorian past. Seven historic, 1880s-era houses and an old Jewish temple have been moved to the hillside site and beautifully restored. ~ Juan and Harney streets.

provided Juan Rodríguez Cabrillo an excellent place from which to contemplate his 16th-century discovery of California. Naturally, **Cabrillo National Monument**, featuring a statue of the navigator, stands facing his landing site at Ballast Point. The sculpture itself, a gift from Cabrillo's native Portugal, isn't very impressive, but the view is outstanding. With the bay and city spread below, you can often see all the way from Mexico to the La Jolla mesa. The visitors center includes a small museum. The nearby **Old Point Loma Lighthouse** (admission) guided ships from 1855 to 1891. ~ 1800 Cabrillo Memorial Drive; 619-557-5450, fax 619-557-5469; www.nps.gov.cabr.

On the ocean side of the peninsula is **Whale Watch Lookout Point** where, during winter months, you can observe the southward migration of California gray whales. Close by is a superb network of tidepools.

OLD TOWN AND MISSION VALLEY   Back in 1769, Spanish explorer Gaspar de Portolá selected a hilltop site overlooking the bay for a mission that would begin the European settlement of California. A town soon spread out at the foot of the hill, complete with plaza, church, school and the tile-roofed adobe *casas* of California's first families.

Some of the buildings and relics of the early era have been brought back to life at **Old Town San Diego State Historic Park**. Lined with adobe restorations and brightened with colorful shops, the six blocks of Old Town provide a lively and interesting opportunity for visitors to stroll, shop and sightsee. ~ 4002 Wallace Street; 619-220-5422, fax 619-220-5421.

The park sponsors a free walking tour at 11 a.m and 2 p.m. daily, or you can easily do it on your own by picking up the *Old San Diego Gazette*. The paper, which comes out once a month and includes a map of the area, is free at local stores. You can also hop aboard the **Old Town Trolley** for a delightful, two-hour, narrated tour of Old Town and a variety of other highlights in San Diego and Coronado. The trolley makes eight stops, and you're allowed to get on and off all day long. Fee. ~ 4040 Twiggs Street; 619-298-8687, fax 619-298-3404; www.historic tours.com.

As it has for over a century, everything focuses on **Old Town Plaza**. Before 1872, this was the social and recreational center of the town; political meetings, barbecues, dances, shoot-outs and bullfights all happened here. ~ Couts and San Diego avenues.

Shoppers seem to gravitate in large numbers toward the north side of the plaza to browse the unusual shops in **Bazaar del Mundo**. Built in circular fashion around a tropical courtyard, this complex also houses several restaurants.

The original mission and Spanish Presidio once stood high on a hill behind Old Town. This site of California's birthplace now

Text continued on page 196.

Legoland

After mountains of ice cream and rivers of chocolate, a kid's biggest fantasy is probably the existence of a giant-sized toy paradise. Well, one out of three ain't bad. Legoland is a life-size box of these classic childhood play things. Colorful bricks are everywhere—in scale-model cities, make-believe jungles, medieval castles and, of course, scads of places where you can pull up a chair and build your own landscape.

Though it's geared toward little ones (roughly ages 12 and under), parents will like it, too. Unlike passive-style offerings at most theme parks (and despite bells and whistles, most amusement parks are really a kind of trumped-up armchair experience), Legoland is—if you'll pardon the overused term—an interactive experience. To be sure, there's the occasional roller coaster and boat ride. But by and large, this is a place to *do* things—drive a miniature car, pedal a multiperson cycle or steer a boat.

Dozens of rides are spread across the 128-acre park that starts with—what else?—**The Beginning**. Here's where you'll find a market for snacks and all of your services—First Aid, Stroller and Wheelchair Rentals, Guest Services, Lost Parents, etc. You will, however, want to maneuver your child around The Big Shop. As at all theme parks, Legoland is booby-trapped with merchandise outlets everywhere, the biggest of which is, you guessed it, The Big Shop.

Once through The Beginning, your best bet will be to turn left at the lake. Consider it a time-saving detour; attractions to the right can hang up your group for the day before you've made it to a single ride (more on that later).

Traveling this path will take you first to **The Ridge**. Here's where you'll find two of the park's most eye-catching features: the Kid Power Tower (haul yourself and a friend to the top with a rope and then free-fall back down) and the Sky Cruiser (Dr. Seuss–looking contraptions in which you can pedal a lap around a raised track).

Farther on, the **Village Green** offers a safari through a jungle of Lego animals (complete with sounds), a Water Works wet play area, and a couple of theaters. Also in Village Green, Duplo PlayTown and the Duplo Train cater to the youngest children in the park (roughly under 5).

Fun Town, the next step on your circuit, is a definite highlight. Two Driving Schools (one for children 6 through 12, a junior version for ages 3 through 5) put kids behind the wheel of colorful (and slow-moving) Lego mobiles that they can actually gas, break and steer. The junior circuit travels a simple circle. The older-kids version requires attention to stoplights and right of way—and drivers may even find themselves in that ubiquitous Southern California occurrence—the traffic jam. Other attractions to look for in Fun Town include the Adventurer's Club (a Lego rainforest), Skipper School (a boating opportunity) and the Flight Squadron ride.

Medieval princes and princesses will feel positively royal on **Castle Hill**. Apart from the fact that it's the only area with a roller coaster in it (the pint-sized Dragon), it has some of the park's best scenery, not to mention a cute show featuring members of the "court." There's also the absolutely adorable Royal Joust ride. If your kids have a penchant for playing dress-up at home, you might want to meander through the unmatchable King's Treasure shop.

Make sure to leave plenty of time to appreciate the marvelous miniatures at **Miniland**. These elaborate scale-model cities—produced by tireless (and obviously patient) artisans with millions of Legos—are remarkable for their attention to detail. Moving parts include a shark in a shipwreck, a marching band outside the Capitol Building in Washington, D.C., and police cars patrolling the streets of New York. Looking is a treat in and of itself, but there are also buttons to push to make the gadgets run.

Finally, end your visit in the **Imagination Zone**. Though there is one ride here—the diabolical Aquazone Wave Racers, where riders dodge water cannons fired by their loved ones—the hallmark is Lego play. Build and program computerized Lego models (this one is by reservation, so ask when you enter the park), tinker with Lego software, or just find a corner and create masterpieces with the bottomless supply of Lego bricks. As mentioned earlier, this is a good spot to wrap up your visit—or perhaps stop for a midday respite—since once kids get going, they may never want to leave.

Throughout the park, food is another of the features that sets Legoland apart from other amusement parks. Fresh pastas at Ristorante Brickolini's (Village Green) are surprisingly tasty and a world away from your average theme-park hot dog. Also look for barbecue, salads and, the all-important theme-park staple, ice cream.

If there's a down side to this booming Lego-opolis, it's crowds. During school vacations, lines can get painfully long. If it's really busy, you might want to use the middle of the day for non-line attractions such as MiniLand. Better yet, bring little ones when school is still in session, or wear a sweater and come during the colder winter months. ~ Take the Cannon Road exit off Route 5. Go east, following signs to Lego Drive; 877-534-6526; www.legoland.com.

houses **Junípero Serra Museum**, a handsome, Spanish Colonial structure containing an excellent collection of Mexican and Spanish artifacts from the state's pioneer days and relics from the Royal Presidio dig sites. Open Friday through Sunday. Admission. ~ Presidio Drive; 619-297-3258, fax 619-297-3281; www.san diegohistory.com.

Within five years after Father Serra dedicated the first of California's 21 missions, the site had become much too small for the growing numbers it served. So **Mission San Diego de Alcala** was moved from Presidio Hill six miles east into Mission Valley. Surrounded now by shopping centers and suburban homes, the "Mother of Missions" retains its simple but striking white-adobe facade topped by a graceful campanile. There's a museum containing mission records in Junípero Serra's handwriting and a lovely courtyard with gnarled pepper trees. Admission. ~ 10818 San Diego Mission Road; 619-281-8449; www.missionsandiego.com.

San Diego County, measuring 4261 square miles, is as large as Connecticut.

LA JOLLA   Another center of interest lies at the northern end of San Diego in the luxurious town of La Jolla. The best beaches are here, stretching from the ritzy La Jolla Shores to the scientific sands at Scripps Beach. The latter strand fronts Scripps Institute of Oceanography, the oldest institution in the nation devoted to oceanography and the home of the **Birch Aquarium at Scripps**. Here you will find 45 marine-life tanks, breathtaking exhibits of coastal underwater habitats, a manmade tidepool, interactive displays for children and adults, and displays illustrating recent advances in oceanographic research. Admission. ~ 2300 Expedition Way; 858-534-3474, fax 858-534-7114; www.aquarium.ucsd.edu.

LODGING   **SEAWORLD AREA**   Pacific Beach boasts the San Diego County motel with the most character of all. **Crystal Pier Hotel** is a throwback to the 1930s, and this is only fitting because that's when this quaint-looking assemblage of 29 cottages on Crystal Pier was built. This blue-and-white woodframe complex, perched over the waves, features tiny little cottages. Each comes with a kitchen and a patio over the sea. A unique discovery that's ideally located for family beachcombing and sandcastle building. ~ 4500 Ocean Boulevard; 858-483-6983, 800-748-5894, fax 858-483-6811. ULTRA-DELUXE.

One particularly pretty four-unit condominium, **Ventanas al Mar**, overlooks the ocean in Mission Beach. Its contemporary two- and three-bedroom units feature fireplaces, jacuzzi tubs, kitchens and washer-dryers. They sleep as many as eight people. In the summer, these rent by the week only. Families with small kids will appreciate fenced patios and the resort's proximity to the waterfront as well as a wide variety of restaurants and shops. ~ 3631

Ocean Front Walk; 858-488-1580, 800-869-7858; www.bill luther.com, e-mail info@billluther.com. ULTRA-DELUXE.

Most of the hotels within sprawling Mission Bay Park are upscale resorts in the deluxe to ultra-deluxe price range. But there's relief to be found at the **Western Shores**, located just across the street from Mission Bay Golf Course. This quiet, 40-unit court simply can't be matched for value anywhere in the area. ~ 4345 East Mission Bay Drive; 858-273-1121, fax 858-273-2944. BUDGET.

Only one Mission Bay resort stands out as unique—the **San Diego Paradise Point Resort**. Over 40 acres of lush gardens, lagoons and white-sand beach surround the villas and cottages of this 462-room resort. Except for some fancy suites, room decor is basic and pleasant, with quality furnishings. But guests don't spend much time in their rooms anyway. At Paradise Point there's more than a mile of beach, catamaran rentals, bike rentals, a fitness center, six tennis courts, six pools, two restaurants and an 18-hole putting course. And if that's not enough to satisfy, this self-contained paradise also boasts a swim-up bar, a fitness center, a sauna, a jacuzzi and a sand volleyball court. If you're seeking a complete family resort, look no further. During Easter week and summer the day camp program for children three to twelve features morning and afternoon recreation as well as evening movies. ~ 1404 West Vacation Road; 858-274-4630, 800-344-2626, fax 858-581-5929. ULTRA-DELUXE.

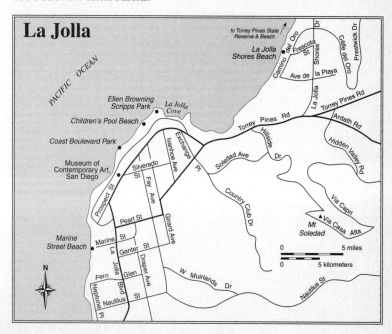

DOWNTOWN SAN DIEGO   The best value for your dollar among reasonably priced downtown hotels is the 67-room **Comfort Inn**. The rooms feature wood furniture, designer color schemes and high-grade carpeting. Families will appreciate the convenience of microwaves and refrigerators in the larger rooms. The inn has a pool-sized jacuzzi and serves a continental breakfast. Conveniently located next to Balboa Park, a few blocks from the city center. Children 18 years old and under stay free. ~ 719 Ash Street; 619-232-2525, 800-228-5150, fax 619-687-3024. MODERATE.

A recommended midtown hotel is **Best Western Bayside Inn**. Small enough (122 rooms) to offer some degree of personalized service, this modern highrise promises nearly all the niceties you would pay extra for at more prestigious downtown hotels, including a harbor view. Furnishings and amenities are virtually at par with those found in the typical Hilton or Sheraton. There's a pool and spa, plus a restaurant and cocktail lounge. ~ 555 West Ash Street; 619-233-7500, 800-341-1818; www.baysideinn.com, e-mail tichotels@sandiego.com. MODERATE.

No downtown hotel has a more colorful past than the **Horton Grand Hotel**. This 132-room Victorian gem is actually two old hotels that were lavishly reconstructed and linked by an atrium-lobby and courtyard. The 1880s theme is faithfully executed, in the hotel's antique-furnished rooms, each of which has a fireplace. A concierge and afternoon tea (served Friday and Saturday) combine with friendly service and perfect location to make this one of the city's best hotel values. ~ 311 Island Avenue; 619-544-1886, 800-542-1886; www.hortongrand.com, e-mail horton@connect net.com. DELUXE TO ULTRA-DELUXE.

CORONADO   Coronado has long been a playground of the rich and famous, and the city's hotel rates reflect its ritzy heritage. **El Cordova Hotel** is in the heart of Coronado. Originally built as a private mansion in 1902, El Cordova's moderate size (40 rooms) and lovely Spanish-hacienda architecture make it a relaxing get-

AUTHOR FAVORITE

Ensconced in a plain-vanilla, two-story former church building, the **Hostelling International—Point Loma** is filled with 60 economy-minded guests almost every night in the summer. Comfortable bunk beds are grouped in 13 rooms housing from two to eight people in youth-hostel fashion. Family and private rooms are also available, and there is a common kitchen and dining area. The courtyard has ping-pong and other recreational activities. ~ 3790 Udall Street, Point Loma; 619-223-4778; www.hiayh.org, e-mail hisdptloma@aol.com. BUDGET.

away spot. A pool and patio restaurant are added features. Family suites are equipped with kitchenettes. The kids will love the location, just half a block from Coronado Beach. ~ 1351 Orange Avenue; 619-435-4131, 800-229-2032, fax 619-435-0632; www. elcordovahotel.com. DELUXE TO ULTRA-DELUXE.

Nothing can detract from the glamour of the **Hotel del Coronado**. With its turrets, cupolas and gingerbread facade, this Victorian landmark is one of the great hotels of California. The last in a proud line of extravagant seaside resorts, the Hotel del Coronado has long been the lodging of choice for United States presidents and Hollywood stars. The 691-room Hotel "Del" has two pools, a long stretch of beach, three tennis courts, a first-class health club and a gallery of shops. On one of the San Diego area's finest waterfronts, this resort is particularly appealing for children. Special programs offer day-long activities for children and teens, including games and beach sports. ~ 1500 Orange Avenue; 619-522-8000, 800-468-3533, fax 619-522-8238; www.hoteldel.com. ULTRA-DELUXE.

The **Coronado Victorian House** is quite possibly the only hotel anywhere to include dance, exercise and gourmet cooking classes in a night's stay. Located in an 1894 historic landmark building near the beach and downtown Coronado, the decor of this seven-room bed and breakfast includes Persian rugs, stained-glass windows and private baths with clawfoot tubs and jacuzzis. Those guests not interested in the extracurricular activities are invited to relax and enjoy such home-cooked specialties as baklava, stuffed grape leaves and homemade yogurt. Two-night minimum. ~ 1000 8th Street; 619-435-2200, 888-299-2822, fax 619-435-4760. ULTRA-DELUXE.

LA JOLLA   Like a Monopoly master, La Jolla possesses the lion's share of excellent accommodations in the San Diego area. Understandably, there are very few budget hotels in this fashionable village by the sea; only a few, in fact, offer affordably priced rooms. Among that scarce number, one stands out as the best value. **Sands of La Jolla** is a small, 39-room motel on a busy thoroughfare. Rooms are not exactly designer showcases, but they are tastefully appointed and neatly maintained. Special two-room family suites feature kitchenettes with microwaves. The kids will enjoy splashing in the pool. ~ 5417 La Jolla Boulevard; 858-459-3336, 800-643-0530, fax 858-454-0922. MODERATE.

Smack dab in the Village is the **Empress Hotel**, a five-story L-shaped building set on a quiet street just a stone's throw from both the beach and the bustle of Prospect Street. A contemporary establishment blending Victorian and European boutique styles, its 67 spacious rooms and suites offer amenities such as hair dryers, coffeemakers, dataports, mini-fridges, and in-room safes; two "Green" suites have filtered air and water. If you're looking to splash out, you probably can't get any fancier than one of the two jacuzzi suites outfitted with a baby grand piano and ocean views. There are also fitness facilities, a sauna, a spa, and a restaurant. Enjoy complimentary continental breakfast on the flower-lined patio. ~ 7766 Fay Avenue; 858-454-3001, 888-369-9900, fax 858-454-6387; www.empress-hotel.com, e-mail info@empress-hotel.com. ULTRA-DELUXE.

Tucked away on the north fringe of the village is **Andrea Villa Inn**, a classy-looking, 49-unit motel that packs more amenities than some resorts. Awaiting you are a pool, spa and continental breakfast service. The rooms are spacious and professionally decorated with quality furniture. Kitchenettes are available. Andrea Villa is located just five blocks from the beach and one block from a city park that's great for kids. ~ 2402 Torrey Pines Road; 858-459-3311, 800-411-2141, fax 858-459-1320; www.andreavilla.com, e-mail info@andrea villa.com. DELUXE.

Numerous movies, including *Some Like It Hot*, were filmed at the Hotel del Coronado.

La Jolla's only true beachfront hotel is **Sea Lodge on La Jolla Shores Beach**. Designed and landscaped to resemble an old California hacienda, this 128-room retreat overlooks the Pacific on a mile-long beach. With its stuccoed arches, terra-cotta roofs, ceramic tilework, fountains and flowers, Sea Lodge offers a relaxing, south-of-the-border setting. Rooms are large and fittingly appointed with southwestern-style furnishings. Most feature balconies, some have kitchenettes and all have access to the usual amenities including pool and tennis courts. Adjacent surf shops that rent boogieboards make this laidback resort popular with families. ~ 8110 Camino del Oro; 858-459-8271, 800-237-5211, fax 858-456-9346; www.sealodge.com. ULTRA-DELUXE.

DINING   **SEAWORLD AREA** Critic's choice for the Pacific Beach area's best omelettes is **Broken Yolk Café**. Choose from nearly 30 of these eggy creations or invent your own. There are soups, sandwiches and salads, too. Pancakes, oatmeal, quesadillas and hamburgers are featured on the children's menu. Breakfast and lunch only. ~ 1851 Garnet Avenue; 858-270-0045, fax 858-270-4745. BUDGET.

DOWNTOWN SAN DIEGO Attracting attention has never been a problem for the **Corvette Diner**. Cool 1950s music, a soda fountain (complete with resident jerks), rock-and-roll memorabilia, dancing waitresses and a classy Corvette have proven a magnetic formula. Simple "blue-plate" diner fare features meat loaf, chicken-fried steak and hefty hamburgers. A special kids' menu offers spaghetti, baby burgers, corn dogs, grilled cheese and peanut-butter-and-jelly sandwiches served with soft drink or milk and an ice cream bar. Young people eager to catch up on their mid-20th-century musical history can place their requests with the resident deejay any evening. In addition, a magician performs on Tuesday and Wednesday, and on Friday and Saturday a guy does balloon tricks. ~ 3946 5th Avenue; phone/fax 619-542-1001; www.cohn restaurants.com. BUDGET.

Everyone likes the warm, friendly atmosphere of a real family restaurant like **Hob Nob Hill**. Here's a place where the waitresses call the kids "hon" and remind them to finish their veggies. Favorites are waffles, homemade breads, chicken and dumplings, potatoes with gravy, lamb shanks and prime rib. Silver-dollar pancakes, burgers, grilled cheese, turkey sandwiches and fish and chips are on the kid's menu. Breakfast is served all day. Wholesome, tasty food. ~ 2271 1st Avenue; 619-239-8176. BUDGET TO MODERATE.

Visitors to Horton Plaza are bombarded with dining opportunities. But for those who can resist the temptation to chow down on pizza, french fries and enchiladas at nearby fast-food shops, there is a special culinary reward. On the plaza's top level sits **Panda Inn**. Here the plush, contemporary design alludes only subtly to Asia with a scattering of classic artwork. But the menu is all-Chinese. Lunch and dinner menus together present more than 100 dishes. Dine on the glassed-in veranda for a great view of the harbor. ~ 506 Horton Plaza; 619-233-7800. MODERATE.

For decades, San Diegans have enjoyed the authentic Mexican dishes at **Chuey's**. Nestled in the shadow of Coronado Bridge, it draws crowds with its great tacos, made the authentic way, crammed with juicy string beef and heaped with grated Mexican cheese. You can also get American fare such as chicken-fried steak and liver and onions here. ~ 1894 Main Street; 619-234-6937, fax 619-235-1816. BUDGET TO MODERATE.

◄ HIDDEN

CORONADO **Peohe's** at the Ferry Landing Marketplace is primarily praised for its panoramic views of San Diego Bay and for its tropical decor. The aqua-accented dining room features green palms, and the children will get a kick out of dining next to rushing cascades of water flowing into ponds of live fish. The dinner menu is mostly fresh fish plus lobster, shrimp and scallops. There are also prime rib and lamb. Featured on the children's menu are fish, chicken, pasta and hamburger plates. ~ 1201 1st Street; 619-437-4474; www.peohes.com, e-mail info@peohes.com. MODERATE TO DELUXE.

POINT LOMA A marine view and whirling ceiling fans at **Humphrey's by the Bay** suggest Casablanca. California coastal cuisine is the fare, which means lots of fresh seafood. Breakfast, lunch and dinner are served. The children's menu features seafood, chicken and that old standby, cheeseburgers. ~ Adjacent to the Half Moon Inn, 2241 Shelter Island Drive, Point Loma;

619-224-3577, fax 619-224-9438; www.humphreysbythebay.com. DELUXE TO ULTRA-DELUXE.

OLD TOWN AND MISSION VALLEY   Mexican food and atmosphere abound in Old Town, especially in the popular Bazaar del Mundo, a great spot for family dining. Two restaurants lure a steady stream of diners into festive, flowered courtyards. **Casa de Pico** is a favorite place to sit and munch nachos. Mexican entrées are served outside on the patio or in one of the hacienda-style dining rooms. Special kids' plates offer a choice of chicken flautas, burritos, tacos, quesadillas or beef taquitos with rice or beans. ~ 2754 Calhoun Street; 619-296-3267, fax 619-296-3113. BUDGET TO MODERATE.

Next door, in a magnificent hacienda built in 1829, **Casa de Bandini** has cuisine that's a bit more refined. Seafood is good here, especially the crab enchiladas. Mariachis often play at both restaurants. There's also a children's menu offering specialties like chicken enchiladas and beef tacos. ~ 2754 Calhoun Street; 619-297-8211, fax 619-296-2557. MODERATE.

HIDDEN ►

Less than a mile from Old Town lies an excellent ethnic takeout shop that few visitors ever find. **El Indio** opened in 1940 as a family-operated *tortillería*, then added an informal restaurant serving quesadillas, enchiladas, tostadas, burritos, tacos, and taquitos. Quality homemade Mexican food at Taco Bell prices; you can sit indoors, out on the patio, or order to go. Open for breakfast, lunch, and dinner. ~ 3695 India Street; 619-299-0333, fax 619-542-0985; www.elindio.net. BUDGET.

LA JOLLA   Illuminated only by the flickering of candles and the incandescent glow of fish tanks, the **Manhattan** at the Empress Hotel features cozy booths, boisterous patrons, and a singing maître d', successfully replicating a New York City family-style Italian restaurant. Popular dishes include cannelloni, veal marsala, and chicken piccata; in addition there are wonderful caesar salads and tiramisu. No lunch Saturday or Sunday. ~ Empress Hotel, 7766 Fay Avenue; 858-459-0700, fax 858-454-4741. MODERATE TO ULTRA-DELUXE.

HIDDEN ►

If, during your shopping foray down Girard Avenue, you come across a line of locals snaking out of a small, unassuming eatery, you've no doubt reached **Girard Gourmet**. You may have to wait to partake of the deli goods (salads, quiches, sandwiches, pastries), but it's worth it. Take it to go, or dine out on the sidewalk or inside in an alpine-like setting. ~ 7837 Girard Avenue; 858-454-3321, fax 858-454-2325. BUDGET.

BEACHES & PARKS

PACIFIC BEACH PARK   At its south end, "PB" is a major gathering place, its boardwalk crowded with teens and assorted rowdies, but a few blocks north, just before Crystal Pier, the boardwalk becomes a quieter concrete promenade that follows scenic, sloping cliffs. The beach widens here and the crowd becomes more family oriented. The surf is moderate and fine for swimming and bodysurfing. Pier and surf fishing are great for corbina and surf perch. South of the pier Ocean Boulevard becomes a pedestrian-only mall with a bike path, benches and picnic tables. Amenities include restrooms, lifeguards and restaurants. ~ Located near Grand Avenue and Pacific Beach Drive.

MISSION BEACH PARK 🚲 🏊 🏖 The wide, sandy beach at the southern end is a favorite haunt of high schoolers and college students. The hot spot is at the foot of Capistrano Court. A paved boardwalk runs along the beach and is busy with bicyclists, joggers and roller skaters. Farther north, up around the old Belmont Park roller coaster, the beach grows narrower and the surf rougher. The crowd tends to get that way, too, with heavy-metal teens, sailors and bikers hanging out along the sea wall, ogling and sometimes harassing the bikini set. This is the closest San Diego comes to Los Angeles' colorful but funky Venice Beach. Facilities include restrooms, lifeguards and a boardwalk lined with restaurants and beach rentals. Surfing is popular along the jetty. ~ Located along Mission Boulevard north of West Mission Bay Drive.

OCEAN BEACH 🏊 🏖 🎣 🛶 Where you toss down your towel at "OB" will probably depend as much on your age as your interests. Surfers, sailors and what's left of the hippie crowd hang out around the pier; farther north, where the surf is milder and the beach wider, families and retired folks can be found sunbathing and strolling. At the far north end is San Diego's first and only dog beach, complete with a doggie drinking fountain. There are picnic areas, restrooms and restaurants. Fishing is good from the surf or the fishing pier. Swimming and surfing is very popular here. ~ Take Ocean Beach Freeway (Route 8) west until it ends; turn left onto Sunset Cliffs Boulevard, then right on Voltaire Street; 858-581-9976, fax 858-581-9956.

BAY WATCH

De Anza Cove, at the extreme northeast corner of Mission Bay Park, has a sandy beach for swimming plus the finest and largest of San Diego's commercial campgrounds, **Campland on the Bay**, featuring 600 hookup sites for RVs, vans, tents and boats. A marina (858-581-4224) rents pedal boats, kayaks, windsurfers, pontoon boats and other seaworthy craft. Rates range from $55 to $275 per night; there's a $4 extra-person fee for more than four people per site. ~ 2211 Pacific Beach Drive; 800-422-9386; www.campland.com.

SILVER STRAND STATE BEACH 🏊 🐟 This two-mile strip of fluffy white sand fronts a narrow isthmus separating the Pacific Ocean and San Diego Bay. It was named for tiny silver sea shells found in abundance along the shore. The water here is shallow and fairly calm on the ocean side, making it a good swimming beach. Things are even calmer and the water much warmer on the bay shore. Silver Strand State Beach is also popular for surf fishing and shell hunting. Facilities include picnic areas, restrooms, lifeguards (summer only), showers and food concessions (summer only). Day-use fee, $4. ~ Located on Route 75 (Silver Strand Boulevard) and Coronado Caves Boulevard between Imperial Beach and Coronado; phone/fax 619-435-5184.

▲ There are 138 sites for RVs and trailers (no hookups); $16 per night.

TORREY PINES STATE RESERVE AND BEACH 🏃 🏊 🏄 🐟 A long, wide, sandy stretch adjacent to Los Peñasquitos Lagoon and Torrey Pines State Reserve, this beach is highly visible from the highway and therefore heavily used. It is popular for sunning, swimming, surf fishing, volleyball and sunset barbecues. Nearby trails lead through the reserves with their lagoons, rare trees and abundant birdlife. The beach is patrolled year-round, but lifeguards are on duty only in summer. Restrooms are available. Surfers might want to steer clear of this beach because there are powerful peaks. Day-use fee, $2 per vehicle. ~ Located just south of Carmel Valley Road, Del Mar; 858-755-2063, fax 858-509-0981; www.torreypine.org, e-mail torreypines@ixpres.com.

SCRIPPS BEACH 🏃 🦭 With coastal bluffs above, narrow sand beach below and rich tidepools offshore, this is a great strand for beachcombers. Two **underwater reserves** as well as museum displays at the Scripps Institution of Oceanography are among the attractions. There are museum facilities at Scripps Institution. ~ Scripps Institution is located at the 8600 block of La Jolla Shores Drive in La Jolla. You can park at Kellogg Park–La Jolla Shores Beach and walk north to Scripps.

KELLOGG PARK–LA JOLLA SHORES BEACH 🏊 🏄 The sand is wide and the swimming is easy at La Jolla Shores; so, naturally, the beach is covered with bodies whenever the sun appears. Just to the east is Kellogg Park, an ideal place for a picnic, swimming and surfing. There are restrooms, a playground and lifeguards. ~ Off Camino del Oro and Costa Boulevard.

▼▼▼▼▼▼▼▼▼▼▼▼▼▼

Outdoor Adventures

SPORT-FISHING

The lure of sportfishing attracts thousands of enthusiasts to San Diego every year. Yellowtail, sea bass, bonito and barracuda are the local favorites, with marlin and tuna the prime objectives for multiday charters. Most outfitters provide bait and rent tackle.

Seaforth Sportfishing uses 36- to 85-foot boats for their runs. Longer trips in summer head out to Mexican waters for albacore. ~ 1717 Quivira Road, Mission Bay; 619-224-3383; www.seaforthlanding.com. **Islandia Sportfishing** offers trips for albacore, mackerel and skipjack. ~ 1551 West Mission Bay Drive, Mission Bay; 619-222-1164; www.islandiasport.com. **H & M Landing** arranges half-day jaunts to local kelp beds or 18-day expeditions past the tip of Baja for giant yellowfin tuna. ~ 2803 Emerson Street, Point Loma; 619-222-1144; www.hmlanding.com. **Point Loma Sportfishing** operates a fleet of ten boats. Their daytrip goes down to Mexico for tuna. ~ 1403 Scott Street, Point Loma; 619-223-1627; www.pointlomas portfishing.com. Also in Point Loma is **Fisherman's Landing**, which takes groups of 6 to 35 on fishing excursions. The 23-day charter winds up in Cabo San Lucas. ~ 2838 Garrison Street, Point Loma; 619-222-0391; www.fishermanslanding.com.

With a population of over one million, San Diego is the sixth-largest city in the United States.

The stately progress of our fellow mammalian creatures in migration is a wonderful sight to behold. A free whale-watching station at Cabrillo National Monument on Point Loma features a glassed-in observatory. To get an even closer look at these mammoth cetaceans, book a charter with one of the many whale-watching companies; most outfitters guarantee marine sightings. The season generally runs from late December to late February (mid-January is the best time).

WHALE WATCHING

Helgren's Sportfishing sets sail from mid-December to mid-April—that's when you'll see California gray whales. ~ 315 Harbor Drive South, Oceanside; 760-722-2133; www.helgrensport fishing.com. **Islandia Sportfishing** serves the Mission Bay area, accommodating up to 147 guests. ~ 1551 West Mission Bay Drive, Mission Bay; 619-222-1164; www.islandiasport.com. In Point Loma, **H & M Landing** takes you out on 60- to 85-foot boats. ~ 2803 Emerson Street, Point Loma; 619-222-1144; www.hmland ing.com. **Point Loma Sportfishing** offers three-hour trips through local waters. ~ 1403 Scott Street, Point Loma; 619-223-1627; www.pointlomasportfishing.com. **San Diego Harbor Excursion** provides three-hour whale-watching tours during winter. ~ 1050 North Harbor Drive; 619-234-4111; www.sdhe.com.

San Diego offers countless spots for diving. The rocky La Jolla coves boast the clearest water on the state's coast. Bird Rock, La Jolla Underwater Park and the underwater Scripp's Canyon are ideal havens for divers. In Point Loma try the colorful tidepools at Cabrillo Underwater Reserve.

DIVING

For diving rentals, sales, instruction and tips, contact **Underwater Schools of America**. ~ 707 Oceanside Boulevard, Oceanside;

760-722-7826; www.usascuba.com. **Ocean Enterprises** teaches a variety of diving classes. They also have dive trips, and rent and sell gear. ~ 7710 Balboa Avenue, San Diego; 858-565-6054; www.oceanent.com. You can also arrange dives with **San Diego Diver's Supply**. They provide instruction, sell gear and do repairs. ~ 4004 Sports Arena Boulevard, San Diego, 619-224-3439. In Pacific Beach, the **Diving Locker** offers open-water certification along with a variety of dive trips. Dives at local kelp beds use two tanks; longer-range and overnight dives include spots such as Los Coronados and San Clemente islands. They also do night dives and rent and sell gear. ~ 1020 Grand Avenue, Pacific Beach; 858-272-1120; www.divinglocker.com.

SURFING & WIND-SURFING

Surf's up in the San Diego area. Pacific, Mission and Ocean beaches, Tourmaline Surfing Park, and Windansea, La Jolla Shores, Swami and Moonlight beaches are well-known hangouts for surfers. Sailboarding is concentrated within Mission Bay.

For surfboard, bodyboard, wetsuit and snorkel rentals and sales, try **Mitch's**. ~ 631 Pearl Street, La Jolla; 858-459-5933. **Hansen Surfboards** rents recreational gear such as snorkel equipment, surfboards, and bodyboards, as well as wetsuits. ~ 1105 South Coast Highway, Encinitas; 760-753-6595; www.hansensurf.com. **C. P. Water Sports** has rentals and lessons for "every watersport imaginable." ~ 1775 East Mission Bay Drive, Mission Bay; 619-275-8945. Surfboards, boogieboards and sailboards are available at **Mission Bay Sportscenter**. They have wetsuits and surfing instruction as well. ~ 1010 Santa Clara Place, Mission Bay; 858-488-1004; www.missionbaysportscenter.com.

BOATING

You can sail under the Coronado Bridge, skirt the gorgeous downtown skyline and even get a taste of open ocean in this Southern California sailing mecca.

Several sailing companies operate out of Harbor Island West in San Diego, including **Harbor Sailboats**. They offer instruction as well as sailboat rentals. ~ 2040 Harbor Island Drive, Suite 104, San Diego; 619-291-9568; www.harborsailboats.com. You can

AUTHOR FAVORITE

Hot-air ballooning is an adventurous activity that has soared in popularity in the Del Mar area. A growing number of ballooning companies offer spectacular dawn and sunset flights, most concluding with a traditional champagne toast. One of the companies in the Del Mar Valley is **A Skysurfer Balloon Company**. ~ 858-481-6800.

also charter, rent or learn from the **San Diego Sailing Club and School.** ~ 1880 Harbor Island Drive, San Diego; 619-298-6623.

Motorboat, sailboat and kayak rentals can be found at **C. P. Water Sports,** where they also teach sailing. ~ 1775 East Mission Bay Drive, Mission Bay; 619-275-8945. Motorboat, sailboat, canoe and kayak rentals are available from **Mission Bay Sportscenter.** In addition, they can teach you how to sail and waterski. ~ 1010 Santa Clara Place, Mission Bay; 858-488-1004; www. missionbaysportscenter.com. **Seaforth Mission Bay Boat Rental** rents motorboats, sailboats, paddleboats, canoes and kayaks. ~ 1641 Quivira Road, Mission Bay; 619-223-1681; www.seaforth boatrental.com. The **Coronado Boat Rentals** has motorboats and sailboats. ~ 1715 Strand Way, Coronado; 619-437-1514.

Charter a yacht through **Hornblower Dining Yachts.** ~ 1066 North Harbor Drive, San Diego; 619-234-8687.

Beautiful **Torrey Pines Municipal Golf Course** is famous for its two 18-hole, par-72 championship courses. ~ 11480 North Torrey Pines Road, La Jolla; 619-570-1234. **Mission Bay Golf Resort** is a public, 18-hole course. ~ 2702 North Mission Bay Drive, Mission Bay; 858-490-3370. A duffer's delight, the 18-hole **Balboa Park Municipal Golf Course** is a par-72 championship course. It also features a nine-hole intermediate course. ~ Golf Course Drive, Balboa Park; 619-235-1184. The **Coronado Municipal Golf Course,** an 18-hole green, runs along Glorietta Bay. ~ 2000 Visalia Row, Coronado; 619-435-3121.

GOLF

San Diego has many private and public hardtop courts. The **Balboa Tennis Club** has 25 outdoor courts, 19 of which are lighted. ~ 2221 Morley Field Drive, San Diego; 619-295-9278; www.tennis sandiego.com. You'll find two unlighted courts at the **Cabrillo Recreation Center.** ~ 3051 Canon Street, Point Loma; 619-531-1534. Three outdoor, lighted courts are found at **Mission Valley YMCA.** ~ 5505 Friars Road, Mission Valley; 619-298-3576; www. missionvalley.ymca.org. If you're in Ocean Beach, try the 12 courts at **Peninsula Tennis Club,** which are outdoor and lighted. ~ 2525 Bacon Street, Ocean Beach; 619-226-3407. Some of the nine outdoor courts at the **La Jolla Recreation Center** are lighted. ~ 615 Prospect Street, La Jolla; 858-552-1658. The **Coronado Tennis Center** has eight outdoor courts, three of which are lighted. ~ 1501 Glorietta Boulevard, Coronado; 619-435-1616.

TENNIS

Cycling has skyrocketed in popularity throughout San Diego County, especially in coastal areas. The **Mission Bay Bike Path** (18 miles) starts at the San Diego Convention Center, winds along the harbor, crosses Mission Bay and heads up the coast to La Jolla. **Balboa Park** and **Mission Bay Park** both have excellent bike

BIKING

routes. Check with Regional Transit about their special "biker" passes.

Bike Rentals To rent a bicycle (mountain, road or kid's) in downtown San Diego, contact **Pennyfarthings Bicycle Store**. ~ 314 G Street; 619-233-7696. **Holland's Bicycles** sells, rents and repairs cruisers, mountain bikes and tandems. Rentals come with helmets and locks. ~ 977 Orange Avenue, Coronado; 619-435-3153; www.hollandsbicycles.com.

WALKING TOURS

Several San Diego organizations and tour operators offer organized walks: **Gaslamp Quarter Historical Foundation** conducts two-hour, docent-led walking tours of the restored downtown historic district on Saturday at 11 a.m. ~ 410 Island Avenue; 619-233-4692.

Walking tours of **Old Town State Historic Park** are offered daily at 11 a.m. and 2 p.m. through park headquarters. ~ 4002 Wallace Street; 619-220-5422.

Join **Coronado Touring** for a leisurely one-and-a-half-hour guided stroll through quaint Coronado. Tours leave from the Glorietta Bay Inn (1630 Glorietta Boulevard) at 11 a.m. on Tuesday, Thursday and Saturday. ~ 619-435-5993.

NINE

Los Angeles Day Trips

From the beaches of the Pacific to the foothills of the San Gabriels, Los Angeles seems virtually inexhaustible. There is so much for families to do and see here that one day trip of the area simply won't seem enough. The second-largest city in the country, Los Angeles rests in a bowl surrounded by five mountain ranges and an ocean and holds within its ambit sandy beaches, hills and wind-ruffled deserts. The 74-mile coastline extending north from Long Beach to Malibu is hard to pass up. Along the way you'll have an opportunity to explore tidepools, visit amusement parks and see the habitat of movie stars. Life here reflects the culture of the beach, a freewheeling, pleasure-seeking philosophy that combines hedonism with healthfulness.

Inland Los Angeles County opens up even more possibilities. First there is Six Flags California, one of today's greatest amusement parks. Then there are the La Brea Tar Pits, dating back to the heyday of the dinosaurs.

Many of the city's best family activities focus around Griffith Park, home of the municipal zoo and planetarium. Of course, no visit to the Los Angeles area is complete without a trip to Hollywood. The NBC and Paramount Studios tours offer a chance to see both television production and motion picture sets. You could become part of a studio audience and see the day-to-day activities of a multimedia complex.

All these features make the Los Angeles area worth a special trip. An intriguing city with colorful murals, folk art, historic adobes and offbeat shops, this is a great place for casual daytripping. If you can't find it in Los Angeles, look again. It's probably just around the corner.

Six Flags California

Spreading across 260 acres and featuring a 4000-seat stadium, Six Flags California encompasses Six Flags Magic Mountain, a quintessential roller-coaster park, and Six Flags Hurricane Harbor, a family-oriented water park featuring water slides and a wave pool open in the summer. Though located adjacent to one another, Magic Mountain and Hurricane Harbor are separate parks with their own entrances and admission fees, not to mention distinct personalities that draw different crowds. To know Magic Mountain is a thrill-ride heaven you only have to look at the mix of hand-holding teens in baggy shorts and high-tops who throng to the park each weekend. By 6 p.m. on a Saturday, anyone over 19 definitely is in the minority. Yet Magic Mountain maintains some family appeal with its less-intrepid rides, a beautifully restored 1912 carousel and a delightful collection of Warner Brothers/Looney Tunes characters. However, it's Hurricane Harbor that most appeals to families, especially those with young kids. The atmosphere is more easygoing, and most attractions are geared toward children.

Summer months are high season when the park reaches an effervescent energy level. The greatest number of shows will be up and operating then, and the crowds will also be colossal. The park is open daily during the summer. During the off-season, from mid-September to the end of March, the park is open weekends and holidays only. Hours vary, so call before setting out.

NUTS & BOLTS

Arrival   The park is in Valencia in the Santa Clarita Valley, a half-hour drive north of Hollywood. Take the Magic Mountain Parkway exit off Route 5. It steers you directly into the park. You'll pay a $7 parking fee and be directed to a lot from which trams will deliver you to the main gate.

Tickets   Six Flags Magic Mountain only offers one-day passes. However, they also have a "Twicket," which allows the bearer a second day of admission for a nominal fee.

Available in the summer is a two-park combo ticket that allows entrance to both Magic Mountain and Hurricane Harbor on a single day. The admission to Six Flags Magic Mountain is $42.99 for adults and $26.99 for children under 48 inches, and adults over 55 years old. Tickets to Six Flags Hurricane Harbor cost $21.99 for adults and $14.99 for children under 48 inches and adults over 55 years old. Two-park combo tickets cost $52.99 for adults (no combo ticket for children). Season passes to Magic Mountain are $90 for individuals, $300 for a family of four. Season passes to Hurricane Harbor are $70 for individuals, $220 for a family of four. Children under 2 are free at both Magic Mountain and Hurricane Harbor.

Game Plan   You'll be one of more than three million people to visit Magic Mountain this year, so it's wise to have a plan. Superman the Escape, Viper and Flashback develop lines within minutes of opening time, especially on summer weekends. If you have teens in your group (there are height restrictions on these rides), you'll want to be in line in your car when the parking-lot gates open, which is an hour before the park begins business.

If you can get through the parking gates within 15 minutes of the park's opening time, catch the tram or walk to the main gate. You won't be bored while standing in line because a Dixieland band performs while you wait. Then, if you can get through the entrance gates in the first ten minutes they're open and head for X, you'll be on the ride by 10:20. Dash over to Goliath, where a small line will already have formed. You may have to wait 20 minutes or so, but it's nothing compared to the one-to-two-hour lines you can expect by the early afternoon. If you want to ride Superman

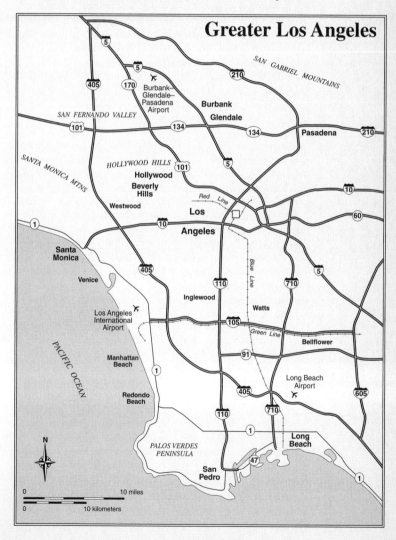

Greater Los Angeles

the Escape, head there now since it draws crowds as well. From there, hit the rides of your choice wherever lines are shortest.

If you're with smaller children who can't make coaster height minimums, you can plan a more leisurely arrival. After coming through the main gate, go straight ahead to the red-brick Guest Relations building and pick up a park map. To help in planning your strategy, we have grouped rides and attractions in Magic Mountain by type rather than geographic location in the park.

Unlike Magic Mountain, there is no strategy for an enjoyable day at Hurricane Harbor. Lines and crowds are not as intense here as they are next door; just show up and have fun!

Guest Services   For general information regarding both parks contact them at 661-255-4100, 818-367-5965 (in the Los Angeles area) or www.sixflags.com/magicmountain.

In Magic Mountain, lockers, strollers and wheelchair rentals are located in Six Flags Plaza behind Guest Relations. Free kennel services are located in the parking lot. At Guest Relations you'll find Lost and Found and Lost Children services. A first-aid attendant is always on duty at First Aid, between the Gotham City Backlot entrance and Magic Moments Theatre. A convenient, free package service lets you make purchases in the park throughout the day, then pick them up before you leave at a shop called Flags near the front of the park. Most ATM cards are accepted at terminals in Six Flags Plaza.

In Hurricane Harbor, lockers are located in Buccaneer Village inside the entrance and to the left. You can rent strollers and wheelchairs at Magic Mountain and bring them into Hurricane Harbor. Guest Relations, also in Buccaneer Village, is where you'll find Lost and Found and Lost Children services. First Aid is located behind the lockers.

Getting Around   Working in a clockwise fashion, you enter the roughly circular-shape park at 6 o'clock. Moving to your left, you'll find the entrances to Viper and Revolution. Following the circle, Roaring Rapids, Ninja and Skytower are spaced inward from the park's perimeter. Psyclone and Déjà Vu are in the far corner, followed by Dive Devil, Batman Action Theatre, The Riddler's Revenge and Freefall at high noon. Batman the Ride, Flashback, Goliath and Colossus are along the opposite edge of the circle, with Superman the Escape in the middle of Samurai Summit.

For an overview, you can hop on the **Metro**, a comfortably modern monorail that stops at three different stations. It's also a good spot for a rest. To avoid a hill-climb, the **Orient Express**, a European-style funicular built in Zurich, takes you to Samurai Summit.

Working your way around Hurricane Harbor in a clockwise direction, you first come to Tiki Falls, the enclosed tube slides.

Near the exit to Tiki Falls are the raft rentals to use in Forgotten Sea, a wave pool. Beyond that is Taboo Tower, three high-speed water slides. Lightning Falls, Black Snake Summit and Lost Temple Rapids, three other water slides, are also located along the perimeter. In the center of Hurricane Harbor are Shipwreck Shores, River Cruise and Castaway Cove.

SIX FLAGS MAGIC MOUNTAIN   The park has nine distinctively themed areas. **Cyclone Bay**, adjacent to the Psyclone wood roller coaster, has the flavor of a beachfront boardwalk and features food areas and specialty shops. **Samurai Summit** with its Oriental theme is home to Superman the Escape, Ninja, the Laughing Dragon Pizza Co. and Skytower. The **Gotham City Backlot**, Batman's home, features Batman the Ride and a Batmobile replica. **Bugs Bunny World** and **Wile E. Coyote Critter Canyon** are planned especially for the small set. The **Six Flags Plaza**, located at the entrance, includes a Guest Relations center, shops and fountains where everyone seems to wait for lost friends.

WHAT TO SEE & DO

Roller Coasters and Thrill Rides   Southern California enjoys a longstanding love affair with coasters, and Magic Mountain caters to that addiction by introducing new terrifiers on a regular basis. These thrillers, from the classic wood varieties to those with cutting-edge technology, run the gamut of roller-coaster excitement.

Goliath is a whipping, turning contraption that unquestionably lives up to its moniker. At 255 feet tall, the steel giant has one the world's tallest drops—a near-vertical plunge down into a smoke-filled black hole at 85 miles per hour.

You can't take the **Riddler's Revenge** sitting down—literally. Riders stand through the 4000-plus feet of track, traveling at a mere (?!) 65 miles per hour. In three solid minutes, look for six inversions including barrel rolls, diving loops and drops.

Déjà Vu straps you into sleek ski lift–style chairs and sends you flying face-down out of the station to the top of a 20-story tower. After a stomach-churning freefall, you race to the top of a second tower and take the fall again—backwards. (Thus the

FLASHBACK

The relentless Flashback coaster employs all the ingenuity of Swiss design to create a ride acclaimed as unique in the world. Each 20-person train carries four riders in each row who sit side by side and experience the feeling of falling face first from the height of an eight-story building. Nearly 130 tons of blue steel tubing were needed to build this $4 million thriller.

ride's name . . . though you may not have time to decide if you've seen it all before!)

X is another freefall coaster, only this one has cars that spin 360 degrees on their own axis, independent of all the backflips, turns and twists of the track. This means that while you're hurtling along at 76 miles per hour, you are also spinning unpredictably backwards and forwards. This is definitely one to do *before* lunch.

Unless you've already booked passage on one of the space shuttle launches, **Superman the Escape** has got to be the next best thing. Six Flags has outdone itself with this one: strapped into one of two 15-passenger vehicles, you escape the Fortress of Solitude, a crystalline ice cavern atop the park's mountain ridge. Electro-magnetic motors fire you through a special-effects tunnel and along an L-shaped dual track that spans 900 feet. Accelerating from 0 to 100 miles per hour in seven seconds, the vehicle blasts along the track, hits the curve at 100 mph, rockets straight up the 41-story tower, then free-falls back down. At one point during the ride, you'll experience a force of 4.5 Gs before you go to weightlessness for six and a half seconds. If you're just not up for this one, but would rather watch, the best viewing spot is from the plaza right in front of the Gotham City Gate.

Psyclone, a classic wood roller coaster, is a replica of New York's legendary Coney Island Cyclone built in 1927.

On **Flashback**, the only diving roller coaster in the world, you're hauled upward through what appear to be stacks of track, then dropped from the top with a free-fall effect through six steeply banked, vertical 180-degree dives. Just when you think it's over, you enter a 540-degree upward spiral that seems to defy gravity.

Psyclone begins with an inky-black, 183-foot tunnel complete with maniacal laughter that prepares you for a 95-foot drop angled at 53 degrees. You'll hit 50 miles per hour as you race down ten steep hills and five banked turns. Psyclone got its name because of its reputation for messing with people's minds. Not surprising when you consider how much it looks like a Los Angeles freeway interchange.

In the opinion of many, **Viper** is the most frightening roller coaster in captivity. It turns you upside down seven times. Its snake-green cars seem to slither along the bright-red track, then "strike" with lightning speed. This mega-coaster, the largest looping roller coaster in the world, drops you 18 relentless stories as it spins through a classic corkscrew. Despite all, the ride is remarkably smooth, attesting to its high-tech perfection.

Batman the Ride takes you through hairpin turns, vertical loops, corkscrews and a zero-gravity spin. Experience all of this in a ski lift–style train that lacks a floor. Try to hit this ride early because lines can mean up to a two-hour wait.

Dive Devil combines skydiving and hang gliding into one experience. Strapped into a harness, you're hoisted 150 feet in the air by cables attached to two towers. When one cable is released, you drop and soar in an arc at a speed of up to 60 mph. You can ride solo or with two pals, but you'll need to make a reservation. There's an extra cost to make this daredevil stunt ($28–$48), and divers must be at least 48 inches in height.

Ninja, set high above the park on Samurai Summit, is the West Coast's fastest suspended roller coaster. The out-of-control feeling here is intensified because trains hang from an overhead track and swing from side to side 180 degrees!

Colossus, the largest dual-track wood coaster ever built, is as notable for its architectural style as its ride. With almost two miles of track, this classic is the longest roller coaster in the park. Providing the rattly, clackety ride of a traditional coaster, it drops and flings you with abandon. If you like coaster thrills but aren't interested in being turned upside down, this is the ride for you.

One of the park's oldies but goodies, the **Revolution** is the first looping roller coaster ever built. Despite its age, this thriller hasn't lost a bit of its pizazz. At one point you're looped 360 degrees to find yourself staring down 90 feet at the Grand Carousel. For true coaster aficionados, this ride will have a touch of nostalgia.

The **Gold Rusher** opened with the park in 1971 and is still going strong. Here you board a runaway mine train that turns sharply, drops quickly and executes dual horizontal loops. It's tame compared to Viper and won't develop such long lines, so it's fun even for younger kids. Hit this one when crowds are at their peak.

These all have 42- to 54-inch height restrictions, so check before you stand in line.

Family Rides   How do you feel about jumping off a ten-story building? **Freefall** lets you do it in four-person cars that are cranked to the top of a tower, then pushed off the edge. You plunge at 55 miles per hour with your stomach in your throat, then end up on your back being air-braked to a halt. If the ride has a fault, it's that it's over before true terror has time to register.

You're guaranteed to get wet on the **Tidal Wave**, where 20-passenger boats plunge over a 50-foot waterfall, dunking those in the front seats and splashing onlookers.

You bounce through the waves and cross-currents of **Roaring Rapids** in huge, 12-passenger circular boats that serve as giant inner tubes careening off rocks and boulders. The sign at the entrance says, "You WILL get wet. You MAY get drenched." Count on the latter.

Another ride with a splashy finale, **Arrowhead Splashdown** features jet boats that power up a hill, circle the back country and plummet into Jet Stream Lake via a 57-foot plunge, guaranteeing yet another shower.

On **Log Jammer**, riders float freely in four-person "logs" along a water flume. The final vertical drop looks worse than it is. You'll get damp, but nothing like on Roaring Rapids. Lines move quickly here so do this ride at peak hours.

In the Gotham City Backlot, **Grinder Gearworks** uses centrifugal force to hold you to the wall while you twirl into the air. Another Gotham ride, the ACME **Atom Smasher** is a fast-moving ride that sends you spinning.

For a park overview, **Skytower** lifts you gently 38 stories above the park to an enclosed circular viewing deck for a panorama of the entire Santa Clarita Valley. On windy days you can feel the tower sway.

High above the Colossus County Fair, Buccaneer swings back and forth, defying gravity in a "pirate ship."

All ages seem to take to the **Grand Carousel**. Its location, directly next to Revolution, clearly defines how amusement park rides have changed. This elegant dowager from another era was built in 1912 by the Philadelphia Toboggan Co. For 50 years it delighted guests at Savin Rock Amusement Park in West Haven, Connecticut, before being brought to Magic Mountain in 1971 and refurbished for the park's opening. Boasting 64 horses and two carriages, it glows with more than 1600 lights.

Bugs Bunny World   The totally renovated Bugs Bunny World provides a refuge for the meek (and perhaps wise) ones who would prefer to stay closer to the ground. The six-acre funland for kids features 16 pint-size rides and adventures here in their exclusive Southern California home. Bugs, Sylvester, Yosemite Sam, Pepé Le Pew, et al. are always ready to pose for photos (look for them in **Granny and Tweety's House**, **Taz's House** or **Bugs Bunny's Burrow**).

Don't have the constitution for Goliath? Tame thrills are on tap on **The Canyon Blaster**, a miniature Six Flags–style coaster that kids and parents can ride together. Tea cups take on a new twist at **Pepé Le Pew's Tea Party**. Travel by coal train on **Foghorn Leghorn's Barnyard Railway**. Freefall with the famous cat at **Sylvester's Pounce and Bounce**, or try to escape the feline entirely in a Tweety cage in **Tweety's Excape**. The **Merrie Melodies Carousel** is a new take on an old classic while the **Looney Tunes Character Fountain** makes a perfect splash spot to cool off. Other thrills include a ride in a "semi" at **Taz's Trucking Company**, a spin at **Yosemite Sam's Flight School** and a wild bus excursion on **Daffy's Adventure Tours**.

Wile E. Coyote Critter Canyon   From Bugs Bunny World, follow the paw prints to **Wile E. Coyote Critter Canyon**, a see-and-touch petting zoo housing more than 55 species of exotic and barnyard animals. Children here can pet woolly sheep and goats, watch a wallaby and admire the beauty of a regal golden eagle. Kids can see this eight-acre area from electrically powered miniature antique cars on the **Granny Gran Prix**, which takes them on a loop through the canyon.

Shows and Entertainment   At the Valencia Falls Pavilion Bugs Bunny is the president of the **Warner Bros. Kids Club**, a participatory game show suitable for the whole family. Learn about Hollywood stunts and special effects during the **Batman Live Action Stunt Show**, held at the Batman Action Theater. **Just Wingin' It** at the Animal Star Theatre features a menagerie of exotic birds. Celebrating **Looney Tunes Nights**, Bugs Bunny, Looney Tunes Characters and Comic Book Super-Heroes parade through the park, finishing in Six Flags Plaza with a fireworks finale.

Not every show is available at all times of year, so check with the park for the latest schedule.

SIX FLAGS HURRICANE HARBOR   If the soakings from Magic Mountain's Tidal Wave and Roaring Rapids rides aren't wet enough, it's probably time to head next door to Hurricane Harbor, Six Flags' extravagantly themed water park opened in 1995.

One of the nicest things about Hurricane Harbor is how kid-friendly it is. While Six Flags, with its emphasis on super-thrill rides and roller coasters, may not seem a particularly appropriate destination for small children, Hurricane Harbor is different: a fantasy entertainment environment of lost lagoons and pirate coves that was designed with children in mind (one attraction doesn't even allow adults). Of course with the addition of some new attractions, there's a nice balance in the thrill ride department, too, and grown-ups will be plenty pleased with the selection of twisting water slides and daredevil drops.

The park is divided into several themed water areas. **Castaway Cove** is a large water play area for kids under 54 inches and includes waterfalls, water gadgets and swings. There are slides and some nice little pools to splash in, as well as a shady area on the outskirts lined with chaise longues. In **Shipwreck Shores**, a huge skull is mounted on the mast of Red Eye the Pirate's ship. This area is for all kids and adults. The skull dumps gallons of water on "intruders" every few minutes. On a raft, you can float along on **The River Cruise**, a 1300-foot-long lazy river that surrounds Castaway Cove and Shipwreck Shore, past the 45-foot volcano, **Geyser Peak**. A wave pool called **Forgotten Sea** is the park's largest "ocean," generating two-foot waves and measuring up to six feet deep. If you'd prefer to watch, you can take a seat on one of the surrounding lounge chairs. **Lizard Lagoon** is aimed at adult and teenage beach enthusiasts. The 3.2-acre recreation lagoon features water basketball, beach volleyball and comfortable lounge chairs set beneath swaying palm trees. Here's where you'll also find **Reptile Ridge**, a 35-foot-high structure housing five open and enclosed tubes ranging from a 255-foot-long gentle slide (Croc Creek) to a 70-foot-long straight drop (Gator Gorge).

Thrill riders, in fact, have a growing number of attractions to choose from, now that Hurricane Harbor has added to its stock of thrill slides. Most are enclosed- or open-tube slides that gently spiral or twist. One of the busiest themed areas, **Black Snake Summit**, features five slides: **Twisted Fang** and **Coiled Cobra**, at 75 feet high each, the tallest fully enclosed speed slides in Southern California; the **Venom Drop**, an open tube offering a 75-foot near-vertical plunge; and the **Sidewinder** and **Boa Constrictor** slides, both 650-foot-long, fully enclosed tubes. Continuing old favorites include **Taboo Tower**, a crumbling temple with three routes of "escape": **Daredevil Plunge**, which has a 45-degree drop; the bumpy **Escape Chute**; and the **Secret Passage**, a 325-foot enclosed spiraling slide. The other water slides are **Lightning Falls** (twisting, open tubes), **Tiki Falls** (enclosed and semi-enclosed tubes) and **Lost Temple Rapids** (a four-person raft ride).

> The park's most novel attraction may in fact be the Bamboo Racer, an attraction where six riders race along a 625-foot slide (head first, no less) on specially designed water "toboggans."

Hurricane Harbor features changing rooms with showers and lockers (extra charge) and raft rentals. A general admission admits you to all the attractions.

DINING

SIX FLAGS MAGIC MOUNTAIN Don't look for haute cuisine inside the park, but you will find plenty of variety among its 16 restaurants and stands. The **Laughing Dragon Pizza Co.** is probably the most attractive of the sit-down restaurants, as much for its colorful and whimsical decor as for its location atop Samurai Summit, which affords great views of the park. As for the food, the name is a good indicator: individual California-style pizzas, salads and pastas. BUDGET TO MODERATE. The **Mooseburger Lodge** resembles a High Sierra mountain lodge complete with a stuffed moose. The menu, which features the mooseburger, offers ribs and chicken dishes, as well as a buffet and salad bar. BUDGET TO MODERATE. Bright, airy **Food Etc.** near Critter Canyon serves cafeteria-style barbecue, pasta, deli subs and salads. You can eat indoors or out on the patio. MODERATE.

The park's 12 food stands all are adjacent to pleasant patios with outdoor seating. **Eduardo's Grill** has tostadas, tacos and enchiladas, and **Pizza Vector** specializes in pepperoni and sausage pizza. BUDGET. A good bet for dessert is the **Plaza Ice Cream Co.**, where hand-dipped ice cream in super duper–sized cones will satisfy the biggest sweet-tooth. BUDGET. For an instant snack, popcorn and pretzel wagons roam the park. BUDGET.

SIX FLAGS HURRICANE HARBOR Caribbean-style buildings house the food stands and souvenir shops in Hurricane Harbor.

Red Eye's Kitchen, in Buccaneer Village, offers rotisserie chicken, pizza, burgers and hot dogs, salads and soft drinks. BUDGET. Fresh fruit and juices can be found at **Tradewind Treats** in Castaway Cove, while snacks like ices, churros and pretzels are at **Paradise Snacks** next to Forgotten Sea. BUDGET.

LODGING

There are dozens, perhaps hundreds, of hotels and motels in the San Fernando Valley within 20 to 30 minutes of Magic Mountain, ranging from super-budget to moderately elegant. Hotels here, all within five minutes of the park, have higher rates in summer.

The 250-room **Hilton Garden Inn** is practically in Magic Mountain's lap. It's the most upscale of the close-to-the-park hotels, and is also the nearest (just a ten-minute walk from the gate). The two-story Spanish hacienda–style inn has oversized rooms with vaulted ceilings. The pool gives the place a resort-like feel, as does the small workout center overlooking the pool and spa. The restaurant serves breakfast only. ~ 27710 The Old Road, Valencia; 661-254-8800, 800-445-8667, fax 661-254-9399; www.hiltongardeninn.com. MODERATE TO DELUXE.

Best Western Valencia Inn is across the freeway from the park, about a 15-minute walk away. This two-story hostelry is made up of four different buildings. Room prices depend on which building you're in, with the least-expensive ones closest to the freeway. Rooms are homey and comfortable, if not particularly stylish. A spa and two pools make it family-friendly. Children under 17 stay free. ~27413 Championship Way, Valencia; 661-255-0555, 800-944-7446, fax 661-255-2216; www.bestwestern.com/valencia. MODERATE.

The **Hampton Inn** is three miles south of the park. Its rooms are fresh and pleasantly furnished in muted-tone Southwest style. Nightly cookie service in the lobby offers families a chance to defervesce after a busy day. There's no restaurant on the premises, but the California breakfast buffet, included with rooms, is appealing and extensive. The palm-fringed pool, spa and patio area adds a Southern California touch. ~25259 The Old Road, Santa Clarita; 661-253-2400, 800-426-7866, fax 661-253-1683. MODERATE.

The **Comfort Inn** offers reasonably priced, no-frills accommodations in a nondescript, two-story building. It's located five minutes north of the park, and although lacking in architectural grandeur it has an uncommonly helpful staff. The continental breakfast, included in the room rate, is more than adequate. ~ 31558 Castaic Road, Castaic; 661-295-1100, 800-228-5150, fax 661-295-0379. MODERATE.

▼▼▼▼▼▼▼▼▼▼▼
Long Beach

Long Beach ranks together with neighboring San Pedro as one of the largest manmade harbors in the world and is a popular tourist destination. It's a revealing place, a kind of social studies lesson in modern American life. Travel Ocean Boulevard as it parallels the sea and you'll pass from quaint homes to downtown skyscrapers to fire-breathing smokestacks.

SIGHTS

Anchoring the southern end of Los Angeles County is Long Beach, one of California's largest cities. Here you can visit the enclave of **Naples**, which was conceived early in the century. Modeled on Italy's fabled canal towns, it's a tiny community of three islands separated by canals and linked with walkways.

Adding to the sense of old Italia is the **Gondola Getaway**, a romantic, hour-long cruise through the canals of Naples. For a hefty price (less, however, than a ticket to Italy), you can climb aboard a gondola, dine on hors d'oeuvres and be serenaded with Italian music. ~ 5437 East Ocean Boulevard, Long Beach; 562-433-9595; www.gondolagetawayinc.com.

The Queen Mary carried so many troops across the Atlantic Ocean that Adolf Hitler offered $250,000 and the Iron Cross to the U-boat captain who sank her.

But the high point of any Long Beach tour is a visit to the **Queen Mary**. Making her maiden voyage in 1936, the *Queen Mary* was the pride of Great Britain. Winston Churchill, the Duke and Duchess of Windsor, Greta Garbo and Fred Astaire all got to know her charms. Today this 1000-foot-long "city at sea" has been transformed into a floating museum and hotel. An art-deco classic, the vessel was known as the "Ship of Beautiful Woods." An elaborate walking tour carries you down into the engine room (a world of pumps and propellers), out along the wooden decks and up to each level of this multistage behemoth. Dioramas throughout the ship realistically portray every aspect of sailing life during the great age of ocean liners. The *Queen Mary*, expertly refurbished and wonderfully laid out, is an important addition to the Long Beach seafront and the anchor attraction for Queen Mary Seaport, which also includes The Queen's Marketplace shopping and dining area. Admission. ~ 1126 Queen's Highway, Port of Long Beach; 562-435-3511, fax 562-437-4531; www.queenmary.com.

Queen Mary's neighbor is the world's largest clear-span geodesic dome. The dome, now empty, once housed Howard Hughes' *Spruce Goose*, the largest plane ever built.

The **Long Beach Aquarium of the Pacific**, part of the waterfront Rainbow Harbor development in downtown Long Beach, has three major permanent galleries designed to lead visitors on a "journey of discovery" through the waters of the Pacific Ocean. One exhibit—the tropical Pacific gallery—also features the huge Tropical Reef Tank, where microphone-equipped scuba divers swim along with schools of brilliant fish and sharks, answering questions for visitors. Kids will enjoy the touch tank full of marine creatures. Admission. ~ 100 Aquarium Way, Long Beach; 562-590-3100, fax 562-590-3109; www.aquariumofpacific.org.

The Pacific Ocean may be Long Beach's biggest natural attraction, but many birds in the area prefer the **El Dorado Nature Center**. Part of the 450-acre El Dorado East Regional Park, this wildlife sanctuary offers one- and two-mile hikes past two lakes and a stream. About 150 bird species as well as numerous land animals can be sighted. Though located in a heavily urbanized area, the facility encompasses several ecological zones. There is also a quarter-mile paved, handicapped-accessible nature trail. Closed Monday. Parking fee. ~ 7550 East Spring Street; 562-570-1745.

Ports O' Call Village in the nearby town of San Pedro is a shopping mall in the form of a 19th-century port town. In addition to shops and restaurants, it houses several outfits conducting harbor cruises. ~ Entrance at foot of 6th Street; 562-831-0287. The boats sail around the San Pedro waterfront and venture out for glimpses of the surrounding shoreline; for information, contact **Spirit Cruises**. ~ Ports O' Call Village, San Pedro; 562-548-8080; www.spiritmarine.com.

For a view of how the waterfront used to look, stop by the **Los Angeles Maritime Museum**. This dockside showplace displays models of ships ranging from fully rigged brigs to 19th-century steam schooners to World War II battleships. There's even an 18-foot re-creation of the ill-starred *Titanic* and the ocean liner model used to film *The Poseidon Adventure*. Closed Monday. ~ Berth 84; 562-548-7618; www.lamaritimemuseum.org, e-mail museum@la maritimemuseum.org.

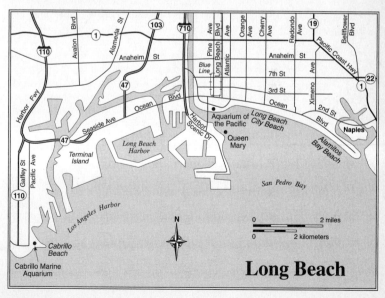

Nearby at the **Cabrillo Marine Aquarium** there is a modest collection of display cases with samples of shells, coral and shorebirds. Several dozen aquariums exhibit local fish and marine plants. Closed Monday. Admission. ~3720 Stephen White Drive; 562-548-7562; www.cabrilloaq.org, e-mail info@cabrilloaq.org.

Of greater interest is **Point Fermin Park**, a 37-acre blufftop facility resting above spectacular tidepools and a marine preserve. The tidepools are accessible via steep trails from the park and from the Cabrillo Marine Aquarium, which sponsors exploratory tours. Also of note (though not open to the public) is the **Point Fermin Lighthouse**, a unique 19th-century clapboard house with a beacon set in a rooftop crow's nest. From the park plateau, like lighthouse keepers of old, you'll have open vistas of the cliff-fringed coast and a perfect perch for sighting whales during their winter migration. ~ 807 Paseo del Mar; 562-548-7756; e-mail parkoffice@sanpedro.com.

DINING   What more elegant a setting than aboard the *Queen Mary*, where you will find everything from snack kiosks to coffee shops to first-class dining rooms. The menu at the **Promenade Café** focuses on steak, chicken and seafood. They also have salads, sandwiches and burgers. The coffee shop is a lovely art-deco room featuring wicker furnishings and period lamps. Kids will enjoy the harbor view and a special menu featuring burgers, fish and chips, nachos and grilled ham and cheese. ~ 1126 Queen's Highway; 562-435-3511, fax 562-437-4531; www.queenmary.com. MODERATE.

For a true taste of regal life aboard the old ship, cast anchor at **Sir Winston's**. The Continental cuisine in this dining emporium includes rack of lamb, veal, duck, venison, swordfish and lobster. Sir Winston's is a wood-paneled dining room with copper-rimmed mirrors, white tablecloths and upholstered armchairs. The walls are adorned with photos of the great prime minister, and every window opens onto a view of Long Beach. Men must wear a jacket and women must wear a dress or pantsuit. Reservations required. Dinner only. ~ 562-499-1657, fax 562-437-4531; www.queenmary.com. ULTRA-DELUXE.

HIDDEN ►   Southern cooking at the **Shenandoah Café** is becoming a tradition among savvy shore residents. The quilts and baskets decorating this understated establishment lend a country air to the place. Add waitresses in aprons dishing out hot apple fritters and it gets downright homey. Dinner and Sunday brunch are special events occasioned with "riverwalk steak" (sirloin steak in mustard caper sauce), shrimp in beer batter, salmon on wild-rice pancake, gumbo, "granny's fried chicken," and Texas-style beef brisket. The budget-priced kids' menu features chicken-fried steak, pasta and barbecued ribs. Try it! No breakfast or lunch Monday through Saturday. ~ 4722 East 2nd Street; 562-434-3469, fax 562-438-4299. MODERATE TO DELUXE.

Santa Monica is *in*. Its clean air, pretty beaches and attractive homes have made it one of the most popular places to live in Los Angeles. As real estate prices skyrocketed, liberal politics ascended. Santa Monica is, in a manner of speaking, Southern California's answer to Berkeley.

Santa Monica

The capital of the Los Angeles beach scene is the resort city of Santa Monica, where white-sand beaches are framed by bald mountain peaks. The highlight of the beach promenade (and perhaps all Santa Monica) is the **Santa Monica Pier**. No doubt about it, the place is a scene. Acrobats work out on the playground below, surfers catch waves offshore, and street musicians strum guitars.

SIGHTS

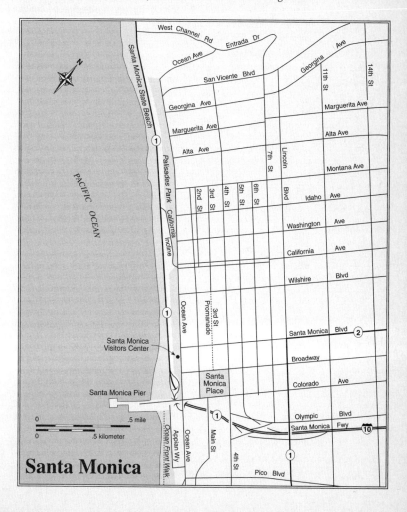

Santa Monica

And we haven't even mentioned the official attractions. There's a late-19th-century carousel with hand-painted horses that was featured in that cinematic classic, *The Sting*. There are video parlors, pinball machines, skee ball, bumper cars and a restaurant. ~ Foot of Colorado Avenue.

From here it's a short jaunt up to the **Santa Monica Visitors Center** information kiosk. Here are maps, brochures and helpful workers. ~ 1400 Ocean Avenue; 310-393-7593, 800-544-5319; www.santamonica.com, e-mail smcvb@santamonica.com.

The **Museum of Flying** is a miniature Smithsonian. Tracing the history of aviation in a single, brightly painted hangar, the museum houses everything from a 1924 Douglas World Cruiser (built in Santa Monica, it was the first plane to circle the globe) to vintage flyable World War II fighters. Open Saturday and Sunday only. Admission. ~ 2772 Donald Douglas Loop North; 310-392-8822; www.museumofflying.com.

An enchanting version of the Old West awaits at **Paramount Ranch,** a 335-acre park that once served as the film location for Westerns. Paramount owned the spread for two decades beginning in the 1920s, using it as a set for *Broken Lullaby* (1932) with Lionel Barrymore, *Thunder Below* (1932) with Tallulah Bankhead and *Adventures of Marco Polo* (1937), the Samuel Goldwyn extravaganza that included a fortress, elephants and 2000 horses. During the heyday of television Westerns in the 1950s, the property was a location for "The Cisco Kid," "Bat Masterson" and "Have Gun, Will Travel."

Today you can hike around the ranch, past the rolling meadows, willow-lined streams, grassy hillsides and rocky heights that made it such an ideal set. "Western Town" still stands, a collection of falsefront buildings that change their signs depending on what's being filmed. If you're lucky, a film crew will be shooting a commercial, a television show, or even producing the last of that dying breed of movie, the Western. ~ In Santa Monica Mountains National Recreation Area; 818-597-9192, fax 805-370-1850; www.nps.gov/samo.

LODGING

Ocean Avenue, which runs the length of Santa Monica paralleling the ocean one block above the beach, boasts the most hotels and the best location in town. Among its varied facilities are several generic motels.

One such establishment is the **Bayside Hotel**. Laid out in motel fashion, this two-story complex offers plusher carpets and plumper furniture than motels hereabouts. More important, it's just 50 yards from the beach across a palm-studded park. Some rooms have ocean views and fully equipped kitchens; no pool. ~ 2001 Ocean Avenue; 562-396-6000, 800-525-4447; www.baysidehotel.com, e-mail info@baysidehotel.com. MODERATE.

Just off Ocean Avenue and a little quieter than most, the **Sea Shore Motel** has 19 guest rooms and one suite located two blocks from the beach and within walking distance of all Santa Monica sights. The rooms have terra-cotta tile floors, granite counter tops and refrigerators. There's a sundeck and off-street parking. ~ 2637 Main Street; 310-392-2787, fax 310-392-5167; www.sea shoremotel.com. MODERATE.

Shutters on the Beach, perched directly on Santa Monica Beach, is cozy and sedate. The lobby has two large fireplaces and the 198 green-and-white rooms are well appoint-ed with dark walnut furniture. Most rooms have coastal views; all feature, yes, shutters, as well as marble baths with jacuzzis. The hotel has a lovely pool terrace, two restaurants, and an oceanview bar. ~ 1 Pico Boulevard; 310-458-0030, 800-334-9000; www.shuttersonthebeach.com, e-mail info@shutterson thebeach.com. ULTRA-DELUXE.

Santa Monica has been a popular resort town since the 1870s.

Loews Santa Monica Beach Hotel, a peach, blue and seafoam-green "contemporary Victorian," features a mock late-19th-century design. Its spectacular five-story glass atrium lobby and most of the 343 rooms provide views of the famed Santa Monica Pier. Rooms are furnished in rattan and wicker and offer special amenities. One-bedroom suites are ideal for families. Baby-sitting service is available. Non-beachies love the shallow ocean-view indoor/outdoor pool. ~ 1700 Ocean Avenue; 562-458-6700, 800-235-6397, fax 562-458-6761. ULTRA-DELUXE.

Next door to Santa Monica, the **Inn at Venice Beach** offers a quiet and comfortable retreat on the edge of Venice's famed canals. Rooms are bright and beachy, with high-beamed ceilings and colorful handpainted designs on the walls. The flower-filled central courtyard, complete with fountain, is a popular spot to relax or to sample the generous complimentary continental break-fast. Located just two blocks from the beach, the hotel is close to bike and 'blade rentals and a host of restaurants. Kids will love the families of ducks that waddle through the parking lot on their way from canal to canal. ~ 327 Washington Boulevard, Venice Beach; 310-821-2557, 800-828-0688, fax 310-827-0289; www.innatvenicebeach.com, e-mail info@innatvenicebeach.com. MODERATE TO DELUXE.

There's a sense of the Mediterranean at the sidewalk cafés lining Santa Monica's Ocean Avenue: palm trees along the boulevard, ocean views in the distance and (usually) a warm breeze blow-ing. Any of these bistros will do (since it's atmosphere we're seek-ing), so try **Ivy at the Shore**. It features a full bar, serves espresso and, if you want to get serious about it, has a full lunch and dinner menu with pizza, pastas and Cajun dishes. ~ 1541 Ocean Ave-nue; 562-393-3113. MODERATE TO ULTRA-DELUXE.

DINING

Every type of cuisine imaginable is found on the bottom level of **Santa Monica Place**. This multitiered shopping mall has an entire floor of take-out food stands. It's like the United Nations of dining. ~ Broadway between 2nd and 4th streets. BUDGET.

A number of excellent eateries line Santa Monica's vaunted Third Street Promenade. This three-block-long walkway, filled with movie theaters and located in the downtown district, boasts some of the best coffeehouses and restaurants in the area.

Gotham Hall serves California cuisine, including free-range chicken marsala and seared ahi tuna. But the real show here is the decor—from the oblong mirrors and wavy-looking paint job in hues of aqua and pink on the walls to the purple pool tables and spotlights shining at odd angles from the beamed ceiling, this restaurant's look couldn't be more unique. ~ 1431 3rd Street Promenade; 310-394-8865; www.gothamhall.com. MODERATE.

Broadway Bar and Grill features spacious booths indoors and curbside tables outside. A perfect spot for checking out the scene, this classic bar and grill serves steaks, fresh fish, and grilled chicken. Kids get their own menu, which features spaghetti, chicken fingers and quesadillas. ~ 1460 Third Street Promenade; 310-393-4211, fax 310-393-5215. MODERATE TO DELUXE.

HIDDEN ▶

The spot for breakfast in Santa Monica is **Rae's Restaurant**, a diner on the edge of town several miles from the beach. With its formica counter and naugahyde booths, Rae's is a local institution, always packed. The breakfasts are hearty American-style feasts complete with biscuits and gravy. At lunch they serve the usual selection of sandwiches and side orders. Come dinner time they have fried shrimp, liver, fried chicken, steaks and other platters at prices that seem like they haven't changed since the place opened in 1958. ~ 2901 Pico Boulevard; 310-828-7937. BUDGET.

BEACHES & PARKS

SANTA MONICA CITY BEACH 🏖 🏊 ⛵ If the pop song is right and "L.A. is a great big freeway," then truly Santa Monica is a great big beach. Face it, the sand is very white, the water is very blue, the beach is very broad, and they all continue for miles. From Venice to Pacific Palisades, it's a sandbox gone wild. Skaters,

AUTHOR FAVORITE

One of the best places in Southern California for stuffing yourself with junk food while soaking up sun and having a whale of a good time is the **Santa Monica Pier**. There are taco stands, fish and chips shops, hot dog vendors, oyster bars, snack shops, pizzerias and all those good things guaranteed to leave you clutching your stomach. ~ Foot of Colorado Avenue. BUDGET.

strollers and bicyclists pass along the promenade, sunbathers lie moribund in the sand, and volleyball players perform acrobatic shots. At the center of all this stands the Santa Monica Pier with its amusement park atmosphere. If it wasn't right next door to Venice this would be the hottest beach around. Lifeguards are on duty, and facilities include picnic areas, restrooms and snackbars. Swimming and surfing are good, and anglers usually opt for the pier. Parking fee, $7. ~ Route 1, at the foot of Colorado Avenue.

WILL ROGERS STATE BEACH 🚲 ⛵ 🏊 Simple and home-spun he might have been, but Will Rogers was also a canny businessman with a passion for real estate. He bought up three miles of beachfront property that eventually became his namesake park. It's a sandy strand with an expansive parking lot running the length of the beach. Route 1 parallels the parking area and beyond that rise the sharp cliffs that lend Pacific Palisades its name. The South Bay Bike Trail makes its northernmost appearance here. You'll find good swimming, and surfing is best in the area where Sunset Boulevard meets the ocean. Lifeguards are on duty. Facilities include restrooms, volleyball courts and playgrounds. Day-use fees vary from $3 to $10, depending on crowds expected. ~ Located south along Route 1 from Sunset Boulevard in Pacific Palisades; 310-451-2906, fax 310-230-1049.

WILL ROGERS STATE HISTORIC PARK 🚶 🚲 🐎 The former ranch of humorist Will Rogers, this 186-acre spread sits in the hills of Pacific Palisades. The late cowboy's home is open to visitors and there are hiking trails leading around the property and out into adjacent Topanga Canyon State Park. Facilities include picnic areas, a museum and restrooms. Day-use fee, $6. ~ 1501 Will Rogers State Park Road, Pacific Palisades; 310-454-8212, fax 310-459-2031.

Los Angeles

Los Angeles is a city that one comes to love or scorn. Or perhaps to love and scorn. It is either Tinseltown or the Big Orange, Smogville or the City of Angels. To some it is the Rome of the West, a megalopolis whose economic might renders it an imperial power. To others Los Angeles is the American Athens, an international center for cinema, music and art.

Culturally speaking, the sun rises in the west. L.A., quirky but creative, sets the trends for the entire nation. It has been admired and self-admiring for so long that the city has swallowed its own story, become a reflection of its mythology. Beautifully crazed, pulsing with electric energy, Los Angeles is living its own dream.

SIGHTS

DOWNTOWN The historic heart of the city is centered around Olvera Street. The actual 1781 founding site of the city is nearby; the settlement was moved to the Olvera Street site after a flood in 1815. Olvera Street is the oldest surviving section of the city, with 27 historic buildings, some dating from the early 19th century, clustered around an old plaza and Mexican market street. Come here on a sunny weekend morning, as vendors put out their wares. Watch tortillas being made by hand and families arriving for a wedding or baptism at the Old Plaza Church.

The **visitors center**, providing maps, brochures and walking tours, sits in one of the pueblo's vintage buildings, a brick-faced Victorian built in 1887 called the Sepulveda House. Walking tours are offered Tuesday through Saturday mornings; two-hour bus tours of historic Los Angeles begin here on the third Wednesday of every month. Closed Sunday. ~ 622 North Main Street; 213-628-1274, fax 213-485-8238.

Heart of hearts is the **Plaza**, a tree-shaded courtyard adorned with statues and highlighted by a wrought-iron bandstand. A colorful gathering place, it's a frequent site for fiestas and open-air concerts. ~ North Main and Los Angeles streets.

Anchoring one corner of the plaza is **Firehouse No. 1**, Los Angeles' original fire station. Today it's a miniature museum filled with horse-drawn fire wagons, old-time helmets and an ample inventory of memories. ~134 Paseo de la Plaza. **Old Plaza Church,** first established as a chapel in 1784, also faces the square. ~ 535 North Main Street.

For the full flavor of Spanish California, wander down **Olvera Street**. Lined with *puestos* (stands) selling Mexican handicrafts, it provides a window on early Los Angeles. The brick-paved alleyway is also one of the West's first pedestrian shopping malls.

For information on Olvera Street and points of interest throughout the city, contact the information center at the **Greater**

sights

AUTHOR FAVORITE

Beauty gives way to the beast at the **Page Museum at the La Brea Tar Pits.** This paleontological showplace features displays of mammoths, mastodons and ground sloths. There are also extinct camels, ancient horses and ancestral condors. Together with over 200 varieties of other creatures they fell victim to the **La Brea Tar Pits**, which surround the museum. Dating to the Pleistocene Era, these oozing oil pools trapped birds, mammals, insects and reptiles, creating fossil deposits that are still being discovered by scientists. American Indians once used the tar to caulk boats and roofs. Today you can wander past the pits, which bubble menacingly with methane gas and lie covered in globs of black tar. Admission. ~ 5801 Wilshire Boulevard; 323-934-7243, fax 323-933-3974; www.tarpits.org.

Los Angeles Convention & Visitors Bureau. There you'll find maps, leaflets and a friendly staff to help point the way through this urban maze. Closed Sunday. ~ 685 South Figueroa Street; 213-689-8822, 800-228-2452; www.lacvb.com.

One fun stop for kids is the **Children's Museum of Los Angeles**, with countless hands-on and hands-all-over-everything exhibits. There are a bus and police motorcycle for kids to ride; make-up rooms for them to paint their faces; a dinosaur cave with holograms and sound effects; a water exhibit that lets kids get in touch with creatures inside aquariums; and a recording studio and video cameras to tape their own antics. Closed for renovations until 2004. Admission. ~ 213-687-8800, fax 213-680-7877; www.chimula.org.

EXPOSITION PARK A multiblock extravaganza bounded by Exposition Boulevard, Menlo Avenue, Martin Luther King Jr. Boulevard and Figueroa Street, Exposition Park is long on exposition and short on park. There *is* an enchanting **sunken garden** with a fountain, gazebos and almost 20,000 rose bushes representing nearly 200 varieties of roses. Otherwise the park blooms with museums and sports arenas.

The **California Science Center** is one of those hands-on, great-for-kids-of-all-ages complexes. It has halls devoted to health and economics and displays demonstrating everything from simple laws of science to the latest advances in high technology. ~ 213-744-7400; www.casciencectr.org, e-mail 4info@cscmail.org.

In the Science Center's **Air and Space Gallery** there are exhibits explaining the principles of aerodynamics as well as planes, jets and space capsules suspended from the ceiling in mock flight. Climbing a catwalk-like series of staircases, you'll have a bird's-eye view of a 19th-century glider, Air Force T-38, an F-20 Tiger Shark and Gemini II spacecraft. Satellites and space telescopes are also on display here, including scale models of Sputnik and the Hubble telescope.

Also at the Science Center, an **IMAX Theater** with a seven-story-high screen takes viewers on film adventures of stunning, you-are-there realism. Several different films are screened daily. You might find yourself cruising with whales, sledding through Alaska or grazing with African wildlife. Admission. ~ 213-744-7400; www.casciencectr.org, e-mail 4info@cscmail.org.

The **Natural History Museum of Los Angeles County** is a world (and an afternoon) unto itself. Among the dozens of galleries are rock and gem displays; dioramas of bears, wolves and bison; set pieces from the American past, including a cut-away Conestoga wagon demonstrating life on the frontier; and, of course, the dinosaur skeletons required of every self-respecting natural history museum. If this is not enough, the museum contains bird specimens and a "discovery center" where kids can play scientist. The insect zoo features 30 live displays of critters from around the world. Admission. ~ 900 Exposition Boulevard; 213-763-3466, fax 213-743-4843; www.nhm.org.

Prettiest of all the buildings in this museum park is the **California African American Museum** with its glass-roofed sculpture court and bright, airy galleries. Devoted to black culture and history, the center displays the work of artists from around the world. Closed Monday. ~ 600 State Drive; 213-744-7432, fax 213-744-2050; www.caam.ca.gov.

HOLLYWOOD Maps of the stars' homes are sold on street corners and in shops throughout Hollywood. But perhaps the best place to begin a visit to the film capital of the world is the **Hollywood Wax Museum**, where you can "see your favorite stars in living wax." Here they are—Marilyn Monroe and Elvis Presley, Clint Eastwood and Sylvester Stallone—complete with that classic grin or sneer frozen forevermore. Admission. ~ 6767 Hollywood Boulevard; 323-462-8860, fax 323-462-3993; www.hollywoodwax.com.

Mann's Chinese Theater is a 1927 movie palace fashioned in "Oriental Baroque" style with pagoda roof, Asian masks and beautiful bas-reliefs. Though the architecture is splendid, the theater is actually known for its sidewalk. Embedded in the cement forecourt are the handprints and footprints of Hollywood's greatest stars. Tom Hanks, Robin Williams, Susan Sarandon and Denzel Washington have left their signatures in this grandest of all autograph collections. Not every celebrity simply signed and stepped, however: there are also cement images such as Donald Duck's webbed feet. ~ 6925 Hollywood Boulevard; 323-464-8111, fax 323-463-0879; www.manntheatres.com.

HIDDEN ► The **Hollywood Entertainment Museum** is dedicated solely to the history, technology and artifacts of Hollywood and the entertainment arts. The central gallery is a rotunda, where a multimedia presentation about Hollywood is shown at intervals throughout the day. Radiating from the rotunda are interactive displays employing interactive computers, video clips and a few special effects. Visitors can actually step onto the bridge of the U.S.S. *Enterprise*, one of the sets from the television series "Star Trek." Then it's on to the set of "Cheers," whose cast members carved their names into the bar as a farewell when the show ended. Closed Wednesday. Admission. ~ 7021 Hollywood Boulevard; 323-465-7900; www.hollywoodmuseum.com, e-mail info@hollywoodmuseum.com.

Throughout this area—extending for three and a half miles along Hollywood Boulevard from Gower Street to La Brea Boulevard and on Vine Street between Sunset Boulevard and Yucca Street—is the **Walk of Fame**, a star-studded terrazzo commemo-

Hollywood in Action

The ultimate Hollywood experience is a visit to a studio. The **NBC Studio Tour** provides a brief view of the television industry. Though only 70 minutes long, it takes in a special-effects center and visits a mini-studio where visitors participate in a mock game show. The wardrobe area, set-construction shop, and make-up room are also on the itinerary. Closed Saturday and Sunday. Admission. ~ 3000 West Alameda Avenue, Burbank; 818-840-3537, fax 818-840-3065.

The **Warner Brothers Studios**, by contrast, takes you behind the scenes to see the day-to-day activities of a multimedia complex. It's also home to the Warner Brothers Museum, where memorabilia from the 75-year history of the studio is displayed. The studio accepts only small groups (over the age of eight); tours are mostly technical and educational and change daily. Reservations required. Closed weekends. Admission. ~ 4000 Warner Boulevard, Burbank; 818-954-1744, fax 818-954-2089.

Paramount Studios operates weekday tours in a behind-the-scenes fashion with a historical overview. Because this is a working studio, no two tours are alike. What you see depends on what is being filmed that day. Tours generally run half-hourly on a first-come, first-served basis, but at press time tours were suspended due to heightened security; call ahead to check status. However, you may join the audience on one of Paramount's TV talk shows or courtroom shows. Show tickets are free and are available up to five days in advance. You must be over the age of ten. Closed weekends. Admission. ~ 5555 Melrose Avenue; 323-956-1777, fax 323-862-8534; www.paramount showtickets.com.

KCET, the Los Angeles public television station, also conducts technical tours of its studio. You must be over ten years old. Closed weekends. ~ 4401 Sunset Boulevard, Hollywood; 323-953-5530, fax 323-953-5331; www.kcet.org.

Dozens of television programs are taped in Los Angeles. The prime production season runs from August through March. For information on tickets call: **Audiences Unlimited** ~ 818-506-0067; **Paramount Guest Relations** ~ 323-956-1777; and **NBC-TV** ~ 818-840-4444.

That's Hollywood!

rating notables from the film, television, radio, theater and music industries. The names of more than 2180 legends appear on brass-rimmed stars embedded in the sidewalk. Pride of Hollywood, it represents the only walkway in Los Angeles to be washed several times weekly.

The Hollywood street scene centers along Sunset Boulevard, a flashy avenue studded with nightclubs and fresh-cuisine restaurants. During the 1930s and 1940s, the section between Crescent Heights Boulevard and Doheny Drive formed the fabled **Sunset Strip**. Center of Los Angeles night action, it was an avenue of dreams, housing nightclubs like Ciro's and the Trocadero. As picture magazines of the times illustrated, starlets bedecked with diamonds emerged from limousines with their leading men. During the 1950s, Ed "Kookie" Byrnes immortalized the street on the television show "77 Sunset Strip."

Another vestige of Tinseltown's history stands across the street from the Hollywood Bowl. Back in 1913, a young director named Cecil B. De Mille found a farm town called Hollywood with a horse barn he could use as a studio. The barn, a kind of wood-frame keepsake, moved around with De Mille over the years, seeing use as an office, a set and even a gymnasium for stars like Gary Cooper and Kirk Douglas. It was here that Paramount Pictures was born. Eventually moved to its present site, the historic building became the **Hollywood Heritage Museum**, a showplace dedicated to the era of silent films and containing a replica of De Mille's original office. Open weekends only. Admission. ~ 2100 North Highland Avenue; 323-874-4005, fax 323-789-7281; www.hollywoodheritage.org.

HIDDEN ▶

Los Angeles has little space for idyllic retreats. One of the city's more placid places is **Lake Hollywood**, a forest-framed reservoir created by the Mulholland Dam. Popular with hikers and joggers, the lake is surrounded by a chain-link fence but still offers splendid views. Scenes from *Chinatown* (1974), the movie that exposed the civic corruption behind Mulholland's project, were shot around the lake. The dam was also used in *Earthquake*, another 1974 flick in which the dike collapses, inundating the city.

sights

AUTHOR FAVORITE

The little ones can play with hands-on exhibits at **Kidspace Children's Museum**. This innovative facility has a television studio, a 17-foot ant hill and everything else a futuristic child might desire. Closed Monday. Admission. ~ 390 South El Molino Avenue, Pasadena; 626-449-9144, fax 626-449-9985; www.kidspacemuseum.org.

~ Southern entrance is at Weidlake Drive; northern entrance is at Lake Hollywood Drive.

To learn more about the architectural history of Los Angeles, visit the **Hollyhock House**. A masterwork by Frank Lloyd Wright, it is a sprawling 6200-square-foot home that represents his California Romanza style. Constructed of poured concrete and stucco, the house incorporates a geometric motif based on the hollyhock. Guided tours of the house are available. Closed for renovations until spring 2004. Admission. ~ 4808 Hollywood Boulevard; 323-913-4157.

PASADENA   One of the Southland's most spectacular complexes and certainly the premier attraction in the Pasadena area is the **Huntington Library, Art Collections and Botanical Gardens**.

The focal point of the 207-acre aesthetic preserve, the **Huntington Gallery** was originally philanthropist Henry E. Huntington's home. Today the mansion is dedicated to 18th- and 19th-century English and French art and houses one of the finest collections of its kind in the country. Another gallery contains Renaissance paintings and French sculpture from the 18th century; the **Virginia Steele Scott Gallery of American Art,** housed in an enchanting building, traces American painting from 1730 to 1930. Moving from oil to ink, and from mansion to mansion, the **Huntington Library** contains one of the world's finest collections of rare British and American manuscripts and first editions.

This describes only the *buildings* on the property! There are also the grounds, a heavenly labyrinth of gardens ranging from a verdant jungle setting to the austerely elegant desert garden. Rolling lawns are adorned with Italian statuary and bordered by plots of roses and camellias. The **Shakespeare garden** is filled with plants mentioned by the playwright, and the **Japanese garden** features an arched bridge, koi pond and 19th-century house. Closed Monday. Admission. ~ 1151 Oxford Road, San Marino; 626-405-2141; www.huntington.org, e-mail webmaster@huntington.org.

The **Arboretum of Los Angeles County** in neighboring Arcadia may be the most photographed location in the world. Everything from Tarzan movies to weekly television shows have been filmed in this 127-acre garden. With plants from every corner of the globe, it has portrayed Hawaii, Burma, Africa, Samoa and Devil's Island.

The history of the surrounding region, captured in several historic structures still standing on the grounds, long precedes the movies. There are **wickiups** similar to those of the original Gabrieleño Indians who used the local spring-fed pond as a watering hole. Representing the Spanish era is the **Hugo Reid Adobe,** an 1839 structure built with over 3000 mud bricks. Crudely furnished in 19th-century Spanish fashion, the adobe dates to the days when the area was part of a huge Spanish land grant. E. J.

"Lucky" Baldwin, the silver-mining magnate who helped introduce horse racing to Southern California, bought the ranch in 1875 and built a **Queen Anne Cottage**. His castle-in-the-sky dream house is a gingerbread Victorian that was often featured on the "Fantasy Island" television show. Also part of this never-ending complex is the **Santa Anita Depot**, open on Tuesday, Wednesday and Sunday. Built in 1890, it's a classic brick train station filled with equipment and memorabilia from the great age of railroads. Admission. ~ 301 North Baldwin Avenue, Arcadia; 626-821-3222, fax 626-445-1217.

HIDDEN ▶   **SAN GABRIEL MOUNTAINS**   Set in the foothills, **Eaton Canyon** is a 190-acre park laced with hiking trails that traverse an arroyo and four different plant communities. Trails meander through the park and lead deep into the adjacent Angeles National Forest. In 1993 about half of Eaton Canyon, including the interpretive center, burned in a fire. Since then, the park has built a new Nature Center, and a fire ecology trail shows the amazing regeneration of foothill flora. ~ 626-398-5420, fax 626-398-5422.

Another of the region's botanic preserves, **Descanso Gardens** stretches across 160 acres at the foot of the San Gabriel Mountains. This former estate has the largest camellia garden in the world, numbering over 60,000 plants, as well as a rose garden where strains of species are cultivated. You'll also find a Japanese garden and teahouse (tea is served weekends only) and a section devoted to native California plants. Admission. ~1418 Descanso Drive, La Cañada; 818-952-4400, fax 818-952-1238; www.descanso.com.

To explore the **San Gabriel Mountains** fully, follow the Angeles Crest Highway (Route 2) in its sinuous course upward from La Cañada. With their sharp-faced cliffs and granite outcroppings, the San Gabriels form a natural barrier between the Los Angeles Basin and the Mojave Desert. A side road from Route 2 leads to 5710-foot Mount Wilson, from which you can gaze across the entire expanse of Los Angeles to the Pacific Ocean. **Mount Wilson Observatory**, the area's most famous landmark, supports a 100-inch reflecting telescope. The telescope can be viewed through a window; there's also a museum here. The observatory is open weekends only. ~ 626-793-3100, fax 626-793-4570; www.mt wilson.edu.

GRIFFITH PARK   Every great city boasts a great park. Consider New York's Central Park, Golden Gate Park in San Francisco and in Los Angeles, Griffith Park (entrances near Western Canyon Road, Vermont Avenue, Riverside Drive and Route 5). Set astride the Hollywood Hills between Westside and the San Fernando Valley, this 4000-acre facility offers a flatlands area complete with golf courses, playgrounds and picnic areas, plus a vast hillside section featuring meadows, forests and miles of mountain roads.

Hooray for Hollywood!

Hollywood & Highland is the latest evidence that Hollywood is coming into a renaissance. An enormous entertainment, shopping, and dining complex, **Hollywood & Highland** is part mall, part theater, and part street scene. Mann's Chinese Theater is here, as is the Kodak Theater (the new home of the Academy Awards), the Grand Ballroom (an upscale venue for catered parties, run by L.A.'s favorite chef, Wolfgang Puck), and a six-screen multiplex cinema. The shopping area features many of the usual suspects (Banana Republic, the Gap) alongside boutiques offering everything from diamonds to blue jeans. The restaurants range from chains like California Pizza Kitchen (323-460-2080) to unique, upscale spots like The Grill on Hollywood (323-856-5530).

This huge outdoor mall dominates the neighborhood and displays a completely different aspect depending on the angle from which you approach it. Coming down Highland Avenue from the north, the enormous four-story Babylonian Arch is the first thing to catch your eye. Its size is impressive, but most arresting is its diagonal positioning. If you enter through the arch, towering above you are two 20-foot pedestals with a life-size elephant sculpture atop each one. Cruising along Hollywood Boulevard traveling east or west, the wraparound, fully animated billboard at the top of the building will make you think you're in the Ginza in Tokyo or Times Square in New York. (The effect is most successful after dark, of course.) Approaching this $615 million dollar extravaganza from underneath, you rise out of the metro station to Hollywood Boulevard, the glittering sidewalk embedded with the names of entertainment stars. The whole complex offers something that's been missing in Hollywood for a long time: glamour. ~ Hollywood Boulevard and Highland Avenue; 323-960-2331; www.hollywoodandhighland.com.

If you like it so much here that you want to stay, you can book a room at the **Renaissance Hollywood Hotel**. With its cool curves and white mirrored facade, this 22-story hostelry evokes the sleek modern design of '50s L.A. Inside, the 640 rooms and suites are appointed in classic '50s fashion, complete with Eames-style chairs and a muted green and yellow color scheme. Amenities include a terrace-top pool and bar, a fitness center, and a restaurant serving eclectic California cuisine. ~ 1755 North Highland Avenue; 323-856-1200, fax 323-856-1205; www.renaissance hollywood.com. ULTRA-DELUXE.

Toward the southern edge of the park, you'll see the **Griffith Park & Southern Railroad**, a miniature train ride. In the winter, you can ride with Santa. A nearby track offers **pony rides**. Hours vary. Admission. ~ 323-664-3266.

The **ranger station** will provide maps and information while directing you across the street to the **merry-go-round**, a beautiful, 1926 vintage carousel, which is open weekends only.

Featuring real-life versions of these whirling animals, the **L.A. Zoo** is among the highlights of the park. More than 1200 animals inhabit this 113-acre facility, many in environments simulating their natural habitats. The African exhibit houses elephants, rhinos, giraffes and monkeys; Eurasia is represented by tigers; there are also jaguars and spectacle bears and, from Australia, kangaroos and koalas. The adjacent **Adventure Island** is where newborn mammals are bottle-fed. You can see the baby animals in an exhibition area. Admission. ~ 5333 Zoo Drive; 323-644-6400, fax 323-662-9786; www.lazoo.org.

Travel Town is a transportation museum featuring a train yard full of cabooses, steam engines and passenger cars from the railroad's glory days. The exhibit also includes a fleet of 1920-era fire trucks and old milk wagons. For the kids there are narrow-gauge train rides here (fee). Admission. ~ 5200 West Zoo Drive; 323-662-5874.

For Hollywood's version of American history, there's the **Autry Museum of Western Heritage**. The focus here is more on Westerns than the West, but it's great fun for kids nonetheless. There are displays of saloons and stagecoaches, silver saddles and ivory-handled six-shooters, plus photos and film clips of all your favorite stars. Closed Monday. Admission. ~ 4700 Western Heritage Way; 323-667-2000, fax 323-660-5721; www.autry-museum.org.

Standing above the urban fray is the **Griffith Observatory and Planetarium**, a copper-domed beauty that perfectly represents the public-monument architecture of the 1930s. With its bas-reliefs and interior murals, this eerie site also resembles a kind of inter-

FARMERS MARKET

Back in 1934 local farmers created a market where they could congregate and sell their goods. Today **Farmers Market** is an open-air labyrinth of stalls, shops and vendor stands. There are tables overflowing with vegetables, fruits, meats, cheeses and baked goods, a total of over 120 outlets. Stop by for groceries, gifts and finger foods or simply to catch Los Angeles at its relaxed and informal best. ~ 6333 West 3rd Street; 323-933-9211, fax 323-549-2145; www.farmersmarketla.com.

planetary temple. In fact it has been the setting for numerous science fiction films such as *When Worlds Collide* (1951). James Dean's *Rebel Without a Cause* (1955) also featured a famous scene here. Apart from a movie setting, the Observatory features a Planetarium Theatre and a space-age Laserium (admission) complete with high-tech light shows. The Hall of Science offers museum displays on astronomy and meteorology. Closed Monday. Admission. ~ Observatory Drive; 323-664-1191, fax 323-663-4323; www.griffithobs.org.

DOWNTOWN   In the reasonable price range it's hard to top the **Figueroa Hotel**. A 1927 Spanish-style building, it offers a beautiful lobby with tile floor and hand-painted ceiling. The palm-fringed courtyard contains a swimming pool, jacuzzi and lounge. The rooms are very large, adequately furnished and decorated with wallhangings. Tile baths add a touch of class to this very appealing establishment. Coffee shop and restaurants on the premises. ~ 939 South Figueroa Street; 213-627-8971, 800-421-9092, fax 213-689-0305; www.figueroahotel.com, e-mail unofig@aol.com. MODERATE.

LODGING

What can you say about a place that became a landmark as soon as it was built? To call the **Westin Bonaventure** ultramodern would belittle the structure. "Post Future" is a more appropriate tag. Its dark-glass silos rise 35 stories from the street like a way station on the road through the 21st century. Within are two shopping levels, 20 restaurants, a revolving cocktail lounge, at least 1300 rooms, and many suites. The atrium lobby furthers the Buck Rogers theme with reflecting pools, glass-shaft elevators and lattice skylights. Considering all this, the guest rooms seem almost an afterthought; because of the building's configuration they are small and pie-shaped but offer good views of the surrounding financial district. The hotel is a short drive from the Natural History Museum and the California Science Center. ~ 404 South Figueroa Street; 213-624-1000, 800-228-3000, fax 213-612-4800. ULTRA-DELUXE.

HOLLYWOOD   The **Hollywood Celebrity Hotel** occupies a 1930s art-deco building just above Hollywood Boulevard. The 40 rooms are nicely refurbished, furnished in neo-deco style and decorated in a Hollywood motif. The rooms are spacious and a continental breakfast is included in the rate. ~ 1775 North Orchid Avenue; 323-850-6464, 800-222-7090, fax 323-850-7667. MODERATE.

The **Hollywood Hills Magic Hotel** is a 40-unit establishment next to the famed Magic Castle, a private club for magicians. Suites with kitchens are furnished in oak and decorated (presto!) with magic posters. They are big and well-maintained. Kids will enjoy the pool and sundeck. ~ 7025 Franklin Avenue; 323-851-0800,

800-741-4915; www.magichotel.com, e-mail info@magichotel. com. MODERATE.

It's as much a part of Hollywood as the Academy Awards. In fact, the very first Oscars were presented at the **Hollywood Roosevelt Hotel**. Built in 1927, the Spanish Revival building offers 335 rooms, plus a restaurant, lounges and a palm-studded courtyard with pool and hot tub. This classic caravansary has many features of the finest hostelries. The lobby is a recessed-ceiling affair with colonnades and hand-painted beams. Guest rooms are small but commodiously furnished with plump armchairs and hardwood pieces. Family suites are available. Across the street from Mann's Chinese Theater, this historic hotel is convenient to the heart of Hollywood. ~ 7000 Hollywood Boulevard; 323-466-7000, 800-950-7667, fax 323-469-7006; www. hollywoodroosevelt.com. DELUXE TO ULTRA-DELUXE.

PASADENA Motel row in Pasadena lies along Colorado Boulevard, route of the famous Rose Parade. **Pasadena Central Travelodge**, a 53-unit stucco complex, is typical of the accommodations. It offers standard rooms with cinderblock walls, stall showers, wall-to-wall carpeting and other basic amenities. The kids will enjoy frolicking in the swimming pool and jacuzzi. ~ 2131 East Colorado Boulevard; 626-796-3121, 800-578-7878, fax 626-793-4713. BUDGET.

The revered **Ritz-Carlton Huntington Hotel** is situated on 23 manicured acres. This 383-room hotel combines modern amenities with the style and charm of another era. There's an Olympic-size swimming pool (reputed to be the first in California) to exercise in or you can wander through the Japanese and Horseshoe gardens. If you are seeking Old World elegance, this is the address. ~ 1401 South Oak Knoll Avenue; 626-568-3900, 800-241-3333, fax 626-568-1842; www.ritzcarlton.com. ULTRA-DELUXE.

DINING **DOWNTOWN** Olvera Street, where the Spanish originally located the pueblo of Los Angeles, is still a prime place for Mexican food. Tiny **taco stands** line this brick-paved alley. Little more than open-air kitchens, they dispense fresh Mexican dishes. You'll also find bakeries and candy stands, where old Mexican ladies sell churros (Mexican donuts) and candied squash. BUDGET.

La Golondrina provides something more formal. Set in the historic Pelanconi House, an 1850-era home built of fired brick, it features an open-air patio and a dining room with stone fireplace and *viga* ceiling. The bill of fare includes a standard selection of tacos, tostadas and enchiladas as well as specialties such as fajitas and crab-meat enchiladas. Children will enjoy specialties like cheese burritos and taquitos. ~ 17 Olvera Street; 213-628-4349, fax 231-687-0800; www.lagolondrina.com. MODERATE.

Across from Union Station, midway between Olvera Street and Chinatown, stands one of the city's most famous cafeterias. **Philippe The Original** has been around since 1908, serving pork, beef, turkey and lamb sandwiches in a French-dip style. With sawdust on the floors and memories tacked to the walls, this antique eatery still serves ten-cent cups of coffee. Open for breakfast, lunch and dinner. ~1001 North Alameda Street; 213-628-3781, fax 213-628-1812; www.philippes.com, e-mail philippe@philippes.com. BUDGET.   ◄ *HIDDEN*

HOLLYWOOD   Hollywood's oldest restaurant, **Musso & Frank's Grill** is a 1919 original with dark paneling, murals and red leather booths. A bar and open grill create a clubby atmosphere that reflects the eatery's long tradition. Among the American-style dishes offered are cracked crab, fresh clams, roast lamb, plus assorted steaks and chops. Closed Sunday and Monday. ~ 6667 Hollywood Boulevard; 323-467-7788, fax 323-467-3360. MODERATE TO ULTRA-DELUXE.

Hamptons Hollywood Cafe may be the world's only hamburger joint with valet parking. This well-known noshing spot has transformed the art of hamburgers to a science, preparing over 340 different combinations. You can order them with sour-plum jam, peanut butter or creamed horseradish. If you disagree with the when-in-Rome philosophy, there are broiled shrimp, chicken, pasta and vegetarian platters. ~1342 North Highland Avenue; 323-469-1090, fax 323-469-0662. BUDGET TO MODERATE.

If Hamptons proves too health-conscious, try **Pink's Famous Chili Dogs**. This popular takeout stand has hamburgers and tamales; but at Pink's, not ordering a dog slapped with sauce is like   ◄ *HIDDEN*

RAGING WATERS

With 50 acres of aquatic attractions, **Raging Waters** is a great place to get all wet on a blazing Southern California day. Located 40 minutes east of downtown Los Angeles, this aquatic hotspot offers roughly 50 attractions from thrill rides to kiddie fare. Extreme slides include the straight-down, seven-story Drop Out. Also here are tube and toboggan rides, wave pools and a water contraption that mimics the experience of skateboarding. Activity areas for smaller children feature waterfalls, swimming areas and a spot where parents and children can explore the nifty Volcano FantaSea (with slide) together. Nine food courts, several activity islands, video arcades and a surf shop make this a complete kid's playland. Closed October to April. Admission. ~ 111 Raging Waters Drive, San Dimas; 909-592-6453; www.ragingwaters.com.

going to Hamptons for waffles. For the meat-free among us, vegan dogs are also available. ~ 709 North La Brea Avenue; 323-931-4223, fax 323-935-7465; www.pinkshollywood.com. BUDGET.

The celebrity photos covering every inch of **Formosa Cafe** tell a tale of Hollywood that reaches back to the 1940s. This crowded café, originally fashioned from a streetcar, has seen more stars than heaven. Over the years they've poured in from the surrounding studios, leaving autographs and memories. Today you'll find a Chinese restaurant, a kind of museum with meals. Dinner only. ~ 7156 Santa Monica Boulevard; 323-850-9050. MODERATE.

Hollywood's prettiest restaurant is a re-created Japanese palace called **Yamashiro**. Set in the hills overlooking Los Angeles, the mansion was built earlier in the century, modeled after an estate in the high mountains of Japan and trimmed with ornamental gardens. Dine here and you are surrounded by hand-carved columns, *shoji* screens and Asian statuary. The courtyard garden contains a waterfall, koi pond and miniature trees. For dinner the kimono-clad servers offer a complete Japanese menu as well as Western-style entrées. Dinner only. ~1999 North Sycamore Avenue; 323-466-5125. DELUXE TO ULTRA-DELUXE.

HIDDEN ►   The Hollywood address for righteous soul food is **Roscoe's House of Chicken & Waffles**, a tiny wood-slat café with overhead fans and an easy atmosphere. Ask for an "Oscar" and they'll bring chicken wings and grits; "E-Z Ed's Special" is a chicken liver omelette; and a "Lord Harvey" is a half chicken smothered in gravy and onions. Very hip. ~ 1514 North Gower Street; 323-466-7453, fax 323-962-0278. MODERATE.

PASADENA   One of the San Gabriel Valley's best food bargains is **Mi Jardin**. Serving classic Mexican dishes, this brick-walled eatery with a patio courtyard offers enchiladas, burritos and tostadas. With three meals daily and a menu numbering over 100 items, it's an exceptional place. ~ 48 Live Oak Avenue, Arcadia; 626-446-0903. BUDGET.

HIDDEN ►   For a great buy, try **Burger Continental**, a congested and crazy café where you order at the counter, then dine indoors or on a patio. Portions are bountiful and the prices ridiculously low. But it's not only the huge, low-priced menu that keeps this establishment packed—the belly-dancing shows also draw crowds. In addition to hamburgers they serve steaks, seafood, sandwiches and an enticing array of Middle Eastern dishes. The best bargain is the "Armenian feast," a combination of kebab dishes and Mid-Eastern appetizers capable of feeding a large family or small army. Breakfast, lunch and dinner are served daily. ~ 535 South Lake Avenue, Pasadena; 626-792-6634, fax 626-792-8520. BUDGET TO MODERATE.

Fish the waters around Los Angeles and you can try your hand at landing a barracuda, calico bass, halibut, white sea bass, white croaker, or maybe even a relative of Jaws.

SPORT-FISHING

L.A. Harbor Sportfishing offers scheduled and chartered trips for yellowtail, bass, tuna, barracuda and bonito. ~ 1150 Nagoya Way, Berth 79, San Pedro; 310-547-9916; www.laharborsport fishing.com. **Pierpoint Landing** has eight charter boats offering half-day to overnight fishing charters. ~ 200 Aquarium Way, Long Beach; 562-983-9300; www.pierpoint.net.

DIVING

If you'd rather search for starfish than stars along L.A.'s coastline, you'll find an active diving scene.

To explore Los Angeles' submerged depths, contact **Pacific Sporting Goods**, which provides lessons and equipment and organizes boat trips. ~ 11 39th Place, Long Beach; 562-434-1604. **Pacific Wilderness** is a PADI training center that sells and rents equipment. ~ 1719 South Pacific Avenue, San Pedro; 310-833-2422. **Blue Cheer Ocean Water Sports** runs trips from Santa Monica to Anacapa and Santa Cruz islands. ~ 1110 Wilshire Boulevard, Santa Monica; 310-828-1217; www.divers4hire.com. For NAUI certification classes and dive trips near the islands contact **Scuba Haus**. ~ 2501 Wilshire Boulevard, Santa Monica; 310-828-2916.

> Santa Monica Bay stretches 30 miles from Redondo Beach to Point Dume.

WHALE WATCHING

If you're visiting Los Angeles from winter to early spring, hop aboard a whale-watching vessel and keep your eyes peeled for plumes and tails.

During the annual whale migration several outfits offer local whale-watching trips. **Pierpoint Landing** will take you out on the briny deep for a three-hour cruise. ~ 2000 Aquarium Way, Long Beach; 562-495-6250. For a one-hour trip call **Catalina Cruises**. ~ 320 Golden Shore, Long Beach; 562-436-5006; www.catalina cruises.com. Out of San Pedro, **Los Angeles Sightseeing Cruise** takes two-and-a-half-hour trips along the coast. ~ Berth 78, San Pedro; 310-831-0996; www.laharborcruises.com. **L.A. Harbor Sportfishing** offers two-and-a-half-hour trips. ~ Berth 79, San Pedro; 310-547-9916; www.laharborsportfishing.com.

SURFING & WINDSURFING

"Surfing is the only life," so when in the Southland, sample a bit of Los Angeles' seminal subculture.

Rent a surfboard, bodyboard, or wetsuit from **Manhattan Beach Bike and Skate Rentals**. ~ 1116 Manhattan Avenue, Manhattan Beach; 310-372-8500. **Jeffers** offers surfboards and boogie-boards. ~ 39 14th Street, Hermosa Beach; 310-372-9492. You'll find surfboard, boogieboard and wetsuit rentals in Malibu at **Zuma Jay Surfboards**. ~ 22775 Pacific Coast Highway, Malibu; 310-456-8044; www.zumajay.com.

SKATING & SKATE-BOARDING

Los Angeles may well be the skating capital of California, and skateboarding, of course, is the closest thing to surfing without waves. Between the two of them, you can't get much more L.A., so find a way to put yourself on wheels.

Spokes 'n Stuff has two convenient locations and rents both inline skates and rollerskates. ~ At the parking lot on Admiralty Way at Jamaica Bay Inn Hotel, Marina del Rey, 310-306-3332; and near the Santa Monica Pier in Loews Santa Monica, 310-395-4748. Along the Santa Monica Pier, **Sea Mist Skate Rentals** has inline skates, rollerskates, mountain bikes and everything else you may need for a day on the South Bay Trail. ~ 1619 Ocean Front Walk, Santa Monica; 310-395-7076.

HANG GLIDING

What better way to let yourself go than by coasting or floating on high? The adventurous can try hang gliding at **Windsports Soaring Center**, which offers lessons and trips off the San Gabriel Mountains. Closed Sunday and Monday. ~ 16145 Victory Boulevard, Van Nuys; 818-988-0111; www.windsports.com.

RIDING STABLES

With its curving hills and flowering meadows, Griffith Park is a favorite spot among urban equestrians. Several places on the edge of the park provide facilities. **Sunset Ranch** offers trail rides on specific park trails, and one that takes you to a Mexican restaurant. Trips are one to two hours. ~ 3400 North Beachwood Drive, Hollywood; 323-464-9612; www.sunsetranchhollywood.com.

In Burbank consider **Circle K Stables** for small group rides. Trail rides can be as short as one hour or as long as five. ~ 914 South Mariposa Street; 818-843-9890. Another Burbank offering is **Griffith Park Horse Rentals**, which takes you on one- to two-hour rides into the hills of Griffith Park. Maximum group of 20. ~ 480 Riverside Drive; 818-840-8401.

Rent horses from **Bar S Stables** and lead yourself through the Glendale portion of the park. Guides can be arranged beforehand. You must be at least seven years old to ride. ~ 1850 Riverside Drive, Glendale; 818-242-8443.

GOLF

The beautiful **El Dorado Park Municipal Golf Course** has two putting greens and a driving range. ~ 2400 Studebaker Road, Long Beach; 562-430-5411. The 18-hole **Skylink Golf Course** is a duffer's delight with club and cart rentals, a driving range, night lighting and a sports bar on the premises. ~ 4800 East Wardlow Road, Long Beach; 562-421-3388. The hilly **Recreation Park** offers both an 18-hole and a 9-hole course. ~ 5000 Deukmejian Drive,

Long Beach; 562-494-5000. If you are in Pasadena, stop by the two 18-hole courses at the public **Brookside Golf Course**. Located right next to the Rose Bowl, this green features many lakes and trees. They rent only clubs. ~ 1133 North Rosemont Avenue; 626-796-0177. In Los Angeles, **Wilson and Harding Golf Courses** are both 18-hole, par-72 public greens. ~ Griffith Park; 323-663-2555; www.griffithparkgolfshop.com.

TENNIS

There are 15 lighted courts available at **El Dorado Park**. ~ 2800 Studebaker Road, Long Beach; 562-425-0553. The **Billie Jean King Tennis Center** offers eight lighted courts. ~ 1040 Park Avenue, Long Beach; 562-438-8509. In Santa Monica, it's a good idea to call for reservations at public tennis courts. **Reed Park** has six lighted courts. ~ Wilshire and Lincoln boulevards; 310-394-6011. **Memorial Park** offers four lighted courts. ~ Olympic Boulevard at 14th Street, Santa Monica; 310-394-6011. Also try one of the six courts at **Ocean View Park**. ~ Barnard Way south of Ocean Park Boulevard, Santa Monica; 310-394-6011.

L.A.'s largest greensward, **Griffith Park** has many outdoor lighted courts. ~ 4730 Crystal Springs Drive, Los Angeles; 323-662-7772. **Elysian Park** has two unlighted courts. ~ Near the intersection of Route 5 and Route 110, Los Angeles. For more information on other local parks and their facilities, contact the Los Angeles City and County Parks and Recreation Department office. ~ www.ci.la.ca.us/rap.

Tennis clubs dot the county; one such club is the **Racquet Center**. The Pasadena location has nine lighted courts and seven racquetball courts. They also rent racquets and have lessons. ~ 920 Lohman Lane, South Pasadena, 323-258-4178. For further information about clubs and tournaments, contact the **Southern California Tennis Association**. ~ P.O. Box 240015, Los Angeles, CA 90024; 310-208-3838; www.usta.com/scta.

BIKING

Though Los Angeles might seem like one giant freeway, there are scores of shoreline bike trails and routes for scenic excursions. Foremost is the **South Bay Bike Trail**, with over 22 miles of coastal

AUTHOR FAVORITE

The **Venice Beach Bike Path** is a casual, two-mile ride where a host of kooky characters and performers line the promenade, vying for your attention. Try to visit grand open-air carnival on the weekend. It is a world of artists and anarchists, derelicts and dreamers, a vision of what life would be if heaven were an insane asylum.

vistas. The trail, an easy ride, is extremely popular and runs from RAT Beach in Torrance to Will Rogers State Beach in Pacific Palisades. The path intersects the Ballona Creek Bikeway in Marina Del Rey, which extends seven miles east and passes the Venice Boardwalk, as well as piers and marinas along the way.

Naples, a Venice-like neighborhood in Long Beach, provides a charming area for freeform bike rides.

The **Santa Monica Loop** is an easy ride starting at Ocean Avenue and going up San Vicente Boulevard, past Palisades Park and the Santa Monica Pier. Most of the trail is on bike lanes and paths. It's a ten-mile roundtrip.

Over 14 miles of bike routes wind through Griffith Park. Two notable excursions skirt many of the park attractions: **Crystal Springs Loop**, which follows Crystal Springs Drive and Zoo Drive along the park's eastern edge, passes the merry-go-round and Travel Town; **Mineral Wells Loop**, an arduous uphill climb, passes Harding Golf Course, then coasts downhill to Zoo Drive, taking in Travel Town and the zoo.

For a look at the good life, check out the route from **San Gabriel Mission to the Huntington Library**, which winds from San Gabriel through the exclusive town of San Marino.

A strenuous but worthwhile excursion is a bike ride along **Mulholland Drive**. Not recommended during commute hours, this route traverses the spine of the Santa Monica Mountains and offers fabulous views of the city and ocean.

For maps, brochures and additional information on bike routes in Los Angeles contact the **Department of Transportation**. ~ 205 South Broadway; 213-485-4277.

Bike Rentals   **Spokes 'n Stuff** offers mountain bikes, tandems and cruisers. ~ Near the pier in Loews Santa Monica; 310-395-4748. Also in Santa Monica, **Sea Mist Skate Rentals** has mountain bikes and helmets. ~ 1619 Ocean Front Walk, Santa Monica; 310-395-7076.

Index

Lodging Index

Dining Index

HIDDEN GUIDES

Adventure travel or a relaxing vacation?—"Hidden" guidebooks are the only travel books in the business to provide detailed information on both. Aimed at environmentally aware travelers, our motto is "Where Vacations Meet Adventures." These books combine details on unique hotels, restaurants and sightseeing with information on camping, sports and hiking for the outdoor enthusiast.

THE NEW KEY GUIDES

Based on the concept of ecotourism, The New Key Guides are dedicated to the preservation of Central America's rare and endangered species, architecture and archaeology. Filled with helpful tips, they give travelers everything they need to know about these exotic destinations.

Ulysses Press books are available at bookstores everywhere. If any of the following titles are unavailable at your local bookstore, ask the bookseller to order them.

You can also order books directly from Ulysses Press
P.O. Box 3440, Berkeley, CA 94703
800-377-2542 or 510-601-8301
fax: 510-601-8307
www.ulyssespress.com
e-mail: ulysses@ulyssespress.com

Order Form

HIDDEN GUIDEBOOKS

____ Hidden Arizona, $16.95

____ Hidden Bahamas, $14.95

____ Hidden Baja, $14.95

____ Hidden Belize, $15.95

____ Hidden Boston & Cape Cod, $14.95

____ Hidden British Columbia, $17.95

____ Hidden Cancún & the Yucatán, $16.95

____ Hidden Carolinas, $17.95

____ Hidden Coast of California, $18.95

____ Hidden Colorado, $14.95

____ Hidden Disneyland, $13.95

____ Hidden Florida, $18.95

____ Hidden Florida Keys & Everglades, $12.95

____ Hidden Georgia, $16.95

____ Hidden Guatemala, $16.95

____ Hidden Hawaii, $18.95

____ Hidden Idaho, $14.95

____ Hidden Kauai, $13.95

____ Hidden Maui, $13.95

____ Hidden Montana, $15.95

____ Hidden New England, $18.95

____ Hidden New Mexico, $15.95

____ Hidden Oahu, $13.95

____ Hidden Oregon, $15.95

____ Hidden Pacific Northwest, $18.95

____ Hidden Salt Lake City, $14.95

____ Hidden San Francisco & Northern California, $18.95

____ Hidden Southern California, $18.95

____ Hidden Southwest, $19.95

____ Hidden Tahiti, $17.95

____ Hidden Tennessee, $16.95

____ Hidden Utah, $16.95

____ Hidden Walt Disney World, $13.95

____ Hidden Washington, $15.95

____ Hidden Wine Country, $13.95

____ Hidden Wyoming, $15.95

THE NEW KEY GUIDEBOOKS

____ The New Key to Costa Rica, $17.95

____ The New Key to Ecuador and the Galápagos, $17.95

Mark the book(s) you're ordering and enter the total cost here ⇨ [   ]

California residents add 8.25% sales tax here ⇨ [   ]

Shipping, check box for your preferred method and enter cost here ⇨ [   ]

❏ Book Rate   **FREE! FREE! FREE!**

❏ Priority Mail $3.50 First book, $1.00/each additional book

❏ UPS 2-Day Air $7.00 First book, $1.00/each additional book   [   ]

Billing, enter total amount due here and check method of payment ⇨ [   ]

❏ Check   ❏ Money Order

❏ Visa/MasterCard _____ Exp. Date _____

Name _____ Phone _____

Address _____

_____

City_____ State _____ Zip_____

Money-back guarantee on direct orders placed through Ulysses Press.

ABOUT THE AUTHOR

LISA OPPENHEIMER and her seasoned team of researchers—Alexis, 11, Melissa, 8, and Steve, 43—have embarked on numerous Disney World fact-finding missions, braving the perils of the Jungle Cruise, the peaks of Space Mountain and the virtual dog slime of Honey I Shrunk the Audience. Working at Disney and elsewhere, she's earned bylines in several travel books, as well as on the pages of *Disney Magazine*, *Parents* and *Family Life*.

ABOUT THE ILLUSTRATOR

GLENN KIM is a freelance illustrator residing in San Francisco. His work appears in numerous Ulysses Press titles including *The New to Key Ecuador and the Galápagos*, *Hidden Southwest* and *Hidden Arizona*. He has also illustrated for the National Forest Service, several Bay Area magazines, book covers and greeting cards, as well as for advertising agencies that include Foote Cone and Belding, Hal Riney and Jacobs Fulton Design Group.